THE FRENCH WAR ON TRADE:
PRIVATEERING 1793-1815

To
John Bromley
and to my family
Helen, Lesley
and
Janet

The French War on Trade: Privateering 1793-1815

Patrick Crowhurst

Scolar Press

Published by

Scolar

Gower Publishing Company Limited,
Gower House, Croft Road, Aldershot,
Hants. GU11 3HR, England

Gower Publishing Company,
Old Post Road, Brookfield, Vermont 05036
USA

Published in association with Leicester Polytechnic

Printed and bound in Great Britain at
The Camelot Press Ltd, Southampton

British Library Cataloguing in Publication Data

Crowhurst, Patrick
The French war on trade: privateering 1793–1815 – (Studies in naval history)
1. France. Foreign trade. Role of privateering, 1793–1815
I. Title II. Series
382'.0944

ISBN 0 85967 804 0

Contents

Preface

The present study began as a small part of the research on the nature of British trade defence in the period 1689-1815. It took shape as it became clear that although much had been written about the *guerre de course*, far less was known about the period of the Revolutionary and Napoleonic wars. The years of research and writing owe much to a number of people and the generosity of research foundations. My principal debt is to the late Professor Bromley, who generously gave advice at every stage and whose unequalled knowledge of French privateering in general and of the years 1689-1713 in particular provided a deep understanding of the problems faced by all who participated in it. More general help and encouragement has been given by many colleages and friends.

The work would not have been possible without the financial assistance of the Social Science Research Foundation and the Nuffield Foundation. Many visits to archives throughout France were generously funded by the Social Science Research Foundation. The Nuffield Foundation helped at a later stage, when it became clear that visits to the Schweizerische Wirtschaftsarchiv in Basel would prove helpful. Research at the Public Records Office at Chancery Lane and Ashridge were also paid for by the Social Science Research Council.

Much help was also given by the staff at the different record offices and I should like to thank in particular M. Castel, the archivist at Toulon, and Dr. Mentha and his successor Dr. Sulser, the archivists at Basel for their particular assistance. I should also like to thank Pat Crerar, Roy Freer and their colleagues at Leicester Polytechnic in Computing Services, this book could not have been produced in its current form without their assistance. Finally the work could never have been carried out without the support of my family, to whom the book is dedicated.

Introduction

For over a century there has been considerable interest in French privateering on both sides of the English Channel and within the last decade the pace has quickened. In consequence much is now known about the laws and decrees that provided the legal framework for what was at best a very risky undertaking. The work of Bromley, Delumeau and his pupils has concentrated attention on the wars of the League of Augsburg and the Spanish Succession, when more corsairs were at sea than in any other period and when French commerce raiding appeared to constitute a major threat to the financial structure of England. It is also evident that there was considerable variety in methods of financing ventures as between St Malo and Marseilles and that Dunkirk and St Malo constituted the major threat to English and Dutch commerce. Of the two, Dunkirk had one major advantage; her merchants could draw on Flemish seaman who were not subject to the French naval conscription and who had a reputation for aggressive behaviour that raised the prestige of Dunkirk's privateers. It is also evident that privateering was strongly influenced by factors such as the effectiveness of British methods of commerce defence, notably by convoys. During the mid eighteenth century the French attempt to organise a strong navy to challenge British command of the sea and the failure to provide adequate defence for French trade and overseas colonies quickly led to the collapse of French commerce while denying merchants the opportunity of organising commerce raiding. It is also agreed that at the end of the eighteenth century there was a revival in privateering.

But important questions remained, which this study seeks to answer. None of the earlier research showed whether the revival in privateering between 1793 and 1815 matched the efforts of a century earlier. There was no information on whether those who financed these ventures did so consistently in both wars or even from year to year. There was no information on whether, and to what extent, other ports also sent ships to sea. There were also questions concerning the type of ship used and whether ships cruised in particular areas: Dunkirkers in the North Sea and Malouins in the Channel Soundings, for example. A detailed examination was needed of the available evidence on profits, for there were conflicting claims on profitability in general and of the claim that some individuals had made vast fortunes from it. The reputation of Surcouf as successful managing owner at St Malo needed a close examination, to see if his efforts at organising ventures matched his earlier success in the Indian Ocean as the captain of privateers. Most important, an effort had to be made to try and establish why men put their capital in ventures which were generally regarded as very risky, and whether their motives were influenced more by their expectation of profits or by the collapse of the commercial boom of the 1780's, which had sharply restricted the opportunities open to merchants.

Privateering had to be set against the background of the economic conditions of the two wars: the collapse of the economy, the slow recovery leading to stagnation and the evolution of Napoleon's attempt to cripple British financial stability by cutting her trade. Closely related to this was the question whether, and in what way, the social consequences of the Revolution were reflected in changes within the commercial community at the ports and whether the change was permanent. Faced with these questions it was clear that this study should be confined to the activities of French merchants within metropolitan France and European ports, for French privateering in the Caribbean and North America was clearly of a different nature, and sufficient research on commerce raiding in the Indian Ocean had already been done to make that reasonably clear. These are the broad questions which this study seeks to answer. Readers may judge for themselves whether they find the answers satisfactory.

1 The economic background

Privateering as a form of economic activity cannot be separated from the life of the community in which it takes place. Previous studies have tended to regard commerce raiding as an aspect of naval strategy or the work of men who were motivated primarily by patriotic zeal or the desire for riches. This study takes a different approach and it is the view of the present writer that the men -and occasionally women - who organised and invested in privateering ventures did so principally because they saw it as a substitute for trade when that collapsed. This is not to say that merchants invested all their available capital in commerce raiding. Most spent comparatively small amounts on a regular basis while it offered any prospects, though there were some gamblers who invested a great deal. To understand why merchants felt compelled to engage in these risky ventures it is necessary to analyse the pre-war boom, the economic collapse and partial recovery, the stagnation and finally Napoleon's attempt to crush British power through denying her opportunities to trade.

In the 1780's, between the end of the War of American Independence and the outbreak of the French Revolution, French commerce enjoyed a period of unprecedented prosperity. The main aspect was trade with the French colonies in the West Indies, linked in some degree with trade with the United States which had developed while the two had been allies in the last four years of the war. This colonial trade was dominated by Bordeaux, which not only acted as the entrepot for the distribution of colonial goods throughout northern Europe, but also possessed a range of industries situated along the tributaries of the River Garonne which produced the household goods and plantation utensils which were shipped to the colonies. Some parts of this manufacturing industry had been modernised along English lines shortly before the Revolution, but in general they were not able to compete with industries within France when their colonial markets collapsed. Nantes and La Rochelle also played a part in the West India commerce, supplying slaves for the plantations and importing sugar and other colonial commodities. Neither however enjoyed a trade that was as diverse as Bordeaux's. Another, more specialised trade from Bordeaux was that with the East Indies, organised through the Ile de France, the modern Mauritius. This demanded not only larger ships but also considerable risk capital. Whereas commerce with the West Indies required ships of around 100-150 tons, the East Indiamen were upwards of 400 tons, and were similar to naval frigates in size and armament. West India merchants could engage in commerce with relatively little capital - though many merchants invested large sums - but the East India trade demanded more costly ships, larger investment in trade goods and a much slower return on investment. Early in the eighteenth century St Malo merchants had engaged in this long distance trade, but by the 1780's it was dominated by Bordeaux and Marseilles, both of which possessed much greater resources.

Much of the energy of the Marseilles merchants was channelled into the Levant, Barbary, Italian and Antilles trades, which not only provided an outlet for French industrial goods but also supplied the commodities required for the industries of Lyons and Marseilles. Of these, silk spinning and weaving at Lyons and soap manufacture at Marseilles were the most important. The expansion of Marseilles' trade with the Levant during the eighteenth century, which had been helped by the creation of Marseilles as a free port in 1669, had been largely at the expense of the British and commerce with the Barbary ports had developed in spite of religious differences which at times threatened to halt it. Marseilles merchants were also able to take advantage of the Rhône-Saône valley to distribute goods throughout eastern France and link with trade routes from the Rhine and Switzerland to Central and Eastern Europe. This geographical advantage encouraged some Marseilles merchants to engage in commerce with the West India colonies in order to develop trade with the north and east and bypass Bordeaux. In general however this remained a relatively minor part of Marseilles' trade.

These three ports, Bordeaux, Marseilles and Nantes controlled the bulk of French commerce. In second place stood a variety of smaller ports whose development had been hindered by geographical disadvantages. La Rochelle, an important port in the seventeenth century, had links with the West Indies and North America but failed to develop partly because it lacked a harbour which was accessible to large ships under all weather conditions. It also lacked good communications with the interior and relied largely on coastal trade to distribute the goods it imported. It remained overshadowed by Bordeaux. Another port which suffered a similar fate was Bayonne, situated a short distance inland at the confluence of the rivers Adour and Nive. In the seventeenth century Bayonne seamen had been famous in the whale fishery and this established the reputation of Bayonne seamen as hardy and courageous. This had been enhanced by the activies of the men who had joined the gangs of freebooters in the Caribbean. Bayonne merchants were also active during the seventeenth and eighteenth century in the trade with northern Spain for wool and iron, which was brought to the annual fair and thence distributed throughout France. Bayonne's success was also enhanced by its privileges as a free port, although it had lost them early in the eighteenth century and did not regain them until 1784, in spite of strenuous efforts by its merchants in 1738 and 1774.[1] However, early in the eighteenth century the river estuary began to silt up and it became more difficult for the larger ships to enter the port. Trade gradually moved north to Bordeaux, though many merchants kept links with both ports and continued to use the ship building and repair facilities at Bayonne. This drift of trade away from Bayonne was a serious matter, for the port stood on a comparatively narrow coastal plain where agriculture did not provide adequate employment and all that remained was some commerce with Spain, a little whaling, some offshore fishing and the reputation for daring, imagination and vigour. This led many men to engage in privateering during the wars from the late seventeenth century through the eighteenth and the Bayonnais and the men of the neighbouring port of St Jean-de-Luz saw themselves as the inheritors of a tradition that in many ways was comparable to that of Dunkirk and St Malo.[2]

In the north east stood three important ports, two of which enjoyed the reputation of being leaders in the commercial war against Britain: St Malo, Dunkirk and Le Havre. In 1789 St Malo was the principal deep water fishing port in France. Every year it sent a large fleet to the cod fisheries off Newfoundland where French rights to fish offshore and establish drying stations during the fishing season were guaranteed by treaty. St Malo was regarded as the main nursery of seamen and it supplied many of the men who served in the navy at Brest and elsewhere. During peace the fishery acted as a focus for a wide-ranging coastal trade. Salt for the fishery was imported from Marennes on the Atlantic coast and was carried to Newfoundland with the annual fleet. The sale of dried and salted cod in the Mediterranean created a commerce in Mediterranean goods which were imported at St Malo and thence carried by small coaster to ports in northern France and the Baltic. St Malo's other commercial role was to ship sail cloth made in the area round Vitré to ports in France and the Mediterranean. In other respects St Malo was a commercial backwater in 1789; the hinterland was poor, agriculture was backward and the port was isolated from the main markets in France. The only other important aspect of St Malo's commercial history had been the opening of trade early in the eighteenth century with the Spanish colonies. This had produced considerable revenue, but had been halted when the French decided to improve relations with Spain and found this illegal trade an embarrassment. But the reputation of Malouin seamen as adventurous freebooters and experienced deep water fishermen was similar to that of Bayonne and the two ports shared the same interest in privateering.

To the east of St Malo lay the important port of Le Havre, which during the seventeenth century had been, with Rouen, the port through which Spanish wool entered for making fine draperies.[3] These enjoyed a good market throughout France and the same port served the manufacturers of coarse linens that were sent to Cadiz for making into clothing for slaves in the Spanish colonies. By the end of this century the woollen textile industry had moved to Louviers, Elbeuf and Darnetal and cotton had begun to take its place, though linen manufacture stayed until the Revolution. The cotton industry flourished at Rouen until the late 1780's - it was distressed in 1789 - and the town was also famous for the manufacture of faience and a variety of other goods, including playing cards, hats and ribbons, pipes, stocks and books. These formed the basis for an extensive trade with Holland, Britain and the Hanse towns, though the bulk of the imports at Le Havre and Rouen consisted of Spanish wool and cotton.[4] The growth of trade with the French colonies complemented this and enhanced the position of Le Havre and Rouen for the distribution of colonial commodities in northern Europe, though this was on a smaller scale than Bordeaux.

At the extreme north east of France, close to the frontier with the Austrian Netherlands, stood the port of Dunkirk. In many respects its position was most unsuitable for anything except fishing. It lay at the edge of a wide, marshy plain on a coast where constantly changing sand banks made navigation hazardous. However, the port proved to be ideally situated for trade with Britain and northern Europe as well as being a base for attacking shipping in wartime. Its sandbanks, hazardous for commerce, proved an excellent defence against a direct assault from the sea and the extensive fortifications, planned by Vauban, complemented the natural defences of canals and marshlands until demolished under the Treaty of Utrecht. Dunkirk, acquired by France towards the end of the seventeenth century, was granted the rights of a free port to develop trade with the Austrian Netherlands and Holland. One consequence was the development of Dunkirk as a fishing port, sending ships to south west Ireland and the North Sea as well as off the French coast. In 1786 a commercial treaty was signed with Britain. This was welcomed initially by Dunkirk merchants because they believed, wrongly as it turned out, that it would lead to a significant increase in French trade. In practice it worked to Britain's advantage and this was one of the factors which later made many Dunkirkers welcome the outbreak of war against Britain in 1793. Dunkirk's lack of a densely populated hinterland and good communications created serious difficulties whenever war broke out against Britain. Dunkirk's trade was threatened by the British navy, which could intercept shipping off the port. When trade collapsed, the only alternative was to turn to commerce raiding. Privateering thus forms an important aspect of Dunkirk's history under both Spanish and French rule. The reputation of Jean Bart, its most famous citizen, had been established in the Dutch wars before privateering reached its peak in the wars of 1689-1714. This period gave Dunkirk its reputation as the leading privateering port. Dunkirk's development as a commercial port came later and Dunkirk reached its peak in the 1780's.

Behind the prosperity of Bordeaux and the other ports which traded with the West India colonies lay a very serious problem. Many of the plantation owners were heavily in debt. Productivity was falling; the soil was becoming exhausted and there was no new land to bring under cultivation. It was becoming increasingly difficult and expensive to achieve a high yield and the plantation owners, though continuing to import large quantities of goods from France, often could not pay for them in full. Some of the Bordeaux merchants tried to resolve this problem by taking control of plantations but this had little effect on productivity and the imbalance in trade. Companies such as Romberg, Bapst et Cie in Bordeaux found that they could not make the former owners work any harder and that their new financial commitments over-extended their financial resources.[5] Commercial disquiet was not confined to the leading colonial merchants. The textile industry in Normandy was also facing serious difficulties. In 1779 trade at Elbeuf had been stagnant and six years later the industry was again at a standstill. This was the beginning of the pre-Revolutionary crisis.[6]

The outbreak of the Revolution thus caught sections of French commerce when they were already facing severe difficulties. But worse was to come. The introduction of *assignats* which became legal tender in September 1790, rapidly disrupted much of trade as their value declined. It became increasingly difficult for merchants to engage in commerce, for they were unwilling to accept *assignats* whose value was falling and they could not easily calculate a price which would provide adequate compensation for the normal delay in payment by bill of exchange. Within two years of the outbreak of the Revolution in Paris there was a major slave revolt in the north of Saint Domingue, and imports of sugar, coffee and other colonial goods fell. Even where the slaves were not in revolt plantation owners and managers were unwilling to take any action which might antagonise their slaves. For the commercial community the situation became worse when elements in the white population tried to introduce revolutionary measures into the government of the colonies. 1792 saw the final collapse of Romberg, Bapst et Cie and others under the continued pressure of these events. Although prices temporarily rose as imports declined, merchants soon found that they could not sell all their stocks.

Inflation brought trade to a halt. The peasants were unwilling to bring their produce to sell for currency they considered worthless. Merchants were unwilling to sell them for the same reason. They tended to keep their stocks in the hope that they would rise in value; this was normal commercial practice and speculative profits formed an important part of the income of many merchants. The situation became worse in 1792 with the outbreak of war with Austria and the attempt to raise additional revenue by taxation. Under normal circumstances taxation would not have been a serious burden; the officials used income returns which merchants had completed. But under these straitened circumstances it was a different matter. Merchants paid their taxes in *assignats* and were doubtless glad to be rid of them but they had very little income. During the invasion of France in the autumn the first steps were taken by the Convention to regulate trade, but when the crisis was past the orders were dropped.

The following year inflation reached dramatic proportions as prices and wages rose steeply. Put simply, there was not enough wheat to feed the population and merchants everywhere in France were suspected of holding stocks that they were unwilling to sell and profiting from the misery of their fellow citizens. At the end of January, after the execution of Louis XVI, Britain declared war on France. This provided merchants and ship owners with the opportunity to fit out privateers and raid British shipping. This was a normal measure at the beginning of any war because both Britain and France tried to capture seamen and weaken their enemy's naval power. In 1793 this was the motive of the Convention, but merchants and seamen desperate for food saw the opportunity to capture cargoes and crew's provisions - in fact anything that could be eaten or sold. In May 1792 the Convention had decreed an end to commerce raiding and Franklin had followed this by a similar plea in January 1793 before war had been declared. After the outbreak of war however the Convention took steps to encourage it along commercial lines. On 1 February a law was passed under which the state abandoned its former right to a share in prize money and the following day it decreed that premiums would be paid for fitting out corsairs and compensation would be given for losses.[7] A further decree of the 6th stated that captains who had commanded privateers for five years could be appointed *lieutenant de vaisseau.* This raised the prestige of successful captains and provided replacements for the naval officers who had fled to Britain. The final step was taken on the 20th when prize goods were exempted from all duties.

These measures were taken on the assumption that patriotism alone might not provide enough men to fit out ships to raid the enemy. A different view is presented in the memoirs of Pierre-Edouard Plucket, a Dunkirk seaman who held the rank of naval lieutenant during this war and was appointed to the Legion of Honour. In his memoirs, published in 1843, he recounts that he was in Nantes in February 1793 and heard the drum beat in the streets announcing the outbreak of war with Britain.[8] His companion, Laporte, who had sailed on a Dunkirk privateer during the War of American Independence, proposed that they should fit out one of the slavers at Nantes and attack the British. Plucket claimed that though he had been imprisoned by the British during the war he was instantly motivated by patriotism and a hatred for the 'European freebooters'.[9] He went to Paris, was given the first letter of marque and quickly raised sufficient funds to fit out a ship, which he renamed the *Sans Culotte Nantais*.[10] According to Plucket's account, the crew of the vessel included about fifteen Dutch sailors whose ship had just arrived at Nantes. On 19 February the corsair slipped down river and in the course of the next ten days captured one British, two Dutch and five other ships which he brought back in triumph to Brest. These were, he claimed, the first to be brought into that port. This may be an accurate account, but it was written many years later when patriotic accounts of this nature formed part of the folk lore of popular French history. The truth is probably more mundane. Plucket never commanded or armed a privateer again and the episode was probably less successful than he claimed. There were some men who placed patriotism before all other considerations and were motivated by a spirit of adventure; others expected to make a profit and many of the officers and men during the early months of 1793 wanted to earn a living at a time of acute crisis.

The figures for the number of ships fitted out demonstrate the immediate popularity of commerce raiding: ports where it was traditionally practised, Dunkirk, St Malo, Bayonne and St Jean-de-Luz sent out 49, 23, 9 and 9 ships respectively. However, merchants at other ports also prepared vessels: 13 at Boulogne, 3 each at Calais and Cherbourg, 2 at Dieppe, 7 at Le Havre, 10 at Nantes, 27 at Marseilles and single vessels from tiny harbours along the northern and western coasts. Patriotism and hunger combined to force men to go to sea in this way.

At the same time that this attack had been launched on enemy trade, the Convention tried to ensure the continuation of French commerce by opening the colonial trade to Americans on 19 February.[11] The British countered this by restating the Rule of the War of 1756 which decreed that no neutral should be allowed to engage in trade in wartime that was denied him in peace.[12] On 1 March the Convention banned the import of all British goods and decreed that from 1 April all items imported into France would have to be accompanied by a certificate of origin signed by a French consul. At the same time efforts were made to keep the coasting trade open by organising convoys under the protection of one or more small naval warships. This proved impossible. In March for example, no ships could be found to carry coal from the mines at Littry to Dunkirk.[13] The agents of the state who needed coal to make cannon at Dunkirk were forced to transport coal via Granville, which entailed a longer journey by cart from the mines to the sea. The shortage of ships also made the grain crisis worse and British naval patrols stopped imports of grain by sea. This helped to force the Convention to attempt to impose a maximum price on grain sales in June after detailed considerations in the previous two months.[14] This is the period when popular fear of famine helped the Jacobins to overthrow the Girondins. At times the fear was not fully justified; at Marseilles where the fear of famine was strong, a stream of small boats arrived from Genoa and during the summer wheat also arrived from Sète, probably from the Barbary States.

The halting of commerce-raiding by the Convention in the summer caused widespread distress, because it removed a form of livelihood. The Convention wanted to strengthen the navy and stopped privateering so that seamen could be recruited to provide naval crews. But there were large numbers of men at Dunkirk and by no means all could be found employment in this way. At Dunkirk 1,449 ships had entered the port in 1789 and the fisheries had employed between 15,000 and 16,000 seamen.[15] Another 5,000 - 6,000 men had been employed in processing tobacco that had been sent to Germany, Switzerland and northern Italy. As these trades collapsed under the embargo so too did the industries which had relied on imported raw materials. Other ports suffered as their trade and commerce-raiding also came to a halt. In the summer the fall of the Girondins was followed by the outbreak of the Federalist revolts, accompanied by the Terror, in many parts of France and in the repression which followed popular vengeance was meted out to many of the richer merchants. In Marseilles and Bordeaux in particular they were regarded as the leaders of the opposition. The revolutionary tribunals also considered that they should provide funds to support the revolutionary army and employment for the starving workmen.[16] These measures, together with other forms of punitive taxation, collectively destroyed the economic power of the leading merchants or forced them to flee.

But these measures did not provide food for the population. The Convention unwillingly passed legislation fixing the prices of grain in April but this measure did not command universal support and was difficult to enforce. Under pressure from the Enragés and disorders in Paris in June a law was passed the following month forbidding hoarding. By this time there was already a shortage of food in Paris - the result of food supplies for the capital being raided in Normandy on their way to the capital. On 27 July a law was passed once again forbidding hoarding and any attempt to combine to fix prices. This law specified that merchants holding stocks of primary necessity - a long list which included not only basic food but also a variety of raw materials - should report these to agents appointed by the Convention. These agents were also empowered to search property for these commodities and fix prices if the merchants refused to do so. The penalty for breaking this law was death. But the Convention shrank from decreeing prices for all commodities. Such a measure was in any case difficult to enforce and did not command universal support. The famine which followed changed the nature of government and placed the merchants in even greater difficulties. It was becoming clear by the end of April that the havest would be poor, partly because of draught and partly because many peasants had abandoned their land. On 9 August the Convention decreed that *greniers d'abondance* should be created to store grain for general use, and an attempt was made to estimate the likely size of the harvest. This was followed by a tax on grain and in September discussions were held on the creation of a scale of maximum prices for a wider range of articles. In October these were imposed by a new law, though merchants were given twelve days grace to organise their affairs.[17] The effect of this Maximum was to force merchants to sell their goods at a heavy loss and prices were set at a half to a third of those which had been in current use before the law was passed. It was soon followed by other measures: requisitioning of stocks, the suppression of the *réserve familiale* and the introduction of ration cards for meat and bread. Other commodities followed, including oil, soap, sugar and salt and general rationing was introduced; this put the control of trade into the hands of revolutionary committees and municipalities.[18] This brought commerce to a halt. Food shortages remained severe and at Marseilles the stocks of corn were lower than in 1793.[19]

In an effort to establish a new and more efficient means of organising trade a commission was created which in three and a half months had drawn up a new table of maximum prices. This showed the prices that goods had been sold for in 1790, the new proposed prices which represented an increase of a third and an allowance for the cost of transport. It also included an allowance to wholesale and retail merchants which amounted to another ten per cent.[20] The law on hoarding and price fixing was eased by ending the death penalty; retail merchants were exempted and only wholesale merchants continued to face stiff penalties. In Germinal Year II (March-April 1794) the revolutionary army was also suppressed. Efforts were also made to revive trade by a series of decrees passed at the end of Ventôse (March) which allowed the export of primary commodities, though merchants were ordered to exchange their foreign currency and bills of exchange for *assignats* which amounted to a loss of 50 per cent.[21] Coffee, sugar, brandy and wine as well as luxury goods in warehouses at the ports could all be exported and the embargo on foreign ships was lifted. This allowed neutral vessels, which had been in French ports since the spring of 1793, to return with cargoes. But the Committee of Public Safety was not concerned solely with reopening trade for the benefit of the population. The Committee also wanted to mobile the stocks of commodities which could be exported and raise money to buy food and war supplies. At Bordeaux there were many merchants with family connexions with Hamburg, Holland and elsewhere in northern Europe. An agency was formed to organise the shipment of commodities, but the plan failed. It is now clear that it could not have produced the grain which was so badly needed; the Dutch took vigorous measures to stop provisions being exported to France.[22] It had been assumed that large stocks of wine and other goods were stored at Bordeaux, but much had already been requisitioned by the army and hospitals.[23] A similar agency was created at Sète , but this was not successful either.[24] The Committee of Public Safety was attempted to raise money through a voluntary loan, but although it produced over five million *livres* much of this was in the form of *assignats* of little real value. Exports produced another four millions and bills on foreign houses two more.[25] At the same time merchants were still unpopular; at Bordeaux there was some anti-Semitism and they were accused of hoarding grain.[26] Bordeaux merchants demonstrated their loyalty to the Revolution by making a generous contribution to the loan, but it cost them around 30 million *livres*.[27]

Under these conditions - commercial uncertainty, unpopularity and lack of funds - it is hardly surprising that commerce was virtually at a standstill in Year

II. Conditions were not better in Amsterdam; in March Herzog, a merchant, wrote to Bourcard a merchant at Nantes, that trade was stagnant.[28] The records of Benoît Bourcard, a merchant of Swiss origin, who had settled at Nantes before the Revolution, shows that his total profit in this (revolutionary) year amounted to 20 *livres* and his expenses to 545 *livres* 12 *sous* 2 *denier*.[29] The decision of the Committee of Public Safety to end the privileges of the free ports on 11 Nivôse Year II (31 December 1794) on the grounds that they were incompatible with the principal of national unity, can have made little difference in the light of economic stagnation.[30] 1794 also saw the beginning of another period of serious food shortage that continued to September 1796.[31] The general lack of food effectively destroyed any hope of a commercial recovery, for although prices were controlled by a third Maximum law most people, especially in the north where the conditions were most severe, were concerned primarily with survival. Conditions in Year III were little better, and it is likely that the Committee of Public Safety raised the embargo on privateering on 23 Thermidor Year III (15 August 1795) partly to try and give men the chance to seize food from foreign ships as well as reopening the attack on enemy shipping.

Initially the results from these new regualations were unimpressive: only twelve ships sailed from Dunkirk and one each from Bayonne, Brest, Calais, Le Havre, Nantes, Roscoff, Socoa and St Jean-de-Luz. Dunkirk's dominance reflects the desperation at a port isolated from the main supplies of grain. The ships which did put to sea were under-manned -the average was lower than at any other time during the war - and the majority were fishermen or foreigners who were not listed in the *Inscription Maritime*. The absence of St Malo is more striking; it can be explained by the naval demand for seamen that had temporarily stripped the port of trained men. The general economic collapse had also played its part; many had gone inland to forage for food or join the bands of lawless men who used the forests to prey on travellers and isolated communities.

In the autumn economic life at the ports was virtually at a standstill. On the Amsterdam exchange the *assignat* had fallen to 2 per cent of its value by the end of June and continued to decline thereafter. It was quoted in the *Nederlandsche Mercurius* between February and May 1796 at between 0.2 and 0.5 per cent.[32] In Vendémiaire Year IV (October 1795) Bourcard received news from another merchant, Louis Biré, that only one shop was open in Bordeaux and that a mutual friend, Palme, could not pay the interest on a loan.[33] Merchants were so short of any form of acceptable currency or bills of exchange that a number tried to barter, or at least, to settle outstanding debts in kind. This however only created new difficulties because it was impossible to agree values for commodities. The pattern of trade also began to break down. Hitherto merchants throughout France had received colonial goods via Bordeaux and Nantes but in October Bourcard was told by the Lyons firm of Rubichon père that the company would be opening an office in Hamburg under the name Eugène Rubichon.[34] When Senn, Bidermann et Cie. of Paris collapsed a new company was formed with headquarters in Paris and a branch in Ostend.[35] This reveals the way in which neutrals, particularly Americans, had switched from Bordeaux and Nantes to the ports of north east Europe. They had done this partly because of the decline of the French market but also because British warships were unlikely to interfere with neutral shipping entering and leaving Hamburg. Much of this shipping also traded with British ports under false papers and it was in British interests to leave these ships alone. Hamburg was popular because it provided access to important European markets through an extensive road and river network. From the point of view of French merchants at the Atlantic ports the most serious aspect was that the Americans were able to sell their colonial goods for lower prices than the French.[36] In any case, while the *assignats* were still legal tender, few foreign merchants wanted to trade with France.

During the winter of 1795-6 inflation reached its peak and in October the value of the hundred franc *assignat* fell to 15 sous.[37] Prices rose by the hour, the printing presses released floods of notes - 39 billion francs were printed in four months, which doubled the number in circulation, and a moratorium was announced to save creditors from ruin. Finally on 30 Pluviôse Year IV (19 February 1796) *assignats* were abolished as legal tender. There followed an attempt to create an alternative form of currency, the *mandat territorial*, but by July this had been abandoned. Conditions in the countryside were appalling; there was little food, banditry was rife and over 10,000 deaths were reported in the department of the Seine alone.[38] But in the summer, when it was evident that the *mandat territorial* would have to be abandoned, metallic currency could now be resumed on a firmer foundation, though it was accompanied by a sharp fall in prices as deflation replaced the former runaway inflation. Under these new conditions commercial confidence began to return, and the evidence of Bourcard's correspondence shows that throughout France merchants once again began to tender for trade with houses that they only knew from heresay.[39] This new sense of optimism helps to explain the renewed interest in privateering: 26 ships were fitted out at Dunkirk 9 at St Malo, 5 at Bayonne and 8 at St Jean-de-Luz, besides a number at other ports. Interests at Dunkirk was motivated partly by the perennial problem of food shortage and of other commodities which commerce raiding seemed to offer. St Malo however had suffered very badly during the Terror; the principal merchants had been imprisoned or had suffered heavy losses; two hundred houses were in ruins and the population had fallen from 16,700 to 9,000. The manufacture of canvas at Rennes, Vitré and Fougêres, which had flourished before the Revolution, was in decay and the iron working and forges at Pontpéan, Paimpont and Martigné had been abandoned in 1795.[40]

Elsewhere an interest in commerce raiding revealed an appreciation that because it was so difficult to import commodities because of British naval activity and the unwillingness of neutral merchants to ship goods to France it was necessary to seize them from British ships. This led merchants to fit out ships elsewhere. Le Havre sent 20 ships to sea, Nantes 4, Cherbourg 6, Brest 17 and Boulogne - to some extent linked with Dunkirk - 11, while most of the other ports along the northern and western coasts sent at least one vessel. But the great ports of Marseilles and Bordeaux only fitted out 5 and 1 respectively, which reflects the continued uncertainty and the destruction of the great merchants. In the case of Marseilles the British naval blockade of the coast was so effective that only the small boats from Genoa could slip along the shore with any hope of escaping the naval patrols.[41] When there was a modest revival of confidence at Marseilles, it proved impossible to import goods because of the British naval patrols. In consequence, Sète emerged as a temporary entrepot for the commerce between the Mediterranean and more distant markets. From Spain came large quantities of *bouchons de Liège* - corks - many of which were shipped to Hamburg, fruit - both fresh and dried; raisins and onions also came from Spain, as did alum, coffee and leather. Some of this alum was later shipped to Denmark. Genoese ships brought starch, corn, olive oil, cork in sheets, soap - much of it shipped to Hamburg - sugar and pottery. American vessels brought refined sugar and tobacco. Other exports to Hamburg included tobacco and olive oil. Silk bonnets were sent to Spain, cloth to Genoa and almonds to Bremen, Hamburg and Sweden.[42] The crucial role of Genoa in this commerce put much of the trade of Marseilles into the hands of Italian merchants, some of whom later moved to Marseilles. There was little interest in commerce raiding there, since the French community had been decimated by the Terror and British trade was carefully protected by convoys within the Mediterranean.

At Le Havre the new interest can be explained by the lack of raw materials for industry at Rouen and Elbeuf. The Rouen soap and candle manufacturers needed animal fats which had formerly come from Russia and supplies of potash and pearl ash from North America and northern Europe were required by the woollen industry. Although the textile industry had suffered, orders for military uniforms had helped to provide employment for the depleted workforce.[43] Other industries were less fortunate.[44] Elsewhere in northern France there was more prosperity. The cotton textile industry Cotton textile industryof upper Alsace made considerable progress, stimulated by the demand for *Indiennes* - printed cotton cloth of a style first imported from India - and the proximity of the successful Swiss cotton industry also stimulated production and provided technical expertise.[45] Le Havre, the port through which much of the raw material for these industries was imported, shows a remarkable resiliance under these difficult circumstances. Its merchants sent at least six new ships to sea, and the exact information on date of construction shows that many of the others were no more than four years old. By contrast, sixty two vessels had been broken up the previous year, if the marine records are to be believed.[46] One feature of Le Havre however is that merchants traditionally drew their finance for ship building from shares which were sold over a comparatively large area of Normandy, concentrated on the district of Caux and at this critical time it may have enabled them to tap funds that had escaped the general repression. This method of raising money may also have been different from other ports where merchants wherever possible bought ships with money provided by commercial partnerships.[47] This practice of linking the financing of trade with the textile industry is important at this stage for it appears to be concurrent with a revival and modernisation in the fortune of the industry as well.

By 1797 the worst of the economic crisis seemed to be over. The famine had ended and business confidence returned, strengthened by the return to metallic currency and a recovery of demand. At Littry in Normandy the crisis which had closed the coal mines was over by Prairial Year V (May 1797), although metallic currency only reappeared slowly.[48] The recovery encouraged neutral ships to return to the Atlantic ports, though their owners were less willing to risk sending them to ports in the English Channel, where the British naval patrols were more active. La Rochelle was one of the ports to benefit from this new mood of optimism. In 1796 99 neutral ships entered the port and 101 the following year, an average of over 10 per month. The majority were Danish, Prussian 54 and American 30, with a handful from Bremen 19, Oldenburg 5 and Sweden 6.[49] This new concern, first discerned the previous year, was further encouraged by the interest shown by shipyard owners and their workers, sailors, marine officers and their families in privateering as a means of earning a living. To this was added the hope of merchants that commerce raiding would produce the goods that could be sold in the port and in a wider market throughout France and even further east. These factors combined into a powerful and emotive force that encouraged many to buy shares in these ventures, especially since shareholders had the first opportunity to buy prize goods from ships captured by their corsairs and could thus forestall their rivals.[50] Merchants were also encouraged by widely fluctuating prices early in the year which contrasted with the economic stagnation of the previous year.

These factors combined to encourage men to fit out more corsairs than in the previous year and Nantes temporarily emerged as the main commerce raiding port, both in terms of the numbers of ships fitted out and also in terms of the capital investment, for the ships were generally larger than at other ports. But during the course of spring and summer merchants discovered that they had miscalculated. The war and economic troubles of the past years had absorbed a great deal of capital and the market for commodities was quickly satisfied. Another problem was that whereas in peace merchants could estimate the quantity of goods to be imported and calculate prices, the entry of prize goods was irregular and no one could tell how much might be captured. At Bordeaux, which sent 16 privateers to sea in the course of the year, the irregular entry of ships caused prices to fluctuate and merchants were unwilling to buy.[51] Merchants at Nantes and Bordeaux who fitted out large ships were also anxious to intercept Portuguese ships returning from South America, but in Fructidor

(August) peace was signed with Portugal and at least one merchant was reluctant to invest any more money in commerce raiding.[52]

In the spring many men had organised privateering ventures and had bought the prize goods in the expectation that the economic crisis was over. By the summer many had learnt that the initial success had been illusory. Men who had bought goods found that they were still unsold when payment became due on the bills. Balguerie wrote to Bourcard in Prairial (June) that although calf skins were selling well business in general was very quiet.[53] In August there were more reports of bankruptcies and it was becoming difficult to know who still possessed credit. In September there was such a shortage of coin that it could only be obtained at a large premium.[54] Balguerie reported in Brumaire (October) that the best known companies were not selling any goods and that it had proved impossible to sell shares in the *Courier,* a Lorient privateer.[55] Although it was widely believed that the signing of peace with Austria would be a prelude to a general settlement, terms could not be agreed between Britain and France and the war continued. Commerce continued to decline at Bordeaux; goods were only sold at a large discount and merchants did not know whose business was still profitable and who was on the brink of disaster.

The same sequence of events, from optimism to pessimism, was repeated elsewhere in France. Boucard himself was buying calf skins in February from Lepecheux Frères of Laval and subsequently sent them to Bordeaux to be sold.[56] In May he was told that following the signing of peace with Austria trade was very quiet at Le Havre and in July commerce was virtually at a standstill at Lorient.[57] In September another correspondent, Jean le Ray, wrote apologetically from Brest that he was writing a bill of exchange on Bourcard for a greater sum than Bourcard's account on him because he was forced to settle accounts in paper, i.e. in a bill of exchange on a merchant house whose credit was respected.[58] In November Bourcard was told that there was little activity in the textile industry at Rouen and in December coin was again scarce and dear at Orleans.[59] The only way out of this financial crisis was to open trade with merchants outside France who were not affected to the same extent by the decline in French commerce. Bourcard was unusually fortunate, because his father Christophe had business contacts in Switzerland and from mid-summer Benoît was able to begin trading with the wealthy silk manufacturers Merian Frères of Basel, the merchants Gaspard Ott of Zurich and Meuron et Bovet of Neuchâtel. He could also draw on financial support from his father and from mid-summer he was able to extend his commission trade with these men, though by the autumn commerce was quiet in the east as well as in France. Bourcard was also helped by the decree passed in mid-summer that allowed prize goods to be exported; Meuron et Bovet specified English nankins from the *Confederation* prize in October 1797 because these were the best quality.[60] But Bourcard was less successful when he tried to sell prize goods in Amsterdam in November; his prices were too high.[61]

Merchants at ports on the Atlantic coast were able to send goods to northern

Europe on neutral ships and could thus dispose of prize goods more easily than at ports in the English Channel. There were also French ships that sailed in the guise of neutrals: the *Jeune Heinrich* of Ostend sailed as the *Jounge-Heindrick* and the *Deux Amis* of Brest and *Martin* of Dunkirk both sailed under the Danish flag.[62] This facility of disposing of captured cargoes and ships helped to explain the continued interest in privateering in 1798: Nantes 37 ships, Bordeaux 25, and Bayonne (where commerce raiding reached its peak) with 45 ships. Dunkirk still dominated the English Channel ports with 41 and 24 went from St Malo. Between 1798 and 1800 quasi-war with the United States hindered any further recovery in the south west, because it halted much of the colonial trade. But the American ships continued to sail with these goods to Hamburg and merchants in eastern France were able to obtain goods via Strasbourg more cheaply than from Nantes or Bordeaux.[63] The earlier crisis had removed the less stable merchants; those that remained were able to build an adequate business out of selling on commission or, like Bourcard, exploited markets outside France. Reports reached Bourcard in 1798 aand 1799 from Bordeaux, Lyons, Belfort, Tours, La Rochelle and elsewhere which reported the familiar pattern of caution, a little trade and much uncertainty. Only 36 ships arrived at Le Havre in 1798-1800 and 90 at Dunkirk, of which 25 were Danish, 12 had come from another foreign port and the remaining 47 were French.[64] Some merchants took the opportunity to send goods *en guerre et marchandise* to Saint Domingue in 1798 when the British withdrew and the experienced Etienne Coulon of Lorient claimed that a merchant should be able to make at least ten per cent profit on such a voyage.[65] These hopes proved illusory; the demand for large quantities of goods did exist on Saint Domingue but most of the ships that were sent fell into British hands on their outward or return voyage. Merchants found that it was safer to concentrate on European trade and that by widening the scope of their commerce there they were able to stay in business.[66] Whether they were able to match their earlier success is hard to say; all accounts from 1790 had been distorted by inflation. Other merchants retired to country estates and waited for the war to end. The last years of the war brought renewed problems. In 1799 France was again at war with Austria, Russia, Britain, Turkey and Naples and had had to contend with a serious uprising in Belgium in the previous autumn. To meet the desperate shortage of money - the state was effectively bankrupt - a new forced loan was levied but this only produced about one third of the amount anticipated. This was partly because commerce was still at a low level, partly because of profound distrust of the government and partly no doubt because Ramel de Nogaret, the new Finance Minister, had introduced new forms of taxation and was also collecting unpaid taxes. In 1800 famine again reached almost national proportions and gave rise to disorders along the main roads which again interfered with commerce. A German visitor to Bordeaux in August 1801, Lorenz Meyer, noted that the river was full of shipping from America and northern Europe. But he also considered that the loss of privateers had been a heavy blow to the port.[67] At La Rochelle the position was worse; only one French ship entered in 1800 and one in 1801.[68]

The Peace of Amiens brought a temporary recovery. Although it lasted a little over a year this was a period of great activity for merchants as they tried to meet the demand for commodities which the war and privation had suppressed. At Bordeaux, for example, 208 ships were fitted out for the colonies, which was almost as many as during the last days of the Ancien Régime.[69] At Elbeuf peace brought renewed prosperity to the region with the recovery of the textile industry as supplies of Spanish wool again became freely available. When Napoleon visited the town in Brumaire (October), he was pleased with what he saw and received thanks for the peace.[70] This was the scene in France during the relatively short Peace of Amiens. Merchants may have realised that it was likely to be of limited duration and a number at Nantes and Bordeaux opened direct links with American ports. One lesson of the Revolutionary War had been that colonial produce could only reach France on American ships, and the trade also provided excellent cover for illegal activities, since the origin of the goods which passed through American ports was hidden by the nationality of the ship which carried them from there. The experience of the Revolutionary War had also shown that in general the British government did not try to interrupt American trade with Europe, partly because Britain did not want to run the risk of war with the United States but also because Britain herself benefitted from American commerce. The return to prosperity continued after the renewal of the Anglo-French conflict in 1803. The peace had allowed merchants to rebuild their stocks of colonial and American produce and trade with the Americans continued after war had been declared. The Consulate also recognised the part that American ships had come to play in French commerce and allowed them to participate in the French coastal trade. Honorat l'ainé, a neutral merchant who was engaged in trade with other French ports, habitually used neutral ships.[71] Bourcard received a letter from a merchant at Rochefort in Vendemiaire (September) informing him that he had permission to export goods from any port in the department to Bordeaux and Bayonne on a neutral ship.[72] Another wrote from Lille the same month that he had found a ship at Dieppe that would sail for New York.[73] He also said that the Americans had returned to their tactics of the Revolutionary War and were shipping goods via Amsterdam. Many ships had arrived and Louisiana and Georgia cottons were cheap and plentiful. Amsterdam was an ideal port for these goods for they could be transported easily and cheaply to markets in northern Europe by canal. Goods also flooded into Hamburg, Altona, and the small port of Tonningen - many from Britain - and so many ships entered Danish ports that at times Hamburg was relegated to third place.[74]

This prosperity could not last. Even without war the boom would have been followed by a decline. By February 1804 it was evident that merchants at the Atlantic ports were becoming more cautious. At Bordeaux Saint Domingue coffee was beginning to sell well and Havana sugar was popular, as was indigo from Ile de France and Louisiana. But none of the merchants wanted to hold large stocks and consumption had in any case fallen.[75] Large imports of American goods via neutral ports hastened the decline. In Germinal (April 1804), Nicolas Fessart at Paris told Bourcard that so many American ships had arrived that the market for colonial goods was glutted. Trade was at a standstill, partly because demand was satisfied, partly because merchants had lost their nerve and partly because of political considerations.[76] For merchants at the Atlantic ports the only way to counter this diversion of commerce to north eastern Europe was to open direct links with American merchants. One wrote from Norfolk, Virginia in October 1804 that he had discussed trade with the leading houses and was able to quote prices for tobacco, flour, sugar and cotton. Bourcard had already opened negotiations to ship goods direct from Louisiana and communications with Philadelphia were apparently so regular that it was possible to insure ships there.[77] In the autumn the British naval blockade at the eastern end of the English Channel forced many ships to go to St Malo. This blockade had begun with the closure of the Elbe and Weser in June 1803 as a counter to the French occupation of Hanover and the district of Ritzbuttel.[78] In July 1804 the blockade was relaxed to allow coasting trade between the Elbe, Eider, Weser and Jade in neutral vessels and the blockade was raised in October 1805 after the French evacuated Ritzbuttel. The blockade was again imposed from May to October 1806.[79] This blockade increased the pressure on storage space and a merchant at Dinan, approximately 14 miles inland, offered his own warehouses and those of his brother at Cherbourg to merchants seeking to store their goods.[80] Bourcard found that although he could now obtain goods more easily, demand fluctuated. He tried to widen his sales but when he approached Swiss manufacturers he discovered that they were not used to American cotton. Geilinger und Graff, to whom Bourcard offered a sample of Georgia cotton, returned it with the comment that it appeared to be of very ordinary quality and was not popular in Winterthur. A good quality Levant was preferred and was freely available from 'the North', i.e. Hamburg and Amsterdam.[81] It was also possible to exploit the continued continental peace by developing commerce with the German states. Bourcard began trading in Ile de France indigo with Gscheiden und Krimmel at Augsburg in the autumn and the German firm also showed an interest in Georgia and Louisiana cottons and Spanish indigo.[82] Payment was to be by bills drawn on Fulchiron et Cie. of Paris. At ports on the Atlantic coast new opportunities for commerce raiding opened with Spain's declaration of war against Britain. Until that point trade with Spain had been interrupted in October and exports of grain and flour from Bordeaux had been forbidden by the prefect early in December.[83] Spain's declaration of war opened the prospect of supplying grain to the Spanish towns, although it was difficult to transport as most of the carts had been requisitioned. It was not difficult to ship the corn from Nantes; there were sufficient neutral ships and it was possible to disguise cargoes as Prussian by sending them on Prussian account with a certificate signed by the Prussian consul and apparently destined for Lisbon. Insurance would cost 15¼ per cent, reduced to 10¼ per cent for safe arrival, though it is possible that insurance rates at Santander were lower.[84]

During 1805 and much of 1806 trade continued in the same manner. It was relatively easy to send goods from Oporto and Lisbon to Emden, Hamburg or one of the other neutral ports in northern Europe and to divert wool to the textile industry of Rouen. But it was hard to make a profit from this. It was easier and cheaper for merchants and manufacturers elsewhere in France to obtain goods from Amsterdam, Hamburg or Ostend than pay the additional costs of illegal shipment from Portugal and the overland carriage or Rhine transport via Strasbourg. Boucard's commission trade is a useful barometer for commercial activity at Nantes and elsewhere on the Atlantic coast. His profit and loss account shows loses of 18,418 fr., 7 fr., and 14,976 fr. for 1805, 1806 and 1807.[85] It was against this uncertain background that Bourcard tried to continue trading. In September 1805 in a letter to C.F. Koch in Emden, Bourcard first referred to cotton for the account of Martin et Cie. of Rouen and then asked for three unsigned letters to be sent dated 1 March, 2 April and 16 August ordering these consignments. He also asked for five other letters dated 17 March, 16 April, 20 May, 26 June and 30 August stating that goods consigned to Lisbon had been sent on the *Hermione*, Captain Pool.[86] The following February Bourcard was able to offer a range of cottons, including Cayenne, Georgia short staple and Bahia to a firm in Aarau and in the same month told another in Linzburg that trade in cotton had been depressed for a long time.[87] This shows that supplies of cotton had been arriving at Lisbon from the United States to avoid British naval patrols and were being carried north to ports in the English Channel and North Sea on a variety of neutral ships. At the same time much colonial produce was being carried in American vessels to Antwerp, though after a peak in 1804 the level of imports declined.[88]

This evidence shows that the textile industry at Rouen, including Elbeuf and the surrounding district, was not limited by any shortage of Spanish wool or cotton but by a shortage of skilled workmen, for many had been recruited into the Napoleonic armies. The textile master, aware of the difficulties of obtaining suitable supplies had in any case begun to use materials from a variety of sources: wool from France, Portugal, Italy, Bohemia, Moravia, Saxony and Hungary were used to supplement Spanish supplies and the cloth was sent to Nantes, Bordeaux, Lyons and Beaucaire.[89] Unfortunately for the workers in this industry the cloth had to be transported to markets by land and the high prices combined with Spanish protective tariffs hampered exports. During the spring of 1806 there was a decline in demand and workers were laid off at Elbeuf.[90] Economic prosperity was in any case very fragile and tended to be concentrated in those areas where raw materials could easily be obtained and the finished goods transported to a market. In the south there was a different picture. The fair at Beaucaire was in many ways an economic barometer for the commercial prosperity of Marseilles and its hinterland. During peace it attracted merchants from Spain and northern Italy, the Swiss and German Confederations and Holland as well as from France. During the early years of the Revolutionary War the troubles at Lyons, Marseilles, Toulon and elsewhere in the south and west had driven merchants away, but there was a recovery from 1799. Eighty-three ships had arrived at this river port in Year VIII, of which forty-five had been foreign, and the numbers continued to rise: 170 in Year IX, of which 68 were Spanish and 15 Ligurian, 217 in Year X but thereafter the figures began to fall under the effect of renewed war.[91] The imposition of the Continental System dealt a heavy blow to the fair; in 1808 there were only 4 foreign vessels and none in 1809. Total sales fell from over 41 million francs in 1805 to 31 million francs in 1806 and 23 million francs in 1810 when the closing of the Spanish market proved a heavy blow. Though there was a modest rise in 1812 the last years of the war saw a further decline and it was not until 1816 that recovery began.[92]

The Berlin Decree of 21 November 1806 and the first Milan Decree which followed inaugurated the Continental System. It stated that Britain was to be blockaded, that all trade with her should cease, British nationals and goods were to be seized and no ship would be allowed to enter a French port after leaving a British. This was Napoleon's response to the failure of the peace negotiations and the British Order in Council of May which declared that the European coast from Brest to the River Elbe was formally blockaded. It had a direct influence on trade, which had been relatively free up to this point, and again encouraged French merchants to fit out privateers. Until this date there had been little interest in commerce raiding because it had been easy to continue trading by using neutral ships and false papers. From November 1806 this was extremely difficult. The British naval blockade was enforced more efficiently - though British captains and admirals were often at a loss to know whether to arrest a neutral ship which they suspected of carrying French goods unless it was captured entering or leaving a French port. Unless they could discover bills of lading which proved the nature of the cargo it was difficult to prove a case against the master or owner of the ship. But the Berlin Decree did make the owners of neutral vessels more cautious and raised insurance rates. The decrees came at a bad time for merchants at Bordeaux, for they had been able, like Bourcard at Nantes, to send goods to Switzerland and Germany and Napoleon's Jena campaign had disrupted the Leipzig Fair. In November and December merchants complained that their trade with Central Europe would suffer as a result of the decrees.[93] Worse was to follow, for the British Order in Council of 7 January 1807 attempted to stop neutrals from carrying goods between French ports. Merchants were thus impeded by both British and Imperial decrees. To some extent their position was eased by the Imperial order of 4 February which allowed vessels to sail under Imperial licence between ports under Imperial control.[94] Shortly afterwards the British captured Heligoland and began using it as a base for smuggling goods into Europe.

This encouraged merchants who had formerly used neutrals to carry their own goods to attack them when they carried British. Between 1803 and 1806 there had not been more than 9 Dunkirk corsairs at sea in any one year; in 1807 there were 23. St Malo had sent no more than 6 between 1803 and 1805; in 1806 this rose to 15 and in 1807 the total was 19. By comparison with 1797 these were modest figures and reveal a general reluctance to engage in activity which was not only dangerous but also in many cases unprofitable. There was comparatively little change for the next few years, though Boulogne and Dieppe overtook Dunkirk in 1809-10 and interest in commerce raiding declined still further at all ports from 1812.

The years from 1806 to the end of the war were crucial for French commerce and industry. The Continental System virtually closed the ports on the Atlantic coast and isolated them from markets in northern Europe, as well as restricting the supply of imported cotton and cotton thread.[95] In October 1806 an embargo caught about 113 Prussian ships at anchor at Bordeaux; later many were sold to French merchants and in May 1807 they sailed under the Danish flag. From August this avenue was closed because Denmark was included in the blockade and the embargo of 19 August immobilised 109 Danish ships at Bordeaux.[96] In December American ships were also forbidden to trade with French ports. Early the following year it was clear that much English commerce was being carried by ships from Hanse ports and Napoleon took steps to try and stop this. In February, March, May and August he ordered the sequestration of ships from Papenburg, Oldenburg, Mecklenburg, Kniphausen, Bremen, Hamburg and Lübeck. On 2 March Holland annexed Kniphausen and suppressed its flag. However, though this made it difficult for British merchants to trade with northern Europe, it also stopped French merchants sending goods on the same ships and closed an important avenue of commerce.

Merchants had faced this form of crisis during the Revolutionary War but in 1806 the situation was critical for they were also cut off from markets in Central Europe because of Napoleon's military campaigns. The sale of corn in Spain, which had appeared to offer excellent prospects to men at Bordeaux, Nantes and Bayonne ended when the Spaniards rose in revolt in 1808. Only men like Raymond Durand, a French merchant at Barcelona from 1808 to 1814 who sold freely to the French and the rebels and engaged in large scale smuggling could hope to prosper.[97] In 1808 Nemnich, a Hamburg merchant, visited Bordeaux and found the port deserted except for a few ships and grass was growing in the streets.[98] Merchants could not sell their wine and were isolated from all markets. The collapse of trade had severely damaged all the industries associated with Bordeaux: only five of the glass works were still working and a company needed capital of 100,000 - 150,000 fr. to be able to stay in business for ten months.[99] Coopers were without work, only seven or eight tobacco factories were working out of the fifty which had existed before the Revolution and stocks of tobacco had begun to lose their flavour. Paper manufacturers who had made playing cards, books and the paper for commercial correspondence had also been bankrupted as the complex pattern of trade in colonial goods, wine, cod and ship building materials had come to a halt. Some goods continued to arrive at Bordeaux to meet local needs, but her position as a major entrepot had collapsed.

The picture was the same at Nantes. Before the Revolution it had been a flourishing port. In 1808 its industries were in decline and its population had fallen.[100] Corn, vinegar, wine and brandy, refined sugar, leather goods, linen, honey and wax from Brittany were all available very cheaply and the hats and printed cotton cloth formerly sent for the slave trade could no longer find a market. The wines of Anjou, Saumur and Tours were less full bodied than those from Bordeaux and the quality of the brandy was lower than it had been formerly. All pointed to a lack of demand. Nemnich's comments on Bayonne reveal a similar state of affairs, though the traditional links with Spain had survived rather better.[101]

The same year Napoleon conceived the idea that colonial trade could be maintained by small squadrons of fast warships that would evade the British blockading force and leave and return safely. This would serve to revive commerce in the Atlantic ports and sustain the colonies. He was wrong on both counts: the British force kept the three squadrons of Brest, Lorient and Rochefort Rochefport squadronin port. The following March the United States passed the Non-Intercourse Act, which stated that any French ship entering an American port after 20 May 1809 would be confiscated. Napoleon replied with the Rambouillet Decree which ordered that all American ships that had entered French ports since the Non-Intercourse Act would be seized, sold and the proceeds paid into the Imperial Caisse d'Amortissement.[102] But his action of expelling the American ships and severing links with the United States dealt a heavy blow to trade and forced him to consider repealing the Berlin and Milan decrees as far as the United States was concerned. In the summer he allowed French ships to take the nationality of Prussia, America, Holland, Denmark or one of the recognised Hanse ports and in December ships were allowed to fly any but the British flag. American merchants were offered licences to trade with France by the Altenburg letter of 29 August and French merchants were permitted to take out certificates of naturalisation, on the understanding that at the end of the war the ships would return to the French flag. By July there had been over two hundred applications and it was reported in August that fifty ships had exported 7,000 tons of wine and 2,000 tons of grain, flour and clover seed. Merchants at Bayonne, Bordeaux, Rennes and in Angoulême wanted the system to be enlarged to cover manufactured goods for export to north Germany and Russia and a similar number of merchants also took English licences, though these were only valid for six months. Many were able to take advantage of the liberal British licencing system to carry wines and brandy to Britain under papers which simulated voyages to Norway. English imports of brandy reached a peak in 1809.[103] By January 1810 one hundred and fifty one licences of the first type had been issued, of which twenty one had not been delivered.[104] When the system was reorganised in June another three hundred and fifty one were signed and delivered but it still did not meet commercial needs. A decree of 15 June allowed smugglers to use Dunkirk to export French brandy and manufactures and Dutch gin, but in return to import only coin or commercial paper. Napoleon's intention was to force Britain to import goods that she did not want and to export only bullion, thus weakening her economically. The measures were in many ways successful and smuggling was extended to Schiedam, Terveese, Wimeraux and Gravelines.

In July licences were given to Americans and in November Napoleon attempted to create a navigation system which would leave French trade in the hands of French merchants. He allowed colonial goods from French and Dutch colonies to enter free when they were carried on French or Dutch ships but when carried on American ships they had to pay one quarter of the August tariff. Napoleon also introduced a comprehensive agricultural and industrial programme which attempted to control economic activity by tariffs, legal prohibition, commercial treaties, loans and subsidies. New standards were set for industrial production, machinery was introduced wherever possible and the provision of raw materials was improved by naturalising foreign imports of cotton and by producing substitutes - beet sugar, pastel, madder and artificial soda - wherever possible.[105] Steps were also taken to improve internal communications and every effort was made to favour French merchants. This system of licencing was gradually extended to cover the whole of French commerce both in northern Europe and in the Mediterranean and later in March 1811 it was further extended to cover Dutch commerce. As in other cases, the ships were to be Dutch or French and were only to sail to England, though special licences were available for Baltic commerce. Apart from this licenced trade, business at the ports was at a standstill. Only a handful of neutral ships entered or left French ports with cargoes and virtually all goods were transported by land.[106]

Trade restrictions were eased in 1809. In February the Danish government ended its ban on the export of manufactured articles through Hamburg and Lübeck and restrictions on neutral vessels were eased. Shortly afterwards the French announced that they would allow Danish goods to cross the frontier into France. The repeal of the American Embargo Act in March also added to the popularity of the Schleswig Holstein market. Between June and December 150 American ships entered Tonningen with huge quantities of coffee, cotton, tea, dye woods and spices.[107]

This is the system under which Napoleon tried to break Britain's economic power. In many ways it was remarkably successful; 1810-22 forms a period of profound economic crisis for Britain and in 1810 the policy stimulated industrial development along modern lines in north eastern France. But the Trianon and St Cloud tariffs created a shortage of raw materials and the Fontainebleau decrees precipitated the economic crisis of 1810-11 in which the silk industry was the worst hit. One of the results of the policy was that Belgium and the left bank of the Rhine were annexed to the Empire and industrial development was helped by the exclusion of British industrial goods. The wool textile industry of

Reims expanded partly because of the initiative of a number of individuals such as the master weavers Ponsardin fils and Dérodé and partly because of these new markets. Ponsardin fils collaborated with the inventor Cockerill who made new spinning machines and their factory was working night and day in 1812. Dérodé introduced the making of larger pieces of cloth in the styles of Sedan and Louviers.[108] But Ponsardin fils was exceptional; the rest of the Reims wool industry suffered heavy losses in the crisis which hit the city in the winter of 1810-11 and after a modest recovery fell further in 1814.[109] Belgium occupied an important position within the French economic empire. The area Jamappes, Ourthe and Sambre-et-Meuse produced half the coal mined in the Empire and the textile production of Lys was only surpassed by Nord and Côtes-du-Nord. Woollen cloth production was also high and it is a measure of this success that the population increased from between 2.8 and 3 million in 1795 to 3.3 million in 1815.[110]

The areas which suffered most from the blockade were those which had traditionally exported agricultural surpluses and naval stores to England.[111] But it damaged commercial confidence over a much wider area. Bourcard did little business in 1811 and 1812 and made a loss in each of these years of 8,982 fr. and 2,426 fr. on much reduced trade. While the Napoleonic system produced a temporary prosperity for France before 1810, Strasbourg became important as the entrepot for goods passing into and out of the Napoleonic Empire. Strasbourg merchants had important commercial links wityh Paris, Lyons, the Midi, Mainz, Leipzig and Frankfurt as well as markets further east.[112] But the crisis of 1810-10 which affected most of western Europe and the depression which followed put a severe strain on relations between France and her allies. The military setbacks forced Napoleon to demand more men and levy higher taxes and the creation of a set of French tariffs led other states to do the same.[113] Industries such as the Reims textile industry, which produced high quality cloth for the luxury market could only proper when they had access to export markets. When overseas sales declined because of the British blockade the Reims cloth found a market in Germany, Spain and Portugal. These were the benefits of imperial expansion for French manufacturers. When this Empire began to contract, Spain and Portugal were closed and only the Kingdom of Italy remained. When that was lost the manufacturers waited for a change in the regime.[114]

The end of the commercial crisis in Britain coincided with the increased trade between Bordeaux and Britain under the system of licences. It appears from the records of cargo values that this commerce worked to Britain's benefit, though this may be distorted by the addition of duties of over 60 per cent.[115] Colonial goods formed the main category and although it is not certain that these expensive items were all sold it is clear that the merchants whose ships were employed made profits from freight charges. Another aspect of this trade is the way in which the English displaced the Americans, partly because the Anglo-American war made it dangerous for American ships to cross the

Atlantic and partly because of delays in allowing American ships to enter harbour and unload.[116] Nonetheless, Bordeaux imported over half of the goods sent from America in 1811 and 1812 and supported a more diverse range of commodities in return, including a high proportion of manufactured items. Imports of American goods at other French ports were modest and Bordeaux's dominance is emphasised by the large proportion of unrefined sugar, coffee and cotton which she received: 84.36 per cent, 78 per cent and 67.16 per cent respectively of French imports.

Imports of American origin in 1811 and 1812

Ports	Rome	Bordeaux	Bayonne	Nantes
Ships	10	32	6	2
Value, fr.	2,563,984	8,414,799	1,693,351	320,815
Ports	Rouen	Brest	Cherbourg	
Ships	1	2	1	
Value, fr.	223,489	98,614	508,474	

Source: P. Butel, 'Guerre et commerce: l'activité du port de Bordeaux sous le régime des licenses, 1808-1815', *Revue d'Histoire Moderne et Contemporaine* (1972), xix, p 142.

Imports at Bayonne, while more modest, suggest that the port was still relatively safe from British naval attack, while Nantes, Rouen, Brest and Cherbourg were not. More important in the long run was the way the Revolution and subsequent wars had enfeebled merchants who had dominated commerce before 1789. Few took any part in trade or privateering during the Revolutionary War and there was little interest in commerce raiding during the Napoleonic. Only in 1812-13 was there any interest either in commercial speculation, privateering or overseas ventures.[117] Bonaffé, one of the richest merchants before the Revolution, lost a great deal of money after 1789 and in 1802 sold his important vineyard and valuable commercial property to a Prussian merchant Jean-Marcel Maurin. Others, such as Abraham Gradis, retired to their estates. Their place was taken by new men such as John Lewis Brown, who was one of the most successful Bordeaux men in 1810-12 and who had a fortune worth over one million francs.[118] But these few personal successes should not obscure the fact that these two wars from 1792 to 1815 destroyed the great colonial trade, shifted the economic focus from the Atlantic coast to north east France which had access to cheaper raw materials and led to what amounted to pastoralistion of the former flourishing commercial and industrial area of the south west. The period was also marked by a decline in population and a financial contraction.[119]

NOTES

1 F.L. Nussbaum, *Commercial policy in the French Revolution. A study of the career of G.J.A. Ducher* (Washington 1923), p 75.
2 It is reflected in E. Lemaignère, *Les corsaires sous l'Ancien Régime* (Bayonne 1895).
3 D. Miquelon, *Dugard of Rouen; French trade to Canada and the West Indies 1727-1770* (Montreal 1978), p 15.
4 See for example the figures showing the values of goods imported at Rouen in the 1770's and 1780's in P. Dardel, *Navires et marchandises dans les ports de Rouen et du Havre au XVIIIe siècle* (Paris 1963), pp 548-9.
5 The course of events in described in F. Thesée, *Négotiants bordelais et colons de Saint-Domingue. "Liaisons d'habitations". La Maison Henry Romberg, Bapst et Cie, 1783-1793* (Paris 1972)
6 J. Kaplan, *Elbeuf during the Revolutionary period: history and social structure* (Baltimore 1964), pp 100-1.
7 L. Nicolas, *La puissance navale dans l'histoire* (3 vols, Paris 1958, 1960, 1963), i,320.
8 *Mémoires de Plucket (Pierre Edouard) de Dunkerque; ancien lieutenant de vaisseau et Chevalier de la Légion d'Honneur* (Paris 1843, new ed. Dunkirk 1979), pp 162-3.
9 'Flibustiers de l'Europe' - presumably the British.
10 It is unlikely that he was given the first letter of marque; it is probable that he was given the first for Nantes.
11 Nussbaum, *Ducher,* p 70.
12 The statement by Lord Mansfield, the Solicitor-General, is quoted in R. Pares, *Colonial blockade and neutral rights* (1936), p 180.
13 G. Lefebvre, 'Les mines de Littry, 1744-An VIII' in *Etudes sur la Revolution française* (Paris 1954), G. Lefebvre (ed), p 122.
14 For an analysis of the period see A. Mathiez, *La vie chère et le mouvement sociale sous la Terreur* (Paris 1927), pp 162-212
15 L. Lemaire, *Histoire de Dunkerque des origines à 1900* (Dunkirk 1980), p 317.
16 W. Scott, *Terror and repression in revolutionary Marseilles* (1973), pp 298-310; for Bordeaux see A. Forrest, *Society and politics in revolutionary Bordeaux* (1975), passim.
17 For details of the law and its introduction in Paris see Mathiez, *La vie chère*, pp 392-5.
18 Ibid, pp 507-8.
19 C. Carrière, 'Le problème des grains et farines à Marseilles pendant la période du Maximum (4 mai1793, 24 décembre 1974)', *Conférences de l'Institut historique de Provence* (1958), pp 60-1.
20 Mathiez, *La vie chère*, p 562.
21 Kaplow, *Elbeuf during the revolutionary period*, p 112.

22 J.- B. Manger, Jr., *Recherches sur les relations économiques entre la France et la Hollande pendant la Révolution française (1785-1795),* (Paris 1932), p 81.

23 For details, see P. Bécamp, 'Les relations avec les neutres au temps de la Révolution: l'agence commerciale à Bordeaux (23 mars 1794 - 29 janvier 1795', *Revue historique de Bordeaux,* (1955), pp 305-16.

24 R. Meyer, *Une agence de commerce extérieur dans l'Herault sous la Convention* (Paris 1946).

25 Bécamp, 'Agence commerciale', p 312.

26 Forrest, *Revolutionary Bordeaux*, pp 162-3, 197.

27 Bécamp, 'Agence commerciale', p 314.

28 Schweizerisches Wirtschaftsarchiv, Basel, Segerhof Archives (hereafter cited as Segerhof Archives), 420, F 17, Herzog to Bourcard, Amsterdam, 14 Feb. 1794. In September Philippe Lafon wrote to Bourcard that there was little dye at Lyons for the silk industry; Lafon to Bourcard, 4 Vend. Year II, 4 Sept. 1794.

29 Ibid, 420, D5, f 52.

30 Lemaire, *Histoire de Dunkerque*, p 365.

31 R. Cobb, *The police and the people; French popular Protest 1789-1820* (1970), p 261.

32 Manger, *Relations économiques*, Appendix IV.

33 Segerhof Archives, 420 F18, Louis Biré et Verdonnet to Bourcard, 23 Nend. Year IV.

34 Ibid, Rubichon père to Bourcard, Lyon, 29 Vend. Year IV.

35 Ibid, Senn et Cie. to Bourcard, Paris, 8 Germ. Year IV.

36 Ibid, Senn et Cie. to Bourcard, Paris, 23 Frim. Year IV quoted prices for Hamburg and Orleans sugar and Saint Domingue coffee. Since the latter was occupied by British forces, the coffee must have come via London.

37 G. Lefebvre, *The French Revolution from 1793 to 1799* (1967), p 174.

38 Ibid, p 195.

39 See for example Segerhof Archives F41, Veuve Beneat to Bourcard, Carhaix, 1 Brum. Year V; Balguerie Dandiron to Bourcard, Bordeaux, 15 Flor. Year V. This also marks the end of the Vendée uprising and in the autumn Danish ships began to reappear in French ports, 144 in Bordeaux alone. In Year V they brought goods worth 24 million francs to France and returned with 6.4 million francs worth of French produce; Heils, *Rapports économiques Franco-Danois*, pp 29-30.

40 L.Benaerts, *Le régime consulaire en Bretagne; le département d'Illeet-Vilaine durant le Consulat* (Paris 1914), pp 14-15.

41 For details of shipping which did evade the patrols and reached Marseilles, C. Carrière, 'Les entrées de navires dans le port de Marseilles pendant la Révolution', *Provence Historique,* (1957), pp 200-19.

42 Archives départementales de l'Hérault, L1148, Etat général des importations et exportations effectués par le port de Sète, An V.

43 Kaplow, *Elbeuf during the revolutionary period*, pp 118-9.
44 The decline of a number of industries in and around Rouen is also shown in P. Dardel, 'Crises et faillites à Rouen et dans la Haute-Normandie de 1740 à l'An V', *Revue d'Histoire Economique et Sociale,* (1948), p 62.
45 L.Bergeron, *'L'episode napoléonienne; aspects intérieurs 1799-1815'* (Paris 1972), p 201.
46 R. Richard, 'La flotte de commerce du Havre (1751-1816); (Etude statistique d'après les Archives desClasses de la Marine)', in *Aires et structures de commerce français au XVIIIe siècle*, P. Léon (ed), (Paris 1973), pp 206-7.
47 R. Richard, 'Le financement des armements maritimes au XVIIIe siècle. Un approche; le cas du Havre'. *Bulletin de la Societé d'histoire Moderne.* xiv sér., (1969), p 11.
48 Lefebvre, 'Les mines de Litry', p 132.
49 N. Charbonnel, *Commerce et course sous la Révolution et le Consult à la Rochalle* (Paris 1977), pp 39-42.
50 Bourcard sold prizes from the *Henrietta* in Thermidor (July); Segerhof Archives, 420 D45, f 88.
51 Segerhof Archives, F41, Balguerie, Dandiron to Bourcard, Bordeaux, 8 Pluv. Year V, 28 Germ. Year V.
52 Ibid, 10 Fruct. Year V.
53 Ibid, Balguerie, Dandiron to Bourcard, Bordeaux, 26 Prair. Year V.
54 Ibid, 2 Brum. Year VI.
55 Ibid, F44, 30 Pluv. Year V.
56 Ibid, F44, 30 Pluv. Year V.
57 Ibid, Leshure, Dorey et Emeruti to Bourcard, Le Havre, 8 Prair. Year V, Lehir Lafontaine to Bourcard, Lorient, 27 Mess. Year V.
58 Ibid, Jean le Ray to Bourcard, Brest, 3 Vend. Year VI.
59 Ibid, Pierre la Halle to Bourcard, Rouen, 17 Nov. 1797.
60 Nankins were a type of printed cotton cloth which had originated in China; ibid, 29 Oct. 1797.
61 Ibid, Mouchet, Boode et Cie. to Bourcard, Amsterdam, 30 Nov. 1797.
62 Charbonnel, *La Rochelle,* p 50.
63 Segerhof Archives, F44, Bodin Frères to Bourcard, Belfort, 11 Prair, Year VI, 30 May 1798.
64 Heils, *Rapports économiques Franco-Danois,* p 47.
65 Segerhof Archives, F56, Coulon to Bourcard, Lorient, 11 Prair. Year VII.
66 Bourcard developed trade with Parish & Co. at Hamburg, Jacob Dankertz at Amsterdam, Vincent Michaud Bull at Freiburg, Rheinhold & Weichsmann at Elberfeld, Geiger & Co. at Ulm, Jean Beaujardin at Ferrol and Cazelon et neveu at St Croix de Tenerife; ibid, E42, passim.
67 M. de Lapouyade, 'Voyage d'un allemand à Bordeaux en 1801', *Revue historique de Bordeaux,* (1942), p 171.
68 Charbonnel, *La Rochelle,* p 53.

69 P. Butel, 'Crise et mutation de l'activité économique à Bordeaux sous le Consulat et l'Empire', *Revue d'Histoire Moderne et Contemporaine,* (1970), xvii, p 533.
70 Kaplow, *Elbeuf during the Revolutionary period*, p 121.
71 For details of the commercial activity see H. Sée, 'Le commerce de Bordeaux à l'époque napolépnienne d'après la correspondance d'Honorat l'ainé', *Revue d'Histoire Economique et Sociale* (1933), xxi, pp 27-50.
72 Segerhof Archives, 420, F157, Faures, Veuve Chauvet to Bourcard, Rochefort, 4 Vend. Year XII.
73 Ibid, Faucille to Bourcard, Lille, 3 Vend. Year XII.
74 R. Ruppenthal, 'Denmark and the Continental System', *Journal of Modern History*, (1943), xv, p 7.
75 Segerhof Archives, 420,. F157, Fleury Emmery to Bourcard, Bordeaux, 6 Vent. Year XII.
76 Ibid, Nicolas Fessart to Bourcard, Paris, 25 Germ. Year XII.
77 Ibid, Veuve Garan Magagnos to Bourcard, Norfolk, Va., 6 Oct. 1804.
78 Ibid, Nicolas Fessart to Bourcard, Paris, 29 Fruct. Year XII, Faucille to Bourcard, Lille, 1 Mess. Year XII.
79 W.A. Phillips and A.H. Reade, *Neutrality; its history, economics and law, vol II. The Napoleonic period* (New York 1936).
80 Segerhof Archives, 420, F157, J. Gautier to Bourcard, Dinan, 26 Fruct. Year XII.
81 Ibid, 26 June 1804.
82 Ibid, 24 Nov. 1804.
83 Ibid, Gouze et Cie. to Bourcard, Bayonne, 5 Brum., 21 Frim. Year XII.
84 Ibid, 1 Nov. 1894.
85 Ibid, 420, D5, Grand Livre, 1806-16, f 7.
86 Ibid, E45, Bourcard to C.F. Koch at Emden, 15 Fruct. Year XIII, 2 Sept. 1805.
87 Ibid, Bourcard to Saxer et Cie. at Aarau, 14 Feb. 1806, Bourcard to Hunerwadel Frères at Linzburg, 14 Feb. 1806.
88 For the importance of Antwerp see K. Veraghtert, 'The Antwerp port, 1790-1814', in *The interaction of Amsterdam and Antwerp with the Baltic region 1400-1800* (Leiden, 1983), J.M. van Winter (ed), pp 193-9.
89 G. Clause, 'L'industrie lainière rémoise à l'époque napoléonienne', *Revue d'Histoire Moderne et Contemporaine*, (1970), xvii, p 582.
90 Kaplow, 'Elbeuf during the Revolutionary period', p 122.
91 P. Léon, 'Vie et mort d'un grand marché intérnational; la foire de Beaucaire (XVIIIe-XIXe siècles, *Revue de Géographie de Lyon*, (1953), p 324.
92 Ibid.
93 F.E. Melvin, *Napoleon's navigational system. A study of control during the Continental blockade* (New York 1919), p 13.
94 Ibid, p 15.
95 L. Bergeron, *L'episode napoléonienne; aspects antérieurs, 1799-1815* (Paris

1972), p 198.

96 P. Butel, 'Charles Fieffé, commissaire et armateur; contribution à l'étude du négoce bordelais sous la Révolution et l'Empire' (thèse du 3ème cycle, Univ. of Bordeaux, 1967), p 18.

97 The full account of his activities is in Y. Roustit, 'Raymond Durand, Commerçant à Barcelone (1808-1814)', *Estudios de Historia Moderna,* (1956-9), vi, pp 313-409.

98 For his comments on the port, see O. Viennet (ed), *Le voyage du Hambourgeois Philippe-André Nemnich (1809),* (Paris 1947), pp 84-95. For further details of the decline of foreign trade at Bordeaux see Butel, 'Crise et mutation', p 549.

99 Viennet, *Nemnich*, p 99.

100 Ibid, pp 84-5.

101 Ibid, pp 106-9.

102 Phillips and Reade, *Neutrality,* p 187.

103 F. Crouzet, 'Les importations d'eaux de vie et des vins français en Grande-Bretagne pendant le Blocus Continental', *Annales du Midi.* (1953), p 53.

104 Melvin, *Napoleon's Continental System,* p 133.

105 Ibid, p 234.

106 Heils, *Rapports économiques Franco-Danois,* pp 196-203.

107 Ruppehthal, 'Denmark and the Continental System', p 11.

108 Clause, 'L'industrie lainière rémoise', pp 582, 585.

109 Ibid, pp 588-90.

110 R. Devleeshouwer, 'Période de "take off" pour l'économie belge?', *Revue d'Histoire Moderne et Contemporaine,* (1970), xvii, pp 614-5.

111 Segerhof Archives, 420, D5, Grand Livre 1806-16, f 7. Bourcard also made a loss of 3,374 fr. in 1809 and 117 fr. in 1814 and his profits in other years were modest.

112 G.J. Ellis, 'Alsace and the Continental Blockade, 1806-13', (D.Phil., Univ. of Oxford, 1972), pp 58-60.

113 Ibid, p 7.

114 Clause, 'L'industrie lainière rémoise', p 594.

115 British imports of wine and brandy are discussed in F. Crouzet, 'Les importations d'eaux de vie et de vins français en Grande-Bretagne pendant le Blocus Continental', *Annales du Midi,* (1953), pp 91-106.

116 P. Butel, 'Guerre et commerce: l'activité du port de Bordeaux sous le régime des licences 1808-1815', *Revue d'Histoire Moderne et Contemporaine*, (1972), pp 141-9.

117 Butel, 'L'activité économique à Bordeaux', p 557.

118 Ibid.

119 See also Bergeron, 'Problèmes économiques de la France napoléonienne', *Revue d'Histoire Moderne et Contemporaine*, (1970), pp 469-505 and F. Crouzet, 'Wars, blockade and economic chnge in Europe, 1792-1815', *Journal of Economic History*, (1964), pp 567-88.

2 The naval war

The Revolutionary and Napoleonic wars mark a decisive turning point in European history. Earlier struggles had been conflicts in which professional armies and temporarily conscripted seamen had fought for victory which had often proved incomplete. The victors had been those left in possession of the field of battle and there had seldom been any attempt or incentive to destroy the enemy army or fleet completely. During the Revolutionary and Napoleonic wars the attitudes of commanders changed. Nelson, until his death in 1805 at Trafalgar, and Napoleon had both wanted total victory and were satisfied with nothing less. One result was that war was waged on a far greater scale than hitherto. Armies and fleets were larger and all Europe became a battle ground; states could not easily remain neutral and most from time to time were forced to become allies of France and follow Napoleon's dictates on commerce, law and political allegiance. At the same time Britain waged war at sea on a world wide basis. In the period 1794-1815, French and Dutch colonies fell one by one into British hands, which gave Britain for the first time a comprehensive control over commodities and markets all over the world.

At the heart of the conflict on the British side was a struggle to increase the revenue which industrialisation and expanding commerce provided. For this supplied the economic resources with which Britain paid for her navy, army and the large foreign subsidies by which the anti-Revolutionary and anti-Napoleonic struggle was intermittently maintained. The importance of Britain's trade was recognised by both sides and the French attempted to destroy it partly by commerce raiding of the traditional kind and finally by decrees which were designed to exclude British goods from Europe. Ultimately the measures failed though the margin was slim and 1808 and 1811-12 were particularly difficult years for the British economy. The figures for the growth in British trade reveal its crucial nature for the capital with which the wars were fought: imports rose from 39.6m in 1796 to 80.8m in 1814 and exports and re-exports from 30.1m and 8.5m to 45.5m and 24.8m respectively.[1]

The defence of this commerce against French attack was one of the key duties of the British navy surpassed only by the need to crush French naval power and the policy of convoy, first introduced during this period for overseas shipping in 1793, which became compulsory in 1796 and was renewed on the outbreak of war in 1803, proved an adequate defence. Whether the huge volume of British overseas trade was ever seriously threatened is debatable - one account puts the figure for the tonnage of British shipping at over one million for the war years - but contemporaries believed that it was in general well protected.[2] At the heart of the matter was the psychological question whether those in control of the economic resources of the country, merchants and financiers, believed that trade was reasonably secure in the face of an attack which was usually exaggerated. Contemporaries do not seem to have appreciated that the threat from French privateers was at its lowest in the early stages of the war when the French government placed an embargo on commerce raiding and conscripted seamen. The threat to British trade did not reach serious proportions until 1797 and gradually declined thereafter to 1802; during the Napoleonic war there was a slow rise to a peak in 1807-8 followed by a fall in the last few years of the war. Furthermore, the Napoleonic privateering never reached the same level as the Revolutionary. In consequence, in spite of the belief, which is probably erroneous, that almost 11,000 British ships were captured between 1793 and 1814, this was no more than about two and a half per cent of all British shipping.[3] This is closer to shadow boxing than reality and popular fears fed on isolated reports which were close to sensational journalism. Even the Board of Admiralty had no accurate picture of events within the French ports because they were forced to rely on the tales of smugglers for the eastern part of the English Channel, supplemented by intelligence reports from spies sent via Ostend or a Dutch port.[4] These reports stated little beyond the bare facts that ships were being fitted out, were under construction or were ready to sail, and they did not provide any clear indication of the crucial matters of size, armament, captain's name, number of crew or the date when the ship might be expected to sail. In any case, it is quite possible that the information was based on rumour and was inaccurate, as it was easier to write a general report that would supply information of a sort and maintain the supply of funds than risk arrest as a spy by seeking detailed news. The net result was that Admiralty policy as regards the number of privateers at sea was based on experience and inspired guesswork.

The main task was to maintain business confidence. London dominated British commerce; the centre of the colonial trade, the East India Company, the principal merchants trading to America, the Baltic and Russia were there, so too were the underwriters of Lloyds and the few outsiders who played a minor but significant part in marine insurance, in short the principal commercial interests. The result was that commercial representatives could, and normally did, approach the Admiralty for protection of their shipping and if the Admiralty failed, in the opinion of commercial interests, to carry out its duties the Board could be criticised in the House of Commons.[5] This close link between commerce and government was of particular importance in eighteenth century wars because it was the commercial interests which provided the capital for fighting the war. Governments had to keep the support of this diverse group or risk the collapse of its policies as funds dried up. During the Revolutionary and Napolenonic wars this support became even more critical than it had been earlier, for the demand for funds was greater. In consequence the Board of Admiralty provided defence for trade from the first year of war by the first Convoy Act and made this compulsory in 1798. At the beginning of the Napoleonic War the Convoy Act of 1803 again made convoys compulsory. So great was the quantity of shipping however that convoys could be provided only for overseas trade; the coastal and Irish trade was too numerous to be protected and in any case the straight-jacket of a convoy programme would have caused serious problems for the population through alternate glut and shortage on a large scale. These vessels were not entirely defenceless: warships cruising off the south and east coasts captured a number of privateers and coasting trade could join the outgoing and returning trade if the movement of the two coincided.[6] From a practical point of view the coasting trade was never as politically important as the overseas, and provided the losses to coasters did not reach dramatic proportion and interrupt the even tenor of life in the shires, no harm would be done to the government's standing. But the foreign trade was more important; investment was higher, more was centred on London and in some cases, notably the East India Company's ships, each one had to be carefully protected. Many convoys were also very large; West India convoys of up to 800 ships were usual, and the Baltic ones could number up to 1,000, though not all were British. The loss of even one convoy would have had a disastrous impact on the government's standing, much as the loss of the Smyrna convoy had done a century earlier.

The Admiralty saw its principal task as the destruction of the enemy's fleets and commerce defence was subsidiary to this. In one respect the two went together; the blockade of Brest was intened to check the squadron there but it also served to protect British commerce. The blockade was based on the principle, established earlier in the eighteenth century that England's defence depended on maintaining a fleet to the west, at the mouth of the English Channel, to watch the movement of the principal French squadron and prevent it entering and dominating the Channel.[7] The fear of French invasion was raised again during these wars and the blockade formed a principal feature of naval policy. For much of the Revolutionary War the blockade consisted of a small squadron of light naval vessels based on the Island of Ouessant, known to generations of British seamen as Ushant. The task of these ships was to watch the movements of the naval shipping in the dockyard and warn the commander of the Western Squadron if it appeared that the squadron was likely to put to sea of its likely strength. Meanwhile the rest of the Western Squadron remained in the sheltered waters of Torbay. The commander believed that this had the advantage of keeping his fleet ready for action while saving wear and tear on his ships, but it had the serious disadvantage that it encouraged a lack of discipline and inactivity led to disaffection. Officers tended to sleep ashore with their wives while the seamen were unable to go on land and when the time came to put to sea it was found that the fleet was lacking in training, discipline and effectiveness. The disadvantage of the system was revealed in 1796 when the French attempted to land an army in southern Ireland under the command of Wolf Tone. The attempt was made in December and it was only a series of gales which prevented the troops landing and which forced the French to call off the attempt. The British reaction proved that the policy was ill-conceived; news of the intended invasion failed to reach the Western Squadron until the French had returned to Brest. However, the policy was continued until 1800 when Earl St Vincent was appointed commander and instituted a close blockade. This radical change had important consequences. For the first time in the war the squadron was kept at sea close to Ushant while a screen of frigates and smaller craft watched the Brest squadron from a point just outside the range of the defending batteries. This policy had one other result: it was rapidly extended to the coast of northern and southern Brittany and the Atlantic ports. The purpose was to prevent any naval or other stores reaching the port. The blockade of Brest thus became the basis for naval patrols to interrupt coastal shipping and to check the movement of corsairs into and out of port. It was also the means of retaking their prizes, and was extended as far south as the mouth of the River Garonne and in the north to Cherbourg and the Contentin peninsula.[8] This blockade was continued after 1800 and remained the effective policy for the rest of the period to 1814.

The blockade had further indirect effects on privateering. At some stages in the wars French merchants were able to trade in colonial goods by using neutrals as intermediaries. American ships brought produce from the West Indies.[9] The produce was later distributed by neutrals, chiefly Prussian and Danish, to northern ports in the traditional way. For a time this worked well; American ships could carry French produce to American ports and re-export it under new papers which showed a different origin. Ships carrying sugar, coffee, logwood, cotton and other items were able to reach French ports because the Atlantic coast was not effectively patrolled by British naval ships until 1800 and while on the high seas could not be stopped if they had (false) papers which showed the cargo to be intended for a British or neutral port. The procedure was always risky and Britain, aware of fraud, tried to stop it by refusing neutral ships to trade with metropolitan France on the grounds that trade which was closed in peace time should not be opened in war. There was also trouble for French merchants when France and Prussia were at war and Prussian ships no longer came to the Atlantic ports. Embargoes were also placed on the movement of shipping from time to time to enable the authorities to obtain seamen, but the halt in commerce trapped foreign ships in French ports until the embargo was lifted or until the ships could slip out of harbour without a cargo.

It was the decline of this trade during the Revolutionary War which encouraged merchants to seek an alternative supply of goods by raiding commerce and merchants at the Atlantic ports were helped by the loose nature of the Brest blockade until 1800. Corsairs could enter and leave ports with relative freedom and risked capture only at the focal points of British trade, which were patrolled by British naval vessels. In the event this proved a poor substitute for commerce, because prizes arrived irregularly in port and merchants were discouraged from buying, partly because they hoped that more prizes would arrive and depress prices. At the same time there was a serious and persistent shortage of capital for investment.[10] The same was true of ports on the north coast of France, which lay within the area regularly patrolled by British cruisers. Thus it was factors within the French economy - irregularity of supplies from privateering and shortage of money - which influenced decisions regarding commerce raiding and not the British naval blockade, especially in its loose form before 1800. The result was that economic decline had forced many merchants to retire temporarily from commerce before the end of the Revolutionary War, while they anxiously waited for hostilities to cease.

The Napoleonic War, by contrast, produced extremes of commercial activity that were closely related to British naval activity. The close blockade of Brest instituted first by St. Vincent was continued by his successors and cruisers - chiefly frigates, brigs and smaller craft - patrolled the Breton and Atlantic coast. At the same time the fear of invasion from the ports of north east France forced the Admiralty to patrol the seas off Boulogne, Dunkirk and ports to the west and these patrols became linked with the cruisers of the Western Squadron based on Ushant.[11] Nevertheless, it was possible, at least in many of the Atlantic ports, to engage in trade with Americans on a relatively large scale, using American ships, as in the previous war. The links with American commercial houses had been made during the boom of the Peace of Amiens and continued when war re-commenced in 1803. British naval power, especially the close blockade from Brest, could have seriously interfered with this trade, but it was not altogether in the interests of the British government to do so. America was also an important market for British goods and Britain received most of the cotton for her textile industry from the southern states. It was when British naval captains, desperately short of seamen, arrested deserters on American ships at sea, that relations between Britain and the United States became soured. Thus it was not until the passing of the Orders in Council in November 1807 that matters finally came to a head in Anglo-American relations.[12]

French merchants were also able to continue this trade because of the widespread use of false papers. In an age when passes were simply poorly printed pieces of paper, forgery was relatively simple. Furthermore, many officials were prepared to sign documents when they could not be sure that the information, about cargo and destination, was strictly accurate.[13] The availability of false documents is one of the features of the age, when printing was widely available but the means of verification absent. It became the standard practice for neutral ships in European waters to begin their voyages in one neutral port and end in another, but to make an unofficial call at a French port on the way to load or unload cargo. Voyages from Portugal to Hamburg, using papers signed by a Prussian consul, were used as a cloak for illegal trading. There was comparatively little that the captain of a British warship could do unless he had sighted a ship entering or leaving a neutral port. Captains were unable to prove before the High Court of Admiralty that a ship should be condemned as prize without this information, or without the real papers consigning goods to or from a French merchant, or a statement that a bundle of papers had been thrown into the sea on the approach of the naval vessel. There were also cases of ships being 'neutralised' when they were in practice French or even former prize ships and merchants could hide the true origin of the ship by hiring a captain of the appropriate nationality. Even if the ship was stopped at sea and the captain questioned, the deception was difficult to detect, because although there were a set of standard questions which were put to the captain and officers, it was not too difficult to agree a common story in advance. The questions themselves, by concentrating on matters such as where the captain took command of the ship, whether he knew where it had been built and when, left loopholes for men to answer accurately yet at the same time hide the real purpose of the voyage, for captains were often ignorant of details of the ship's construction. Naval captains, faced by a lack of concrete evidence, seldom wished to present a weak case to a sceptical Admiralty court and face a counter charge for damages from the nominal owner if they failed to prove their case.

The consequence of this relative freedom for commerce was that French merchants were able to continue trading for the first few years of the war. But it was Napoleon and not the British naval blockade which interrupted this commerce in 1806 by the institution of an economic blockade through the Continental System. This self-imposed blockade brought widespread distress in French ports and Napoleon was forced to modify it to allow Bordeaux and other ports to dispose of produce through licenced trade, though under strict conditions.[14] The British reaction, expressed in the Orders in Council, tried to control trade to Britain's advantage and Napoleon was gradually forced to dismantle the economic restrictions.

The consequence was that privateering was linked closer to the state of French commerce than to British naval activity. Until 1807 there was comparatively little interest in it during the Napoleonic War at any of the ports, for merchants were able to engage in overseas commerce through neutral shipping. This is also a period in which the balance of French economic activity finally shifted from the Atlantic ports, whose rise had dominated the 1780's, to the north east of France. Because the trade in colonial commodities was in the hands of Americans in this period, it was they who supplied the French colonists with manufactured goods. Consequently the market for French-made items declined except for wines, brandies and provisions and the industrial hinterland of Bordeaux and Nantes, mostly composed of handcraft industries, gradually collapsed. Consequently Bordeaux, Nantes and the other Atlantic ports were no longer the focus for colonial trade as in the 1780's and neutrals, predominantly Americans, shipped colonial produce directly to Hamburg and other ports in northern Europe. This by-passed the former trade via Bordeaux, and produced a number of striking consequences. The Americans bought and sold colonial produce more cheaply than the French had done through Bordeaux, La Rochelle and Nantes and consequently Hprices in northern Europe were lower. In addition, merchants in Switzerland who had formerly bought from Bordeaux and Nantes now purchased goods via Hamburg and Amsterdam at prices that the French merchants could not match. When this elaborate commercial structure collapsed through the Continental System, merchants again looked to commerce raiding for revenue and interest remained high from 1807 to 1811 and declined in the year of Napoleon's invasion of Russia as the internal market declined and profits fell.

This analysis of the relationship between privateering and the naval war may suggest that naval activity had less effect on commerce raiding than the condition of the internal market and the availability of capital. This is overstating the case however. The surge of interest in 1797 during the Revolutionary War also needs to be examined in terms of the general condition of the British Navy. It cannot be purely coincidental that 1797 saw not only a great interest in privateering all over France but also, on the British side, two naval mutinies. One of the factors which influenced investment in commerce raiding was whether a ship might safely return to port with any prize it might have taken. While it was possible to evade the British blockade to some extent by using neutral ships, it was not easy to send French vessels to sea and to return safely to port. The naval mutinies changed the apparent prospect for commerce raiding for it appeared to Frenchmen that fewer British ships would be at sea to defend trade. The actual details of the Spithead and Nore mutinies are less important than the impression they caused among French commercial circles. The fact that the Spithead mutiny collapsed relatively quickly but that the Nore mutiny, which produced the 'Floating Republic' did not and seriously weakened Admiral Duncan's blockade of the Dutch fleet, was of profound significance for French merchants. The naval vessels which were most likely to capture privateers, whether off the coast of South West Ireland, in the English Channel, the Soundings or North Sea were the smaller warships: frigates, cutters and brigs on which living conditions were probably worst. These were the most cramped - the navy always carried more men than was necessary. Also, since they were not in the first line of the navy their provisions were often in the worst condition. These factors, combined with the perennial difficulties of overdue pay and the absence of shore leave, made life in these small ships less bearable than in the line of battle ships. At the same time these small vessels were ordered to cruise at sea in winter when weather conditions were at their worst and when the large ships were laid up in a sheltered anchorage.

However, most of these small ships kept at sea and maintained the defence of British trade contrary to French expectations. The main difference between life on the frigates and cutters and the battle ships was that cruising in the waters of the English Channel provided moments of excitement when a strange sail was sighted and raised the chance of prize money. The crew of a small vessel also formed a closer-knit community than that of a large warship and the regular routine of sailing in the English Channel was preferable to remaining at anchor off the English coast. This explains why, when the mutiny broke out, commerce was still protected by cruisers and during the year many privateers were captured. No doubt this came as a surprise to merchants who had confidently assumed that disaffection was rife everywhere in the navy and there was a prospect of revolution. These men misunderstood the nature of the problem; the root of the Spithead revolt was social - poor food, harsh discipline by a few unpopular officers and boredom. The cause of the Nore mutiny on the other hand was a mixture of these issues and political fervour of a revolutionary kind. It was impossible to tell from outside the navy which way mutinies would end and throughout the summer there was a fear of French invasion and attempts to resolve the matter with the minimum of bloodshed. Equally important, though equally unpredictable, was the way that Earl St Vincent, commander of the Mediterranean squadron, dealt firmly with the first sign of disaffection and prevented mutiny spreading there.[15] The restoration of discipline in the British navy and the high level losses among raiders deterred merchants thereafter, for many of the voyages which had begun with high hopes of reward ended with the capture of the ship by a British vessel.

This elaborate system of commerce defence through convoys and cruisers was based partly on decisions taken by the Board of Admiralty and partly on actions by the port commanders at Portsmouth, the Nore and elsewhere.[16] The prime means of commerce defence was by convoys, organised by the Board of Admiralty in response to requests from the East India Company as well as from interested groups of merchants such as the naval contractors who supplied the Navy Board with Baltic stores, the West India Committee representing the plantation trade and other groups and individuals. The dates of sailing were agreed after consultation or requests and the number and strength of the escorts was decided by the Board of Admiralty. At the same time it was recognised that storms and accidents at sea would sometimes disperse convoys. The escorts appointed to see the ships in safety to their destination could not protect those which became separated through no fault of the master. Yet these stragglers also had to be protected if possible and additional cruisers - generally frigates, cutters and brigs - were appointed to patrol the areas through which trade passed. These convoys and the cruisers whose task was to assist in commerce defence were concerned mainly with overseas trade. To protect the coasting and Irish trades other ships were appointed to patrol the south and east coast of England. These small ships were not appointed directly by the Board of Admiralty but by local commanders who were in any case in a better position to assess the local need.

The captains of these small naval craft, had one of the most thankless tasks in the navy. They commanded a variety of small boats, many of which were hired by the Admiralty from merchants at the beginning of the Napoleonic War because St. Vincent's ruthless economies had led many to be sold. Their task carried no prestige and many of the captains were lieutenants with little prospect of promotion. They faced a number of disadvantages. They were not local men and did not possess local knowledge, though they could take pilots on board when approaching harbour. Their opponents, on the other hand, regularly sailed in these waters where they had chosen to cruise. The captains of privateers were fishermen and commanders of merchant ships in peace time and often possessed a detailed knowledge of tides, winds and currents. Their boats, mostly small and medium sized merchant ships, pressed into service at the beginning of the war, were manoeuvrable. In the English Channel many carried the dipping lug sail which was a more handy rig than that carried by all but the naval cutters.[17] The crews of the privateers, though undisciplined, were fit and experienced young men, supplemented by a handful of landsmen and cabin boys whenever there was a shortage of seamen. The naval vessels, on the other hand, though manned by experienced seamen who were the equal of the French, were commanded by men who did not have the same local knowledge. The commander was not necessarily the man most fitted to pursue an agile enemy. However, if the naval commander was normally no more than competent and able to capture his enemy through the disciplined handling of his ship, there were also men in the navy who possessed the same guile and originality as the best privateer commanders. They realised that although their boats might, by naval standards, be sound and well found they lacked the speed and manoeuvrability of their opponents and set out to trick their enemy by a number of ruses. One was to pretend to be a merchant ship by showing a total lack of discipline and a casualness in handling the ship. The privateer commander was easily misled; the guns were hidden and most of the members of the crew were out of sight below deck. The corsair which approached was unaware of his mistake until he had approached within range of the naval guns. Then the covers were thrown off, the rest of the crew rushed on deck and opened fire on the French vessel. By then it was too late for the corsair to escape. It was a technique which was effective in the English Channel; in the Mediterranean the naval vessel lulled his enemy into a false sense of security by flying the flag of another state until the corsair came within range. Then the flag was run down and a naval ensign raised in its place.

In the Mediterranean the small cruisers had many opportunities to use this deception because of the variety of ships from Italian states, Malta, Spain, the Turkish empire and France as well as Britain and the Barbary states which were found there.[18] The duties of naval cruisers in the Mediterranean were also more varied than in northern waters. British commerce sailed under the protection of convoys organised at Gibraltar. There were fewer hostile privateers, and these tended to attack shipping from the weaker Italian states, which were virtually undefended, rather than the British which always sailed under naval escorts. There was some danger in the eastern Mediterranean at the start of the Revolutionary War when a small number of corsairs were issued with letters of marque at the port of Erakleion in Crete by the French consul. Their object was to attack the important trade with the island of Zante and the Turkish empire. These ships were however protected by escorts on the voyage from Gibraltar and returned with cruisers which saw them in safety to Gibraltar. From the standpoint of the navy the dominant issue in the Mediterranean was to watch the Toulon squadron and, in the Napoleonic War, to prevent the invasion of Sicily. This policy led to the pursuit of the Toulon ships when Napoleon invaded Egypt and Nelson's destruction of them in Aboukir Bay was the logical outcome. Elements of the Mediterranean squadron also played a vital role in the defence of Acre, which effectively blocked the escape route of Napoleon's army. Individual cruisers also prevented supplies reaching Toulon by sea by capturing coastal convoys and during the war in Spain attacked coastal batteries and signal posts as well as destroying coast roads and cooperating with the Spanish guerillas. On a lesser scale British frigates also attacked enemy corsairs and cruised off the focal points for trade when it was time for the British ships to return to Gibraltar in case any became separated from their escorts or sailed independently.

These isolated naval vessels were no more than adjuncts to the main form of commerce defence, which was the convoy. An indication of the size of some of these has already been given, and the figures for the increase in the value of commerce demonstrate the enormous size of some of the larger convoys. Yet they remained the best way of defending commerce. The main reason was that although the number of merchant ships increased - probably doubled by comparison with earlier wars - the number of escorts needed for the task of protecting them remained roughly the same. The reason was that the total area occupied by the new volume of shipping increased at a relatively small rate by comparison with the numbers of ships. Thus only a few more warships were needed to protect a vastly increased number of merchant ships. The organisation of this defence remained as it had been in earlier wars: warships patrolled the sides, rear and front of the convoy much as sheep dogs tried to control a flock and used their relatively greater speed to chase away corsairs.[19] The risk was that a naval vessel might be lured away from its charges in this way and leave a part of the convoy exposed. There was also the danger that a corsair would follow a convoy at a safe distance and cut vessels out at night or if they became disabled and fell behind. If the convoy was a large one the number of ships which could be lost in this way was fairly small in comparison with the total size, but it put a premium on effective patrolling by the naval escorts and on the discipline by the captains of the merchants ships. If either was absent losses could be much higher. Friction between the escort commander and the merchant captains was common; naval captains, who disliked their task, were frequently abrupt and overbearing and sometimes gave scant heed to the ships they were supposed to be protecting. Merchant captains also tended to show a scant regard for naval orders and were tempted to run from a convoy at night to arrive first at the destination and sell the cargo for a better price. It was to prevent this that naval officers were ordered to report infringements of discipline so that action could be brought by underwriters whose policy had been invalidated, but it was never easy to enforce.[20]

The navy also played an important role in restricting the commerce of northern Europe whenever this was felt to be benefitting Napoleon. In practice however the problem proved to be less clear cut than many imagined. In 1803, on the outbreak of war, the Navy instituted a blockade of the Weser and Elbe as a counter to the French occupation of Hanover. But it proved impossible to know what area was included in the blockading zone, in particular whether the Texel was included or not because government policy, and naval instructions, were ambiguous. In theory this should have damaged or destroyed trade which had formerly passed through the ports on these rivers, notably Hamburg and Bremen. It had one unexpected result: it interfered with important British commerce and had to be modified. That only meant that British merchants had greater freedom to trade with the enemy than the British government intended: Admiral Keith complained bitterly that British merchants were trading with ports where the French were constructing invasion craft. After the imposition of the Continental System and the Orders in Council the blockade of the North German coast was conducted in a way that was intended to benefit British merchants. The Foreign Secretary, Canning, asked the Admiralty to lift the blockade on Hamburg and Tonningen, because these were ports through which goods were able to evade the Continental System. The Admiralty's attempt to satisfy the demand for blockade and the need to allow British goods to be smuggled into continental Europe gave rise to a series of contradictory orders. The seizure of Hamburg in 1807 was to provide British merchants with a base for smuggling, and it is claimed that in the last half of 1807 no fewer than 1,475 small vessels entered Hamburg laden with British goods. The actions of British naval vessels off the north coast of Europe also helped restrict the French privateers whose captains were aware of the important British trade and tried to capture shipping there. The imposition of a formal blockade in May 1806 from Hamburg to Brest, and extended in practice to the mouth of the Garonne, coincided approximately with the decline of French trade in American ships and an interest in commerce raiding to recoup their losses.

The *de jure* blockade from 1806 and the blockade which preceded it also helped to restrict privateers by making it more difficult for them to set sail from their home ports. In practice it was difficult to enforce off many of the ports. Dunkirk was protected by an elaborate series of sandbanks, and since the marker buoys were removed as soon as war was declared and the batteries at the end of the entrance channel were powerful and fully manned, it was difficult and dangerous to try and maintain a close blockade. When the wind veered to the north the British vessels had to abandon their post temporarily to avoid running aground and this was the signal for corsairs to prepare to put to sea, and they could normally do this when the wind changed and before the British could return. Jean Bart had used the vantage point of the church tower to tell whether British ships were in position off the port and his successors were able to do the same. When these small craft returned they often approached close in shore, where the water was too shallow for the naval ships to go or waited until night and used their knowledge of local conditions to evade the British ships. While the invasion of Britain was being planned the navy kept a close watch on Dunkirk and neighbouring ports to observe the numbers of invasion barges and gun boats in the ports. This also restricted privateering. Similarly, coastal blockades of Brest and other ports which contained hostile squadrons further limited the opportunities for commerce raiding, even though this was not the main purpose.

It would be misleading to assume that all the vessels engaged in this activity were under the orders of the Admiralty or local commanders. One of the most useful craft in the English Channel in the war against privateers was the revenue cutter. The principal duty of these vessels was to prevent smuggling - a subject on which British opinion was divided because smugglers were one of the main sources of information about life and conditions in the French ports. These revenue cutters were fast and manoeuvrable and unlike the cutters in naval, service, were commanded and manned by men with great experience of navigating in the waters of the English Channel. Theirs was not a task restricted to wartime; on the contrary, they probably had less fewer duties in war, since there was probably less smuggling.

Naval campaigns overseas also contributed to the war on privateers, though in a less direct way. The capture of Tobago, part of Saint Domingue and St Pierre and Miquelon in the first year of the war demonstrated British naval strength while weakening France economically. In succeeding years more possessions of France and her allies or conquests fell into British hands: Martinique, Guadeloupe, St Lucia, the Saints, Marie Galante and Deseada in 1794; Ceylon, Malacca and the Cape of Good Hope in 1795, Dutch colonies in the East and West Indies in 1796, Trinidad and Madagascar in 1797, Minorca in 1798, Surinam in 1799, Goree, Curaçao and Malta in 1800 and Danish and Swedish islands in the West Indies in the final year of the war, when British power in India was also extended by the Wellesley brothers. Most of these territories were returned in the Peace of Amiens, except for parts of India, Ceylon and Trinidad, while Malta was 'neutralised'. After the renewal of war in 1803 many were recaptured. St Pierre and Miquelon, St Lucia, Tobago and Dutch Surinam had fallen into British hands by the time of the Battle of Trafalgar together with more Indian territory and others followed: the Cape of Good Hope in 1806, Curaçao and the Dutch West Indies in 1807, part of the Moluccas in 1808, Senegal and Martinique in 1809, Guadeloupe, Mauritius, Amboyna and Banda in 1811 and Java in 1812. This list includes all of the French overseas possessions, and though French merchants were able to some degree to continue to receive goods from these islands until 1806 by way of neutrals, chiefly Americans, the pattern of trade was disrupted and they were forced to look elsewhere for profit. Thus the capture of these overseas territories, many of which had supplied a particular need in France, tended to drive merchants towards commerce raiding as an alternative.

The naval blockade of the French coast also checked the flow of naval stores to Brest and other ports, though it is not easy to judge the extent.[21] Naval shipbuilding was probably largely dependent on supplies of Baltic materials to construct the ships and keep them in a sound condition. It is not clear how far this also applied to the commercial yards. The naval blockade prevented the movement of these essential stores to Brest and other French ports because these stores were classed as materials of war and neutrals were not allowed to carry them to French ports. At the beginning of war the lack of stores probably had little effect on commerce raiding because there were ships in good condition available for this purpose. However, from time to time these had to be repaired and the rigging, sails and sheathing renewed. It is significant that corsairs on the Atlantic coast tended to go to Spanish ports to be refitted, because stores were available there. On the other hand, they were probably more expensive and it was less easy to control expenditure, even though the work was placed in the hands of a merchant who was a friend or business associate of the owner.[22] But he had to be paid commission. This helps to explain how owners of privateers were able to keep their ships in good condition, but there were others who decided during the course of the war to build ships especially for privateering. These ships were designed for greater speed and had finer lines than the usual merchant ship. It is hard to know what timber was used to build these new ships, because supplies of seasoned timber were unlikely to be available. It seems that under these conditions builders turned to the wood which was readily available in France, which still possessed large forests. In one respect the merchant builders were more fortunate than the naval, for they did not require the huge, specialised timbers that were needed in the naval yards and ships could be constructed out of almost any wood. The only disadvantage of building a ship from a soft wood such as fir was that it had a very limited life but that was relatively unimportant to a merchant who did not expect the war to last very long. Other materials - pitch and tar, hemp and iron - were below the standards of the best Swedish and Russian but may have been perfectly adequate for the purpose of building a corsair. They were some supplies of iron available in the Nantes region in the form of small deposit of ore and the famous Indret foundry used this iron to make cannon. In consequence it was perfectly reasonable to be able to build and repair ships in the merchant yards for this purpose, although the cost of transporting goods over land instead of by river and sea made the task more expensive.

The naval war also posed the problem of manning, for as the war progressed it became more difficult to find suitable crews. As privateers were captured their crews were imprisoned and most remained in Britain for the rest of the war. Some officers were able to escape or were exchanged, but the Admiralty did not wish to return men to active service. Britain had the advantage that there were probably more seamen available and it was easier to obtain replacements, if necessary using foreign seamen, then it was for the French. The consequence for the French was that after 1797 many of the best men were in British prisons or hulks and they were forced to turn to anyone, even renegade British seamen, to make up their crews.[23] Shortage of men had always been a problem while the government tried to maintain its naval forces, and only Dunkirk had been able to draw on additional seamen through attracting Flemish who were not subject to the *Inscription Maritime*. St Malo corsairs were at a particular disadvantage because the Breton seamen were recruited into the Brest fleet in large numbers. The French attempt to maintain a fleet in being during the Revolutionary and Napoleonic wars contributed to the shortage of men for the privateers. A century earlier the French had abandoned their attempt to dispute England's command of the seas after the defeat at La Hogue, apart from small raiding squadrons, and this released many men for commerce raiding. During the Revolutionary and Napoleonic wars the French tried to keep their fleet in being, in spite of the defeats in the Glorious First of June (1794), Camperdown and St Vincent (1797) and Trafalgar (1805) and this kept large numbers of men at Brest, Rochefort and Toulon, although the navy was also short of the men it required. The consequence for commerce raiding was that it became progressively more difficult after 1797 to obtain the men required and it is not clear whether the seamen were quickly released when peace came. Both sides recognised that it might be no more than a temporary peace and probably delayed their return. When war broke out again in 1803 the navy swept up all the French merchant ships that could be found, much as it had done at the outbreak of the Revolutionary War and every war in the eighteenth century.

Seen from the point of view of the French shareholder in privateering ventures, the naval war made it extremely difficult to make a profit from commerce raiding, or even to continue with it after the peak of 1797, although conditions were easier in the second half of the Napoleonic War. There was a shortage of seamen, of capital to finance the voyages, of suitable materials to build and repair the ships and indirectly the naval blockade damaged neutral trade and drove it away from the Atlantic coast. The decision to maintain naval squadrons deprived commerce raiding of many of its potentially important leaders who might have been able to inspire a more permanent resurgance of spirit, though this is unlikely in view of the superiority of the British navy.

NOTES

1 These are computed or declared values; P.M. Kennedy, *The rise and fall of British naval mastery* (1976), p 145.

2 The figures for the clearances of British ships at British ports in 1792; G.J. Marcus, *A naval history of England; vol. 2; the age of Nelson*, (11), p 103. This amounted to over 13,000 entrances and a somewhat larger number of clearances; C.E. Fayle, 'The employment of British shipping' in *The trade winds; a study of British overseas trade during the French wars 1793-1815* (1948), C.N. Parkinson (ed), p 73.

3 Kennedy, *Rise and fall of British naval mastery,* quoting A.H. Mahan.

4 Most of this is contained in Adm 1/6023-40, Intelligence, 1793-1810, 3rd. series.

5 The scale of commerce protection can be gauged from the Register of Applicatiojns for convoy in Adm 7/60, 1795-1801, 1808-14.

6 For information on the methods of organising convoys, see P. Crowhurst, *The defence of British trade, 1689-1815* (Folkestone 1977), pp 72-3 and for the legal implications, ibid pp 96-9.

7 The Western Squadron hade been introduced by Anson in 1747, though its ordinary cruising ground at that point had been between Ushant and the Scilly Isles.

8 For details of the effectiveness of these patrols, see below pp 104-8.

9 Though the trade was subject to many interruptions; P. Butel, 'Crise et mutations de l'activité économique à Bordeaux sous le Consulat et l'Empire', *Revue d'Histoire Moderne et Contemporaine*, (1970), xvii, pp 541-2. For a more detailed study of the effect of changes in the nature of trade, especially of Bordeaux, see R.P. Crowhurst, 'The decline of Bordeaux, 1789-1815' to be published in *Business History*.

10 There was a profound financial crisis in France under the Directory; in 1796 a merchant in Bordeaux, Louis Biré, wrote to a friend in Nantes that trade was almost at a standstill, little business had been done at the annual fair and he was being hard pressed by his creditors; Segerhof Archives, 420, F19, Louis Biré et Verdonnet to Bourcard, Bordeaux, 20 Germ. Year IV.

11 See below, pp 95-6.

12 For the background to these orders, F. Crouzet, 'Groupes de pression et politiques de blocus: remarques sur les origines des Ordres en Conseil de Novembre 1807', *Revue Historique*, (1962), ccxxvii, pp 45-72.

13 In 1804 insurers gave their opinion that it would be possible to send a

cargo from Nantes to Bayonne on a neutral ship with papers signed by the Prussian consul stating that the destination was Lisbon, Segerhof Archives, 420, F157, Gouze et Cie. to Bourcard, Bayonne, 1 Niv. Year XIII.

14 This is discussed in Butel, 'Guerre etcommerce: l'activité du port de Bordeaux sous le régime des licences, 1808-1815', *Revue d'Histoire Moderne et Contemporaine*, (1972), xix, pp 128-49.

15 The ringleaders of the mutiny on the *St George* were tried, found guilty and hanged the next day, in defiance of naval custom; Marcus, *Naval History, vol.2*, p 99.

16 This process can be seen through the In Letters recording requests for convoys from groups of merchants, societies or companies (Adm 1), the subsequent minutes of the Board (Adm 3), Out Letters from the Secretary (Adm 2), especially letters referring to convoys in Adm 2/1097-1114, records of applications for convoys, lists of convoys and registers of applications to sail without convoy in Adm 7. Some information regarding the local activities of commerce defence with small craft is to be found in the letters from commanders of naval stations.

17 This is the view of Marcus, *Naval History of England, vol.2*, p 104. To check this statement would very difficult but an examination of the descriptions of privateers in the *rôles d'armement et de désarmement* in French archives and the records of captured ships in the papers of the High Court of Admiralty tend to supporft this.

18 This will be examined more closely in connexion with profitability, see below, pp 211-31.

19 The principle was the same throughout the eighteenth century; for an example of the attempt to protect the large West India convoys in this way, see Crowhurst, *Defence of trade,* p 191.

20 The issue was a complicated one in law wich gradually became resolved through the efforts of Lord Mansfield. For an explanation of the principal cases, see ibid, 96-100.

21 For more information on the blockade of Brest, see J. Leyland (ed), *Papers relating to blockade of Brest, Vol.1,* (1906), passim.

22 A typical example is that of the privateer *Adélaide* described in R.P. Crowhurst, 'The privateering activities of a Swiss merchant, Benoît Bourcard, at Nantes1793-1814, *Revue français d'Histoire d'Outre-Mer,* (1982), lxix, pp 225-35.

23 One example is the report in *Extrait des dispositions au Havre de l'équipage du corsaire le Custine* that Captain Cochrane paid a guinea to compensate sailors for treason that they were to commit against their fellow citizens, in Archives de la Marine, Cherbourg, 4 P3/17.

3 Privateering: the reality. 1793-1815

French commerce raiding during the Revolutionary and Napoleonic wars was less effective than during the Nine Years War and War of the Spanish Succession. The French had fewer ships at the end of the eighteenth century and the British, with a larger navy, were able to exercise a stronger and more effective defence of their trade. On the other hand the fear remained in the minds of British merchants that the French constituted a serious threat and the Admiralty had to maintain constant vigilance to defend British interests effectively. Fears of the French were exaggerated by rumours and the sighting of supposedly French corsairs off the English coast from time to time and the popular belief that the French ports were a hive of activity in which corsairs were being constantly fitted out and seamen enrolled for their crews. There was also the fear that every corsair was successful and that commerce raiding was constantly being encouraged by the arrival of rich prizes in the French ports. This pessimistic view was supported by the reports sent by English spies via Dutch ports which painted a similar picture. The result of all this fear and often hearsay evidence was that commercial opinion was often convinced that the coastal waters, especially off the south coast of England, were 'infested' - to use a contemporary term - with dangerous corsairs and that English commerce was exposed to attack. The reality was not appreciated: that comparatively few ships were at sea at any given time, that the attack varied considerably from year to year, and reached a peak in 1797-8 in the Revolutionary War and 1809-10 in the Napoleonic.

The basis of the British fear - for English merchants were not alone in their worry about this threat which was a legacy of earlier wars - was the exaggeration of the nature of the commercial war. The fear was certainly not based on any accurate appreciation of the real threat, and was fed by stories about the commercial war a century earlier when English commerce had indeed suffered heavy loss. The British fear was also based on a measure of respect for the men who formed the officers and crews of these private warships and whose knowledge of the British coastal waters was considerable. The knowledge that a handful of men was able to amass a fortune from commerce raiding and become national heroes in France: Robert Surcouf, Jean Blanckman and a number of others, raised the status of privateering in the eyes of the British navy as well. The good fortune of a few Frenchmen encouraged many to seek their fortunes in this way, hoping to emulate the heroes of the late seventeenth and early eighteenth century. The reality after 1793 was different. British naval power was greater, particularly by contrast to the French navy which had been seriously weakened by the desertion and persecution of the officers. The British also suffered from the misunderstanding about the strength of the French attack; there were fewer French ships at sea than in the climax of privateering, though as will be seen later, there were occasional surprises. In 1797, for example, the peak year of the Revolutionary War, there were more ships at sea from Nantes than from Saint Malo. The reputation of the former glory was, at least in this case, less important than the practical opportunities as they were perceived at Nantes.

Of all the qualities required for successful commerce raiding, the most important was imagination. The commercial war was above all a battle of wits between the British Board of Admiralty aided by the officers commanding the naval bases on the English coast and the commanders of privateers. Those who saw commerce raiding merely as a series of short, cross channel raids to capture undefended coastal shipping - which was not covered by the Convoy Acts - or cut stragglers from convoys, were the men whose ships were frequently captured. The more intelligent strategy was to seek an area of sea through which British vessels had to pass but where it was more difficult to protect a scattered mass of shipping. The intelligent captain's greatest asset was his detailed knowledge of the waters of the English Channel, the North Sea and the approaches to the British Isles, together with a thorough knowledge of the times each year when trading vessels set sail and returned to port, together with the course that each trade followed. One student of naval history has stated that many of the men on board these privateers were fishermen "with all the fishermen's inbred skill and resource for ascertaining his position - even without the aid of soundings - in darkness or thick weather; relying on the observation of certain sea birds, seals or fish, and, above all, on the colour and run of the seas".[1] But the coastal fishermen (as distinct from the oceanic) were not fighters. The principal feature of the crews of these corsairs is that they were mostly young men, between the ages of 18 and 28, many of whom had sailed on merchant ships and knew the harbours and their approaches as well as the characteristics of each trade. Most of the fishermen, with the notable exception of the deep sea fishermen who normally sailed to the Grand Banks and offshore fisheries at Newfoundland, remained on their ships because the coastal fisheries in European waters were normally considered by both sides to be neutral and were not attacked. Fishing in wartime was thus comparatively safe and reasonably well paid by the standards of the age. It was only the young men from the merchant ships who lost their livelihood in war and unless recruited into the navy saw opportunities only in commerce raiding for earning a living as well as the chance of getting rich.

Decisions about where the ships should cruise were governed by a number of factors, the most important of which was size and sea going capability. Other factors were the experience of the master and officers and the type of trade that the captain was proposing to attack. The managing owner of a privateer often issued general orders for the conduct of the cruise, but in general he relied on the captain's experience and luck rather than a carefully scheduled plan of campaign. This proved a sensible arrangement since it provided the captain with the chance of using information gained from other vessels while at sea. But inevitably corsairs tended to concentrate in certain key areas through which British shipping passed and the favourite places were those off the English coast where local conditions made it possible for the French vessel to lie in wait unobserved by his intended victims. This is the reason why so many voyages in the English Channel were made in autumn and winter when visibility was poor and when many British warships were laid up for the winter, except for those which, later in the Revolutionary and Napoleonic wars were patrolling the Western Approaches to the English Channel or cruising off the French coast.

There is comparatively little evidence on the French side of where the vessels cruised, and the historian must rely heavily on the records of captures in the papers of the High Court of Admiralty. Here the position is noted in the replies given by the captain and officers to a set of standard questions which were designed to establish the size of the crew, the nationality of the owner, the port where the vessel was fitted out, the year she was built and a number of minor details. In addition the date of capture and the port to which the ship was taken is also recorded, though the latter information is of relatively little value since it seldom bears much relationship to position where the raider was captured. The evidence of these Admiralty court records is comprehensive, for in addition to the details of the capture of the French ship, there are often other papers which had been found on board the corsair : letters of marque, permits for taking prizes to a French or neutral port under prize crew, lists of agents in French and other ports to which prizes could be consigned. Occasionally other papers are found, including the papers listing the crew for the *Inscription Ma-*

ritime and providing information about the ship, occasionally permits for the ship to be used as a merchantman and even on occasion bundles of papers found on board prizes. Taken collectively these reveal much about the ship, where she was fitted out, her ownership, where she was sailing when captured, the size and composition of her crew and how long she had been at sea. The papers do not include sailing instructions and do not show where the ship had already been before her capture, unless details of earlier prizes are available. As evidence of the favoured cruising grounds these Admiralty court papers are valuable and comprehensive, provided it is accepted that the details also represent where the British warships cruised to look for them. This is not a serious disadvantage because the cruising grounds of the privateers and of the warships were the same. The papers also reveal where the Board of Admiralty considered merchantmen to be at risk from commerce raiding. There is one exception: the coastal waters of the Iberian Peninsula and the Mediterranean. In the case of the former there were privateers from the Basque ports in the early stages of the Revolutionary War, though none were captured because there were few British warships and because the French ships did not launch their attack against the well protected British ships but against vessels from other countries which were not defended. In the case of the Mediterranean there were comparatively few corsairs, except in the early stages of the Revolutionary War when there were many in Corsica, and the French ships preyed on the vessels sailing under the flags of the minor Italian states and the kingdom of Austria-Hungary, because these were not defended unless they joined the British convoys.

There is one further, though comparatively minor difficulty in establishing the exact position of capture of a few of the French corsairs. Although statements of capture off the Lizard, North Foreland, or other landmarks can be taken as accurate, there were a few captures made in the Atlantic where the position is stated in degrees of Latitude, and often though not always in degress of Longitude, west of Greenwich and of Paris. The measurement of Latitude can be taken as accurate, since it was comparatively easy to obtain using the navigational instruments carried on even the smallest of British warships, and officers were skilled in using them. Longitude measurement was more problematic. There were two methods available in theory for establishing this. The first was to use some form of lunar navigation, which was elaborate and required mathematical calculation to be completely accurate. The other, using a chronometer was also mathematically based.[2] The method was well established - Cook had made three voyages navigating by chronometer and the Navy had carried out trials in the early 1760's - but the chronometers were very expensive. The East India Company equipped its ships with them by 1790. The consequence of this was that many captains relied too much on the traditional means of measuring position, mainly through a calculation of distance run from simple calculation from the log. This was inadequate because it made no allowance for prevailing currents or winds. As a result it is possible that the position in terms of degrees of Longitude west of Greenwich are inaccurate. Where the position is stated in terms of degrees west of Paris one can only assume that the captain of the British warship had very little idea where he was and took the word of the commander of the French vessel which he had just captured. On the other hand the measurement of Latitude is much more likely to be accurate. In the final analysis it is this measurement which was the more important, for it was the practice of a number of French captains to wait on the line of Latitude of a landfall because the masters of merchantmen sailing independently frequently made their approach to the British Isles in this way.

If navigation in the Atlantic could be complicated for the late eighteenth and early nineteenth century mariners, sailing in the waters of the English Channel was far simpler and required only a chart and a compass. For most of the captains of the small privateers the limit of their navigational skill was the ability to plot a course and mark it as a rhumb line on the chart. It was a practice recognised by the contemporary mapmakers, who covered the charts with an elaborate pattern of lines radiating from the focal points on the coast, so that mariners could easily plot and follow a compass bearing. It was in these restricted waters of the English Channel that raids began on English commerce in the first year of the Revolutionary War. Corsairs were taken along the south coast of England, off the Scilly Isles as well as off the coast of the Austrian Netherlands and Holland.

After the activity of the first year there was a lull, as the French government prepared for an attack on England and imposed an embargo on the movement of all French shipping. After the embargo came a profound commercial crisis and it was only towards the end of 1795 that men began fitting out privateers again. In the following year this recovery continued and was marked by a gradual extension of the cruising grounds to include south west Ireland and the Soundings. The captains of French ships were probing to try to find areas in which the British defence would not be so strong and where there would be fewer rivals to capture isolated ships. The progress of the commercial war thus followed a pattern: French initial attack in the English Channel, countered by the first Convoy Act and the posting of British cruisers in the English Channel. As the losses of isolated ships further west became known British warships were sent to provide additional protection in the areas to the west and the areas near ports in Portugal were also protected by convoy escorts who remained in the vicinity of the ports between seeing their charges safely into harbour and bringing them home. The result was that French ships were also captured off the north west coast of Spain.

Up to the end of 1796 these events provided a prelude to the real attack which came in 1797, a year in which over 130 French privateers were captured in European waters. The majority were in the English Channel, not only off the coast of France. Others were found as far north as the border with Scotland and off the Scilly Isles; the remainder were found far to the westward. This enlargement of the cruising ground may have proved more rewarding for the

French captains but it also became more expensive because the ships that sailed west into the Atlantic were larger and much more costly to fit out and it was difficult to capture a correspondingly large number of richly laden ships to make these voyages a financial success. It was the decline in profits which inexorably followed the expansion of 1797 which led to the decline thereafter. Some tried to remedy the problem by seeking new areas for their raids off the coast of Spain and Portugal and the lines of Latitude along which ships sailed to Lisbon and Oporto. At times captains even took their ships across the Atlantic. By 1799 the pattern of French raiding had begun to change and in the last two years of the war it appears that captains were trying to capture ships from outward bound convoys as well as isolated ships from the western ports, principally Bristol and Liverpool, which were not forced to sail in convoy. This remained the same in the Napoleonic War, though the number of French ships was lower. In the first year of the war approximately the same number was captured off the south coast of England as in the approaches to the English Channel. These remained the main theatres of operations; there was a decline in 1804-6 when merchants were able to trade with the United States with better prospects than raiding British commerce. When this trade declined there was a renewed interest in commerce raiding in 1807 and 1808 but thereafter it was confined to the western approaches to the English Channel.

This brief overview of commerce raiding does not take into account the incidence of privateering at different French ports or what areas were considered the most dangerous for British commerce. The details of the ports of origin of the captured vessels appear in the records of the High Court of Admiralty and this indicates the ports which were the most serious threat to British trade.

Opinion on both sides of the English Channel regarded Dunkirk as the leading privateer port, partly because of its past reputation and partly because it enjoyed many opportunities for attacking trade: it was close to the Straits of Dover, had access to the English Channel and North Sea and possessed men, shipping and capital. In reality however the Straits of Dover were not the focus for this activity, because the narrow straits were also close to the naval base in the Downs, off Deal. Many merchant ships did stop at Deal on the outward voyage to receive passengers or final instructions, and on their return to post news of a safe arrival to merchants in London and set their passengers ashore. This focus for shipping was however also protected by the Goodwin Sands, and it would have been dangerous for French ships to sail to landward of these because the Goodwins would have blocked their escape. It is all the more surprising that one small privateer was captured in these waters; her captain relied on poor visibility to mask his presence but was captured a few miles south east of the Downs in 1805.[3]

The North Foreland attracted others; it was a point past which a variety of shipping sailed between the Thames and ports in northern Europe and the Baltic as well as lying on the coasting route followed by all shipping. It was also possible for a well–handled boat to stand some chance of escape from the larger and more ponderous warships. Nonetheless, five ships were captured, four from Dunkirk ranging from 20 to 48 tons and one, the 25 ton *Quatre Frères*, from Calais.[4] All were seized between 1799 and 1810 between November and February and all fell to small naval vessels, two to gun brigs, one to a sloop and the last to a naval cutter. These naval vessels were all superior in terms of their armament, larger crews and greater discipline, features which provide the key to so many unequal combats. It was not inevitable that these French ships should fall into British hands; the 23 ton *Diane* was a new vessel and presumably fast and manoeuvrable. The captain of the 21 ton *Lyonnais* relied on local knowledge and guile. His ship was not French-built and had the appearance of a small neutral cargo ship. The vessel was so insignificant that Lieutenant Brown of the gun brig *Vixen* who captured her did not bother to send her into port as prize but took the crew out and sank her. Of the remainder, the *Quatre Frères* fell to a third rate warship, which would normally have been slower. In this case however the *Kent* was virtually a new ship, less than a year old.

If the North Foreland was a dangerous area for French ships, the South Foreland was little better. The 60 ton Calais ship *Intrépide* and 46 ton *Sphynx* were caught there in December 1798 and December 1796.[5] Of the two the latter is the more interesting, for she was English built, had been captured as a prize and had been fitted out at Morlaix. Ships from this port did not usually sail so far east but her captain, Felix Lallemand, was a Dunkirker and was familiar with these waters. Other corsairs preyed on the coasting trade and waited off ports at which these called. Two were captured off Dover and another three nearby during the Revolutionary War, though it is significant that there were none during the Napoleonic War, when English naval patrols exercised a strict vigilance off this coast. The two off Dover were both 12 ton Calais boats and were captured by naval cutters in December.[6] Of the other three one was an English prize, the 15 ton *Calaisien*, and another was a 14 ton boat, the *Renard*, also from Calais. Other captains tried their luck in early summer, planning to attack the ships bound for overseas markets. All of these had to join the conveys at Spithead, and there was the chance that some might sail independently and be easy prey. The French corsairs which followed this approach were all small: the 12 ton *Epervier* of Le Havre and 20 ton *Aimable Thérèse* of Dunkirk were both new and the latter carried a polyglot crew of Flemings, Italians and a negro. They were captured in May by a hired, armed cutter the *Flora* and the *Ann*, a new sixth rate.[7]

From Portsmouth eastward to the Downs could be a dangerous lee shore in a southerly gale for there were few places where ships could anchor in safety. Only small, handy craft manned by experienced sailors could cruise off this shore in winter when visibility was poor. The boats captured off Dover were little more than rowing boats, further west off Folkestone slightly larger vessels were found during the Napoleonic War. Apart from one small boat, the 25 ton *Modéré* of Boulogne captured in January 1800 by the, new warship, *Nile*, the other four, from Calais and Boulogne, ranged from 35 to 83 tons and date from

1808-9 and 1812.[8] Westward of Folkstone, Dungeness offered raiders an ideal cruising ground. Ships could lie to leeward of the point and be unobserved by most passing warships. At the same time the flat, marshy ground off Dungeness and Romney was sparsely inhabited and there was little chance that watchers from the shore would see the French boats and sound the alarm. A number of corsairs were seized off this desolate coast; some in winter: the 33 ton *Heureuse* of Cherbourg in 1809, the 31 ton English-built *Requin* of Dieppe in 1797 and the 70 ton Boulogne ship *Renard* in 1800.[9] Two others, the 40 ton *Amis* of Caen and 35 ton *Actif* of Calais were seized in early summer.[10] The *Amis* was an unusal craft to find off the English coast. She had been built at Caen in 1790 as a comparatively shallow draught boat for the river trade and it is unlikely that she possessed the qualities of speed and manoeuvrability that a corsair needed. Another feature of the voyage is the lack of any previous experience of the managing owner in commerce raiding, and the venture has the hallmark of a risky and ill-considered project which did not deserve to succeed. That the *Amis* sailed in 1797 is a further symptom of the general optimism of that year, in which so many tried their hand at commerce raiding, often with disastrous results.

At some parts of the south coast there were particular features which encouraged captains to try their luck. Off Hastings, and some of the other towns, the sea shelved gradually and only the smallest vessels could approach the shore. One of the smallest French prize vessels was the 6 ton *Petit Diable*.[11] The captain hoped to be able to escape by sailing inshore of the British vessels; the other French ships which fell into British hands off Hastings were slightly larger and cruised further off the coast: the 16 ton *Actif* of Dunkirk carried a Spaniard and an Italian in its 14 man crew and another *Actif*, formerly an English vessel, were captured in the winter of 1796.[12]

The most popular cruising ground in the eastern half of the English Channel was off Beachy Head. Here the chalk cliffs rose majestically from the sea and provided a landmark to shipping which was visible over a long distance both in winter and summer. No fewer than twenty French ships were captured here, fifteen of them in the Revolutionary War, half in summer and half in winter.[13] Many were from the small ports to the south west of Dunkirk: Saint Valéry-en-Caux, Fécamp and Honfleur; others were from Le Havre, which had become more important in the years preceding the French Revolution as the outport for Rouen's textile industry. The other ships were from Dieppe, Calais, Boulogne and Dunkirk. The British ships which formed the defensive patrols were mixed: sloops, brigantines, a gun brig and cutters formed the majority but the largest were two fifth rate ships, the *Stag* and *Ann*, which had been built and were sailed like small frigates, being square and not sloop rigged.

Many of the corsairs which were found in the eastern half of the English Channel were small, less than twenty tons. They carried a handful of men which was barely adequate to sail the ship and provide prize crews, and it may have been the intention of captains and managing owners to take ransom notes rather than try and bring any captured vessels back to their home port. These small vessels were able to cruise within a comparatively small radius - they could not carry many provisions and had to rely on raiding isolated farms when these ran low. Their captains were probably men whose experience was limited to the waters of the south eastern coast of England and neither the crew nor the captain wished to venture far from home. Larger ships had a wider range and were not restricted in the same way. Whereas many of the small craft described already had done little more than sail directly across the English Channel, the 65 ton cutter *Fantaisie*, captured off Beachy Head, was from Dunkirk. She had already sailed in the North Sea in March 1793 where she had captured a Dutch prize and sent her to Stavanger, and her captain had been ordered by the managing owner to sail as far as the Irish coast if he made no captures further east.[14] The choice of Stavanger was unwise. Only Bergen and Christiansand, the modern Oslo, were safe from attack and boats from British warships could, and sometimes did, raid small Norwegian ports and carry off privateers and their prizes, which gave rise to strong diplomatic complaint.[15]

Beachy Head marked the dividing line between the cruising grounds of the Dunkirkers and the seamen from Saint Malo and the ports westward from Le Havre. Some of the larger Dunkirk ships were occasionally found west of Beachy Head, but no Saint Malo corsairs ventured east. Shoreham marks the eastern limit for the latter. It was a small port, whose needs were met by coasting vessels. These attracted the captain of the 10 ton Saint Malo *Fine*, which before the war had been employed in this occupation and was captured in October 1796.[16] If the *Fine* was a long way from its home port, the 12 ton *Poisson Volant* of Nantes was even further. This tiny craft carried two small swivel guns and a crew of twenty five and fell to the revenue cutter *Lively* , revenue cutterin June 1797 between Shoreham and the Isle of Wight.[17] Even smaller were the tiny 8 ton *Belle Angélique* of Le Havre taken off Shoreham in the summer of 1796 by the revenue cutter *Hound* , revenue cutterand the 6 ton Calais boat *Vigilant* caught in October 1796.[18] Of the eleven others in the same area the 40 ton *Amis Des Lois* of Dunkirk is unusual because she carried three Americans among its 36 man crew and also because she was a prize, formerly the *Prosperity* of Whitstable and of a type which was common off the south east coast of England. She was a sturdy boat for her size, and carried eight small cannon and six swivel guns when it left Dunkirk in April 1793 to cruise off Middelburg and then turned west to Brighton, where it was captured.[19] Not all were this small; the 45 ton *Revanche* of Calais, which was seized off Bognor in 1806, and the 68 ton *Modeste* of Fécamp represent the larger.[20] The very small craft which were also found in the area tended to sail in winter when visibility was less and it is evident from the small armament carried by many of them that the captain and crew intended to board their prizes rather than draw attention to themselves by gunfire: the 22 ton *Affrique* of Le Havre carried 21 men but only six small swivel guns, twelve stand of small arms, fifty pistols and twentyfive swords when she was captured by the sloop *Spitfire* in March

1793.[21] There were also many small vessels taken in the same area ranging from the 18 ton *Bonheur* of Cherbourg captured in March 1797 to the 38 ton *Entreprenant* of Le Havre seized in February 1793, and it is significant that most of these small craft cruised in winter and that most were captured when privateering was at its peak between the autumn of 1796 and the winter of 1797. During the Napoleonic War corsairs tended to give the area a wide berth.

From the British point of view, the Isle of Wight marked the last point at which merchant ships outward bound for an overseas market were sailing with only light protection, since it was in the sheltered waters in the lee of the island that all the the major convoys assembled. When the convoys were gathering, there was less chance of taking an isolated ship, since under the convoy acts all merchant ships had to sail under the protection of a warship whose captain issued sailing instructions. The opportunities for privateers was thus limited in the early summer. On the other hand, when the convoys returned there were often many ships separated from the main body or whose rigging and sails had been damaged on the return voyage and found it difficult to keep up with the main body. These returning merchant ships were also better prizes, because their cargoes were not readily available in France and could fetch higher prices than the goods carried from England. Consequently privateers were found to the south of the Isle of Wight and the attraction of the area is seen from the variety of the privateers : a 16 ton vessel from Paimpol, the *Alerte*, two 45 ton ships from Dieppe and Calais and a number from ports directly to the south: Cherbourg, La Hogue and Le Havre.[22]

Westward of the Isle of Wight lies the broad sweep of Christchurch and Poole bays. Few merchant ships sailed there unless they were bound for Poole and only two French ships were captured, the 35 ton *Entreprise* of Le Havre and 34 ton *Provisoire* of Dieppe in 1796 and 1798.[23] There was little for them to catch there, though there were better propects near St. Albans Head, which offered some protection from prevailing winds, though the corsair captured there seems to have been on unfamiliar ground. The 100 *Sans Culotte* had been built in Morlaix in 1789, but had been fitted out for commerce raiding at Nantes and later at Brest.[24] It carried a small armament of five two pounder cannon and eight swivel guns and a crew of thirty four but its captain, Peter Long, was probably an American and the owner, John Dyot, was a compatriot although the managing owner was a Frenchman. No doubt Long hoped to be able to use his knowledge of English to bluff his way out of danger and use his local knowledge of the coastal waters to gain success where few Frenchmen cruised.

If the water to the west of the Isle of Wight were generally free from corsairs, Portland Bill was very different, for the shipping which visited Portland Harbour attracted many corsairs. The waters to the south of the Bill were considered very dangerous on account of the tide race formed by the meeting of the tides from both sides of the Bill. Occasionally vessels were swept westwards and driven ashore on Chesil Beach.[25] French captains were aware of this danger and tended to keep well to the south. The Bill was a favourite haunt of French ships because British merchantmen tended to lie in the lee of the Bill for a favourable wind to carry them to Devon or Cornwall or ports in the Irish Sea. Portland Harbour was defended by a castle and ships were safe as long as they stayed there, but when the wind changed there was a rush as captains tried to catch a favourable opportunity to sail. This is what the Frenchmen were waiting for; fourteen corsairs were taken off Portland during the Revolutionary War, though none between 1803 and 1814. They ranged from the tiny 9 ton *Deux Amis* of Cherbourg to the 100 ton Brest ship *Pichegru*, owned jointly by an American, Cowell, of Brest and a well known Saint Malo partnership, Duchesne and Pintedevin. Perhaps the most succinct of all orders to captains were those given to Henri Lecuyer of the *Impromptu* of Cherbourg; he was to observe the movements of shipping in England and take prizes on his return.[26] In the case of the *Impromptu*, as in the case of a number of other corsairs, the vessel was a former English ship, the *Ann* of Dartmouth, which may even have a familiar sight in the coastal waters. She was also a cutter, a fast and manoeuvrable type of ship when handled by an experienced and disciplined crew and it is appropriate that she was caught by a naval vessel of the same type, the *Nimble*, which did have a disciplined crew. Of the ships captured in this area south of the Isle of Wight the majority were from Cherbourg and Le Havre, which were almost directly due south; only two were from Saint Malo.

The main reason why there were so few corsairs from Saint Malo in these waters in mid-channel was that there were excellent prospects to the west, closer to their base. A few sailed to the South Devon coast, seeking the coasters bound for Exeter, Torquay and the small harbours nearby. Only two privateers were captured there, the 26 ton *Alexandrine* from Brest, taken off Torbay in March 1798 and the 25 ton *Etourdis* of Le Havre off Berry Head in February 1797.[27] In most weather Torbay provided a safe anchorage but occasionally a strong easterly wind blew and the coast became a dangerous lee shore. When this happened ships ran for the shelter of Dartmouth or put out to sea.[28] Many more vessels were found off Start Point further south, where the promontory offered protection from the prevailing westerly winds. This attracted ships from Saint Malo, Saint Servan and Granville. The British navy captured twelve ships off this point during the Revolutionary War but surprisingly only two during the Napoleonic, in September 1809 and December 1813, a proof of the deterrent effect of the British blockade and the new opportunities of licenced trade during the latter years.

Historians have emphasised the handy nature of the privateers which were found attacking English commerce in these seas, their speed and manoeuvrability and the distinctive lug sail which many carried. The record of captures of these ships by naval warships and revenue cutters show that they were by no means invincible. There were also a number of features which distinguished the corsairs from Dunkirk and the eastern ports from those in the west of the English Channel. Many of those from the east were cutters and were taken by similar boats in navel and revenue service; it was in the west that many carried the lug sail which for some historians is synonymous with privateering and smuggling. These apparently nimble ships were captured by a variety of British warships: cutters, sloops and occasionally frigates formed the main coastal defences in the eastern half of the English Channel, which matched the French attack. To the west these were supplemented with naval luggers such as the *Speedwell* and a hired schooner, the *Hope*, was also successful. The *Speedwell* was particularly fortunate; she took the 39 ton *Télémaque* and 12 ton *Amis*, both from Granville in four days in October 1797 and the 49 ton *Heureuse Espérance* of Saint Malo in December 1799. The captain was the same man, Lieutenant Robert Tomlinson. It appears from this example that although Tomlinson was a successful master of a small boat he lacked the family connexions to get advancement. It cannot have been pleasant to cruise in the English Channel year after year, winter and summer to try and catch the small ships which slipped briefly across the English Channel and were commanded and manned by experienced seamen. The command of a small ship like the *Arab* should have been the first post of a young man who was bound for promotion. As it is Tomlinson was able enough to pass the exam from midshipman but not lucky enough to catch the Admiralty's eye by a spectacular success and was condemned to serve for years on a small ship in the difficult waters of the English Channel. It was not a fate that was reserved solely for Lieutenant Tomlinson. When the Earl of Dundonald was a young man and still Lord Cochrane he was considered troublesome though brave. He was appointed to a former collier the *Arab* which was taken into naval service, and cruised from Plymouth, rounded Lands End and stretched as far as St George's Channel during the Revolutionary War.[29] Cochrane was less fortunate than Tomlinson, for whereas the *Speedwell* was a fast cutter the *Arab* was a slow and cumbersome ship, built for carrying capacity and strength rather than speed and Cochrane failed even to sight a French craft.

There was also the more serious problem that navigation in the English Channel demanded, especially in winter, considerable knowledge of the currents and tidal races that could not be acquired easily. Westwards of Start Point the coastline today is marked by a series of lighthouses which emphasise the perils of navigation. In the Revolutionary and Napoleonic wars navigational aids were more primitive and British and French alike risked being driven ashore, especially during the winter storms. Under these circumstances it is significant that three French ships were seized in the comparative safe waters off Plymouth and two were far from their home ports: the 25 ton *Prudent* was from Lorient and the 30 ton *Point du Jour* was from Dieppe.[30] The captains of both probably lacked the local knowledge to cruise off the more dangerous though potentially lucrative Cornish coast. Other points which attracted corsairs were the Eddystone lighthouse, three, the Dodman, two, and a single ship off Pendennis Castle.[31] Most of these vessels were comparatively small and preyed mostly on the coasting trade, where vessels sailed independently. The exception was the *Indomtable* of Dieppe. This was much more powerful; she measured 128 tons, carried an armament of 16 guns and had a crew of 125. She was also a former English ship. When she was captured she was on her second cruise and had used a sea fog to sail unobserved among the ships of a returning Mediterranean convoy. She captured one ship by boarding without a shot being fired but the fog suddenly lifted and she was seen and seized by the escort, the warship *Persian*.

The Lizard was a popular, and dangerous, cruising ground for privateers. The main reason for this was that ships returning from the West Indies and North America frequently made for the Lizard at the end of their trans-Atlantic crossing. It was the southernmost point of England and by steering westwards from this the captain could be sure of missing the dangerous rocks off the Scilly Isles. It was also the practice for captains who were short of provisions on returning to England to stand off for Rame Head and Falmouth or Plymouth Sound and their course took them close to the Lizard. Falmouth was popular in this respect because ships could enter and leave at any state of the tide and with almost any wind. It was when the wind veered north that ships could not negotiate Carrick Roads, which formed the approaches to Falmouth harbour, and when this happened ships made for the shelter of the anchorages between St Anthony's Point and the Manacles.[32] More important for outward bound ships, Falmouth was the most westerly port in the English Channel and ships could leave it and steer against the prevailing westerly and south westerly winds to reach the Atlantic. For this reason many convoys assembled at Falmouth, and the port was also used by the packet boats bound for North America, Lisbon, Malta and Gibraltar. Their crews carried valuable cargoes-including species - on their own account and were prepared to fight to the death to defend them. It is for this variety of commerce that the Lizard was so popular with corsairs. No fewer than twenty one were taken there, fourteen in the Revolutionary War, mostly in 1793, 1797 and 1798 and the remainder at intervals between 1803 and 1810. One interesting feature is that more corsairs were seized off the Lizard during the Napoleonic War than off any other part of the English coast, and this indicates the continued attraction of this dangerous, rock strewn point where mist could obscure the coastline. It also explains why so many of the corsairs sailed there in summer rather than winter.

Most of the privateers taken off the Lizard in winter were from Saint Malo and Granville - six of the eight - and one each from Lorient and Dunkirk. These winter cruisers were also larger than the vessels which were found further east in winter; none was under 35 tons and most were nearer 90. One, the 90 ton *Favori* of Saint Malo, put up a determined fight and it took the naval schooner *Pickle* an hour to subdue her.[33] The other ships taken off the Lizard fall into the familiar pattern and range from the tiny 16 ton *Papillon* from the small port of Conquet and the 15 ton former English vessel which became the *Incroyable* of Saint Malo to the 152 ton *Résolu* of Saint Malo.[34] The one ship that does not fit into the general pattern is the 90 ton *Coureur* of Fécamp, which fell into British hands in May 1793. She was an American built ship, constructed in Boston in 1784. It is not clear whether she had a distinctive rig or general appearance but was probably one of the general cargo ships which carried Boston's trade to Europe. These ships were often built in America, sailed to a European port with a cargo and sold.

West of the Lizard was an area which marks the dividing line between the English Channel and the deep water commerce raiding. It was an area through which the Irish trade had to pass and this was the intended prey of three small vessels which were captured off Lands End. Other ships were also found there; the *Bougainville* of Saint Malo, which carried the large crew of 82, spent some time cruising between the Lizard and Cape Cornwall and in December 1800 and January 1801 took the 108 ton brig *Mayflower* laden with butter from Waterford for London, the 168 ton ship *Richmond* with rum from London for Dublin and the 160 ton *Hebe* with corn for the same destination.[35] These were valuable prizes, for there was a shortage of food in Saint Malo and the cargoes could be sold at high prices. The Scilly Isles marked the boundary of these attacks on the Irish trade. East of the Scillies the raiders were comparatively small, seldom more than 40 tons, and many slipped briefly across the English Channel for raids. As one moves westward the average tonnage rose, partly because the seas off the Lizard were rougher and more dangerous and partly because the ships which were pressed into service as privateers - apart from those built specifically for this purpose - were larger than the smaller vessles of Dunkirk and the eastern ports. At the Scilly Isles one meets a different type of ship and the British defence consisted of more powerful ships, usually frigates and smaller line of battle ships. It was in the waters to the west of the Scillies that the larger merchant ships from Nantes, Lorient and above all Bordeaux waited for the returning convoys in the autumn and the outward bound ships in the spring. The difference in shipping can be seen in the records of the capture of privateers in the vicinity of the Scilly Isles. To the east were the boats such as the 12 ton *Terrible* of Paimpol, the 21 ton *Hirondelle* of Morlaix and the 25 ton lugger *Suprême* of Saint Malo.[36] These could shelter in the lee of the Scillies; the ships which cruised to the west had to withstand westerly gales: the 102 ton *Heureux Courier* of Granville was captured south east of the Scillies in June 1800, another eight were taken south of the islands, one to the north and two to the north west.[37] They were all from Brest and Saint Malo except for the 80 ton *Vengeur* of Ostend found north west of the Scillies in January 1797. Of the others six were over 100 tons and the largest, the *Guidelon* of Saint Malo, was a new 250 ton ship. Occasionally privateers went north of the Scilly Isles to look for the Irish trade; the 150 ton Brest sloop *Fantaisie* took the *Arrow* of St Ives bound for London with coal in January 1796, presumably from the important coal port of Whitehaven. The master of the *Fantaisie* did not want to send coal back and agreed a ransom of 450 gns. to be paid in five days.[38] Few Frenchmen ventured far north of the Scillies because it was unfamiliar and it is surprising that the *Sans Souci* , Audacieux and *Espiègle* did. The first was a 150 ton

Saint Malo ship which encountered two British frigates near the mouth of the Bristol Channel in December 1812.[39] The other two ventured close to Milford in the summer of 1797 and represent the confidence of that year.[40] The *Audacieux* was commanded by a Canadian who had come to Saint Malo in 1790; perhaps because the Revolution had ended his employment in the cod fishery, or he was consumed with revolutionary zeal.

West of the Scilly Isles the attackers were found in a wide arc stretching from the south west of Ireland and the Soundings to the Iberian Peninsula. They were trying to capture shipping from the returning or outward bound convoys, depending on the season. The most northerly area where privateers were found was to the west of Cape Clear. This was favoured as the end of many trans-Atlantic voyages during these wars because they provided the captain with the opportunity of making for Cork and landing the major part of his crew to avoid having to hand them over to the press gang on their return to England. East Indiamen also occasionally made their landfall at Cape Clear and it was a simple matter for the captain of a large ship to wait on the line of latitude out of sight of the Irish coast for ships to reach him. In fact, it became difficult to protect stragglers from these raiders for they could always cruise to windward of the British warships, which could not sail too far to the west without leaving the landmarks exposed. Eight French ships were taken off Cape Clear and another off the Skelligs a little to the west, a third off Cable Island and one described in the naval report as being 'in Latitude 46° off the coast of Ireland'.[41] Several of these were very large: the *Duguay Trouin* of Saint Malo, formerly the slaver *Baron Bender*, was a 500 ton ship; she had a crew of 156 and carried 22 cannon. The *Triton* of Nantes and the *Surveillant* of Bordeaux were both of 350 tons with crews of 163 and 157 respectively. Of the others only three were under 100 tons and the 27 ton *Achéron* of Saint Malo was exceptionally small. Cape Clear was sufficiently important as a cruising ground to attract ships from a long way away: Granville, Brest, Saint Malo, Morlaix and Nantes were the main ports but there were also ships from Bordeaux and even Bayonne. These could carry ample stores for a long cruise and could take the cargo of small prizes if necessary. They could also put up a spirited defence against small naval vessels. The sloop *Seagull* escorted a convoy to Cork in August 1803 and then her captain learnt from a Portuguese schooner that a French privateer was cruising off Cape Clear. Captain Burke immediately went in pursuit and sighted the privateer *Bellonne* which he took after a fight. The 350 ton *Surveillant* of Bordeaux, which had been hired for a three month cruise fought the frigate *Alcmene* and about a hundred shots were fired before she surrended.[42] Occasionally small boats were sent to cruise further east to intercept the trade in provisions from Cork. ClorkThis was also an area with which French seamen, especially from Saint Malo were relatively familiar, because Irish provisions had been used on the Saint Malo cod fishing boats for many years, as well as in the trade to the French West Indies. The 60 ton *Eveillé* of Brest was found off Ballycotton Island, a short distance east of Cork, in June 1796 waiting for the ships which put in at Cork for provisions for long voyages.[43] To the west, well out into the Atlantic were other, larger ships which were waiting for the isolated ships making for their landfall. Some of these had abandoned their convoys deliberately to try and reach the market first. The majority probably lost sight of the convoy in a gale or at night when the look out failed to keep a close watch on the escort's riding light or failed to distinguish it from the lights of other ships in the convoy.[44] There were even occasions when escort commanders seriously neglected their duty, and there was often friction between the naval captain and the merchantmen. One particularly serious example of cavalier treatment of merchantmen was that of Sir Richard Strachan. In 1806 he was ordered to escort a convoy of between 250 and 300 bound for the Mediterranean and the West Indies safely into the Atlantic and then seek out a French squadron which was known to be at sea. Strachan proved a wild man who paid little heed to the convoys and appointed the slow *Woolwich* as whipper in. It was hardly surprising that within a week fifty merchant ships had been abandoned, many were disabled by the bad weather and that in general they were left defenceless.[45]

Apart from the efforts of convoy commanders the Admiralty appointed a number of frigates to cruise within specific areas which linked to form a defensive screen. The first ship covered an area from three or four degrees west of the Soundings to 20°W and from 47°N to 50°N. Further west another cruised as far as 25°W and between 48°N and 50°N.[46] To the south another ship cruised between 47°N and the Western Islands.[47] These areas were carefullt chosen and represented the experience of may years in earlier wars. Two of the French ships were taken in 20°West is described as lying in 20°W of Paris - both were from La Rochelle.[48] Of the other two ships also captured in 51°N one was very large, the 300 ton *Georgette* of Nantes.[49]

Most of the merchant ships returning to England were found on 50°N a course which would carry them past the Scillies to the Lizard and the privateers cruised in a long line along this line of Latitude. Closest to the English coast were a few small vessels such, as the 20 ton *Dragon* of Granville, but the majority were found between 9°W of Paris, where the 66 ton *Joséphine* and the 113 ton *Ville de Caen* of Saint Malo were taken and 24°W of Paris where the 120 ton *Epervier* of Bordeaux was captured.[50] A total of thirteen corsairs were found in these waters, three each from Granville and Nantes and four from Bordeaux, which included the 500 ton *Heureux*.[51] Most of these cruised in the autumn for the returning trade convoys through occasionally some ventured out in the spring. They too were successful; the *Joséphine* of Granville captured the *Jane* of Greenock, though the value of the prize is not known.[52]

To the south and west was a vast area in which a variety of ships from the Atlantic ports cruised to attack convoys. It would be tedious to describe in detail the individual ships and the places where they were captured, since the account would by now make familiar reading. More significant are the areas in which they were taken and which indicate the personal choice of the managing owner and captain who were seeking a hunting ground beyond the waters of the English Channel and approaches to it. The Admiralty had to get the merchant ships through a screen of hostile vessels, the exact positions of which could never be known. To try and protect the most valuable convoys additional ships were sent to escort the vessels through this danger zone. On the return voyage additional frigates and other ships were given the difficult task of finding and capturing these raiders, but the evidence shows that they captured sufficient to be able to deter many owners after the first euphoria of 1797. In all thirty five ships were captured in an area bounded by 48°N - 50°N and from the Soundings to 10°W. The majority were from Saint Malo and ranged in size from 50 and 150 tons. They included the 50 ton *Egalité* built for the Newfoundland fishery in 1787 which was fitted out at Saint Malo in 1793 for a merchant company in Rouen to cruise as a privateer.[53] At the other end of the scale were two Nantes ships, the 600 ton *Brave* and 300 ton *Musette* captured in February 1798 and December 1796.[54] The attraction of this area for privateering was not only the prospect of taking prizes, but the variety of goods which they might gain: The *Courier de la Manche*, a 70 ton cutter from Saint Malo, took the American *John and Joseph* off the Sorlings bound from Baltimore to Leghorn with a cargo of sugar and campeachy wood in February and the 120 ton *Sally* in March from Messina for London with wine, mutton and silk.[55] The area even attracted a Calais boat, the 130 ton *Bonheur*, which was taken in 48°33'N and 9°10'W by the frigate *Cerberus* in April 1805.[56]

There were other ships which cruised even further west on the tracks of the outward and homeward convoys. The decision where to cruise was of crucial importance, for the captain had to use his judgment to estimate where the convoys were likely to sail under the prevailing conditions and it was easy to miss even a large, dispersed convoy. These raiders came from ports on the Atlantic coast and Saint Malo and in 1805 there was even a cruiser from Dunkirk, the 125 ton *Hirondelle*, as far west as 48°N and 14°W and before being captured by the large frigate *Venus* the *Hirondelle* sent one prize to a Spanish port.[57] Size and seaworthiness were the two most important features of these larger commerce raiders which at times faced very rough weather in the Bay of Biscay. The 88 ton *Tiercelet* of Rochefort was one of the smallest to be taken so far west; the majority were around 130-180 tons, and the largest were the 330 ton *Victoire* of Bayonne and the 500 ton *Volage* of Nantes.[58] These may have seemed enormous merchant ships; they were poorly armed as warships. The *Volage* carried twenty-two cannons but all but two were eight pounders and the remainder were eighteen. This was little compared with the weight of metal that a frigate could hurl against it. The crew, though large, was similarly lacking in discipline and probably courage.

At the southern end of this arc of commerce raiders were the ships which lay in 47°N: the 160 ton *Scipion Français* from Bordeaux captured an American prize and sent it to Santander during her cruise in Year VIII before being taken by the fourthrate line of battle ship *Endymion* in May 1800 in 47°25'N and 14°46'W of Paris.[59] Most of these ships were from Bordeaux, Nantes and La Rochelle, but there was one from Saint Malo, the 214 ton *Prince Murat*, two from Lorient and a Dunkirk ship.[60] Not all surrendered without a fight; the *Sans Culottes* of Lorient fell in with the sloop in 47°N and her mixed crew of Americans, French and Italians fought for four and a half hours. The final toll was seven killed and eight wounded of the crew of eighty one men but the captain, Jean la Freyte from Bayonne, was evidently able to inspire his men. The two ships were well matched in tonnage, armament and crew and the privateer was only two years old. In the end it was the discipline of the naval crew which tipped the balance. The small vessels surrendered without a fight; the 30 ton *Levrette* of La Rochelle could not hope to match the frigate *Arethusa*.[61] Besides these ships which lay in wait a long distance off the shore there were others which sailed closer to the shore to intercept the coastal traffic. Many of these were either English or bound for an English port or carried goods which could be condemned as fair prize in a court. British warships mounted patrols along the coast between Lisbon and the north west of Spain, occasionally stretching further out to sea whenever there seemed a prospect of capturing French shipping. The coastal waters off northern Spain were normally a safe area for French cruisers, and contained ports to which they could retire to refit, carry out temporary repairs, obtain stores between voyages and condemn prizes. At the same time these waters acted as a thoroughfare for the ships from Bayonne, Bordeaux and Saint Jean-de-Luz when they sailed to and form their cruising grounds off the Portuguese and north west coast of Spain. Occasionally British warships were sent to patrol this area and were sometimes successful in capturing privateers, though in general it was not considered safe to venture beyond Santander. There was no port to the east where British ships could seek refuge from a westerly wind, and there was a danger of being blown ashore on a hostile coast. It was small wonder that commanders of squadrons were unwilling to hazard their ships there except under exceptional circumstances. One example was when Lieutenant Bourne in the schooner *Felix* sailed in June 1804, but his ship was better suited to the conditions there than the other warships. Her fore and aft rig enabled her captain to sail closer to the wind than the square rigged warships, and Lieutenant Bourne was rewarded with capturing three of the four French luggers which piled between Bayonne and Santander. One carried maize; the other two were laden with specie which consisted of 61,529 dollars.[62]

Commerce raiding off the Portuguese and Spanish coast was similar in some ways to that off the south coast of England already described. Privateers lay in wait off landmarks: Cape Ortegal, Cape Prior, Corunna and Finisterre as well as off the ports to which merchant ships were bound: Vigo, Oporto, Lisbon and Cadiz. These landmarks with their familiar shapes, which could be seen far out to sea, provided shelter from gales and contrary winds such as Beachy Head and the other headlands had done in the English Channel. In the case of Portugal there were also merchant ships and Newfoundland fishing boats which made for 'the high land of Viana' at the end of their voyages, such as ships returning from the Caribbean or North America made for Cape Clear or the Lizard. The commercial war off the Iberian peninsula was as much a battle of wits between the naval captain and the master of the privateer as further north, though with the difference that the Bayonne, Bordeaux and Saint Jean-de-Luz men were familiar with these waters and the naval captains were not. Nonetheless, from the British point of view the work was done at least reasonably efficiently and successfully: four privateers taken off Cape Ortegal, two off Cape Prior, one off Corunna, eight off Cape Finisterre, four off Vigo, one off Oporto, five off Lisbon, one off Cadiz Cadizbesides four more at unidentified points on the coast. One of the interesting features of the roll of captives is the almost total absence of any of the small Bayonne and Saint Jean-de-Luz vessels. The reason is that they were shallow draught and able to stay further inshore than the naval captains dared to take their ships, and one of the latter had the opportunity of sending its boats to capture them at anchor off the shore, as was the case sometimes of the Norwegian coast. Another point in favour of these small French vessels is that they carried sweeps and were able to row out and take ships when there was a calm which immobilised the warships and in the same way were able to escape. These small vessels, often little more than rowing boats, were regarded as a particular nuisance by the English naval officers, who were often powerless to protect their convoys in calm weather. Occasionally these small vessels were captured: the 26 ton *Aventure* and 30 ton *Espérance* were seized off Lisbon and Oporto, but in both cases their captors were comparatively fast.[63] The first was seized by the *Aurore* frigate and the second by the armed schooner *Netley*. Although most of the ships which were found off this coast were from ports in south west France there were occasional exceptions: the *Revanche* taken in October 1796 near Cape Prior was from La Rochelle and the *Valeur* captured in the same area two years earlier, was from Brest. These privateers were not threatened by the naval warships alone; occasionally English corsairs were found off this coast: the 72 ton *Valeur* of Brest fell to the *Lord Hawke*, though in general English privateers were merchant ships engaged in trade which also carried letters of marque to enable them to take French merchant ships if the occasion arose.

English commerce with Lisbon, Oporto and the other ports on this coast, though not politically as significant as that with the Carribbean and North America, was still important as the main supplier of wine and citrus fruits and as a market for the Newfoundland fishery. However, it was not an easy trade to protect, for it combined the commerce with England with the arrival of the boats from the cod fishery and their integration in the convoys returning to Britain. To protect this, warships usually patrolled a line from Ushant to Finisterre, which was also the line followed by French convoys sailing from Brest to ports on the Atlantic Coast. In addition ships cruised for French corsairs in an area of which the centre was 46°N 12°W. through which passed much of the outward bound English shipping. This was a considerable distance from the coast and the French ships which sailed there were formidable. It is greatly to the credit of Captain Blake of the sloop *Seagull* that he chased a French vessel for five hours and then fought her through the night in the course of which action "The masts and jury rigging (were) so much cut up, having the larboard fore and main shrouds torn and sprung stays, all the running rigging and sails, the fore yards cut away in the slings, with the shot between wind and water, that I was obliged to haul off to secure the masts and replace the rigging".[64]

Another attraction for French corsairs was the arrival in the autumn of the Newfoundland fishing boats. Though these were under the protection of at least one frigate and sailed in convoy, ships could be separated from the main body and a number were bound for the Straits and markets in the Mediterranean. Because of the attraction for French privateers, British frigates cruised off the coast, especially in the area of Viana and these patrols were strengthened by the frigates which were sent from the Mediterranean sqaudron and the escorts for the Portugal trade. Captain Prowse was given the task of cruising off Cape Finisterre in the *Sirius* for ten weeks in April 1806 and Captain Dundas was told to cruise from 30 to 90 miles off the same cape in May 1805 for the same purpose.[65] This policy paid dividends; the frigate *Triton* captured the 40 ton *Araignée* from Bayonne in September 1798 and the 150 ton *Corunesa* which had been given a French letter of mark at Corunna and had sailed from there in March 1800 was captured in 44°17'N.[66] There were also ships from further afield. After the initial optimism had waned in 1797 masters and managing owners tended to look for areas which might offer better prospects than in the English Channel. The commerce with the Iberian peninsula thus began to attract shipping from further north: the 300 ton *Zoée* from Quimper and 153 ton *César* from Saint Malo fell into British hands in 1797 and 1798. There was even one from Granville, the 130 ton *Bon Citoyen*.[67] The latter is the most surprising capture, because it was not a new ship. It had been built in 1782 at Granville and was sixteen years old when caught by two third rate warships and a frigate in 44°N 13°W two months after the letter of marque had been granted. Another unusual prize was the 20 ton *Vengeance* seized in 1800.[68] This was a ship from La Rochelle whose managing owner was the well known Dunkirk merchant Dauchy, who moved to Paris during the course of the Revolutionary War. This was a small speculation by a man with great experience of fitting out similar ships at Dunkirk, but who had been forced to look elsewhere as the British grip on the English Channel had tightened. The *Vengeance* was captured by the frigate *Minerva* in April 1800 in 42°10'N and 9°48'W.

So far it has been stressed that French raiders were concerned primarily with capturing British merchant ships, and this is the view held in France. But there were other prizes to be gained as well, which attracted less public attention though captains, managing owners and shareholders were well aware of them. These were merchant ships from other enemies of France or vessels carrying goods belonging to them or bound for their ports. During the course of the two conflicts France was at war with a number of other states, including Portugal and Austria-Hungary. The sudden change in alliances could catch captains unawares and one example was perhaps the unnamed 300 ton Danish vessel bound from Cadiz to Hamburg and Altona which was seized by the *Républicain* of Nantes in 38°30'N and 14°W of Paris in April 1793.[69] She was carrying tobacco, cochineal, vanilla, indigo, coffee, sugar, beef, raisins and a variety of other goods and made a rich prize. A similar example was the *Dame Catherine*, another 300 ton Danish ship, taken on a voyage from Marseille to Hamburg by the same privateer in 43°53'N and 16°W later in the same month.[70]

More adventurous privateer captains ventured further afield to attack shipping bound for the West Indies, West Africa and North America and returning from there. The captains of the British convoy escorts often considered that when they had passed the latitude of Gibraltar their convoys were safe, because most French corsairs remained in European waters. Occasionally, however, French corsairs pursued British shipping much further and hoped at the same time to be able to take Spanish and Portuguese ships returning from South America. The 500 ton *Général Dumourier* of Bordeaux took the Spanish *San Jago Apostel* in 35°45'N in April 1793 bound from Lima to Cadiz with a valuable cargo which included copper, cocoa and hides.[71] Other corsairs sailed to the Canary Islands and Madeira, where English shipping called to replenish stores and take wine on board for sale in the West Indies and elsewhere. It was off Madeira that the 100 ton *Revanche* was seized by the fourth rate warship *Endyminion* in April 1798.[72] So too was the 101 ton *Concord* of Marseille in June 1805 and these two illustrate the strategic importance of this island which the British occupied, with Portuguese consent, late in 1807.[73] The area was so important that British warships were occasionally sent to cruise there to intercept Spanish shipping: Cochrane was appointed to cruise off 'the Western Isles' in the *Pallas* frigate in 1804 and had the good fortune to take two rich Spanish prizes which formed part of a convoy homeward bound from Havana to Cadiz.[74] The Admiralty recognised the importance of this area by sending the *Endyminion* to patrol the seas in January 1804. It would be wrong to assume that the larger ships remained in European waters; some only began their cruise there. They carried ample supplies of provisions and were commanded by men with a great deal of experience in trans-Atlantic sailing and a number put this to good use by crossing the Atlantic to seek prizes among the complex pattern of inter-island commerce in the Caribbean. Some managing owners also planned commercial voyages but these ships were carefully chosen for their speed and were well-armed, since merchants who invested in these voyages could not insure them. The slender evidence of these voyages is that they failed to realise the expectations of their backers because they could never realise the very high prices which alone would have made these voyages profitable.

This specialised and restricted form of privateering has its equivalent in the Mediterranean, where there were many opportunities for combining the two.

One significant difference between the Mediterranean and northern Europe as far as commerce raiding was concerned was that the risk of capture was comparatively small in the Mediterranean. At the beginning of the Revolutionary War a number were fitted out in ports in Corsica, Crete and a few at Marseille and Toulon. Later in the war some sailed from Spanish ports using letters of marque issued by French consuls. But in general these ships did not attack British trade. After the initial months of 1793 it became clear that this was well defended, but there were many others which could be attacked and condemned in prize courts: Austro-Hungarians from Trieste when the two countries were at war, vessels from Italian city states which might be carrying goods belonging to enemy merchants, since there were important British commercial interests at Leghorn and elsewhere in Italy whose needs were supplied from elsewhere via the coasting trade in Italian ships. Similarly in the eastern Mediterranean, the British trade with the island of Zante and ports in the Levant attracted commerce from a wider area whose goods might be captured and condemned by French privateers. Captains were thus able to exploit local knowledge of the web of trade which supplied British needs and prey upon it at its weakest points. Many of these voyages by commerce raiders could easily be combined with trade because French ships continued to sail to ports in north Africa for grain and elsewhere for a variety of commodities which were imported at Marseille and elsewhere on the south coast of France until an effective coastal blockade was introduced by the British Mediterranean squadron. But in addition to this the commercial war in the Mediterranean forms part of the long running battle between Christian and Muslim, in which the majority of French and other Mediterranean captains plied their voyages under the threat of capture by the Barbary corsairs, and this induced a wariness which was not found elsewhere. By the end of the eighteenth century the power of these corsairs was in decline, though they were still able to attack the ships from smaller north European states which were less able to call on naval power to protect them and seek redress if captured. Under these circumstances the French trade and commerce raiding in the Mediterranean was carried on under somewhat different circumstances than elsewhere and the British response was also different.

The British measures to counter French commerce raiding elsewhere were not restricted to patrolling the focal points of trade and escorting convoys. Another important aspect was to take the war into French coastal waters. There was a vigorous attempt to check privateering at its source, and in at least one case it was possible to do this while carrying out one of the basic principles of British naval policy: the defence of Britain by stationing a squadron permanently off Brest.[75] This policy was extended by the use of frigates to patrol the north and south coast of Brittany partly to prevent supplies reaching Brest but also to capture privateers while they were in French coastal waters. It was also intended that the squadron should prevent warships from entering or leaving the base. That was the theory; in practice the westerly gales which blew the squadron off station - until it was discovered that part at least could shelter in the bay off Douarnenez - allowed French ships to return when the gales abated and before the British squadron could return. The hopes of a total blockade were seldom if at all realised. The squadron's record against privateers was better. Many, twenty in all, were captured in the vicinity of Ushant - and four others within a short distance of Brest.[76] Six had been fitted out at Brest and all were captured by the frigates from the Western Squadron. The corsairs varied widely, from the 18 ton *Ressource* to the 340 ton *Heureuse Nouvelle*, but it is likely that all were taken when they were trying to enter harbour rather than leave it. The former was more perilous, since ships making for Brest made their landfall at Ushant rather than in the bay on which Brest is situated, or even Camaret. The coastline was rocky and dangerous and a landfall anywhere else than Ushant was courting disaster. The island also served as the starting point for ships sailing westward from Saint Malo in peace time and returning from the Newfoundland fisheries and this practice of using Ushant persisted in wartime. Seven of the ships captured off Ushant were from Saint Malo; this includes the 100 ton *Franklin* of Port Louis which had been fitted out at Saint Servan. Ushant was also used by ships from other ports: two small Cherbourg ships, the 47 ton *PhénixPhénix and 49 ton Succès*, the 48 ton *Messager* from Conquet, the 24 ton *Napoléon le Grand* and 300 ton *Espoir* from Nantes, the 95 ton *Juste* from Lorient and the 110 ton *Ami des Planteurs* from Bayonne were all seized to or from cruising in the Channel Soundings. Not all surrended meekly without a fight; the *Ami des Planteurs* fought the sloop *Speedwell* and frigate *Surprise* for an hour and a half before finally surrending.[77]

The Admiralty records show how the patrolling force was deployed from the records of the captures. A screen of frigates sailed to the west and south of the island of Ushant and in the bay off Brest to watch for any sign that the fleet was planning to put to sea. In so doing they took three small Brest ships between 18 and 69 tons and the large 250 ton *Difficile.*[78] To the north of Ushant smaller craft mounted patrols and it was here that the revenue and naval cutters, sloops and occasionally frigates were used. Patrols were also made further away off the south coast of Brittany and along the Atlantic coast as far as the mouth of the Gironde. Their task was partly to watch the squadron at Rochefort and the Île de Ré, and partly to disrupt coastal traffic. The French tried to counter this by setting up a line of coastal telegraph stations on the coast of the Île de Ré to warn of the presence of British shipping, but these were only defended by militia and could easily be destroyed by a naval landing party. The British ships captured a variety of vessels in these raids: privateers, some naval storeships and a few that had been sent on trading voyages along the Atlantic coast in the belief that the risks of capture were slight. Many captains thought that they could remain at anchor under the guns of coastal artillery by day and sail by night but the British soon learned of this practice. Cochrane for example noticed a brig at anchor off Sables d'Olonne and sent a boarding party to capture it under cover of darkness before it could set sail.[79] Although his men were seen before they could board the brig and troops opened fire with muskets

Cochrane returned the fire from his frigate which he had anchored close to the shore to provide support if necessary and the brig was captured. On another occasion the naval brig *Pique* discovered a convoy off Abervrac'h on 17 December 1805 which was sailing by the light of a full moon. The escort, the 50 ton brig *Pique* of Saint Malo was abandoned by her crew during the action and another French gun brig and five of the convoy were wrecked.[80] A naval patrol off Lorient captured the 50 ton Lorient vessel *Zéphir* in October 1797, the 163 ton Brest privateer *Duguay Trouin* in January 1810 and the *Hirondelle* of Nantes (tonnage unknown) in the same month.[81] Naval vessels cruising off Nantes to intercept ships from there captured three: two from Nantes and one from Saint Malo.[82] The French tried to counter these activities in June 1803 by stationing the gunboat *Venteux* in the Île de Batz roads, where it was protected by coastal batteries. However it was captured by British seamen after a desperate fight in which the coastal batteries played no part, perhaps for fear of killing their compatriots.[83] Further south the British used the Île d'Yeu as a base and ships from there captured three French corsairs: the 90 ton *Aventurier* of Lorient, the 120 ton *Brunette* and the 300 ton *Mars* of Bordeaux in 1797 and 1800. This coastal blockade was also extended to cover Bordeaux; in June 1803 the *Sirius* took ships bound for Guadeloupe, Charleston and the Île de France in 45°53'N and 4°25'W and 5°25'W.[84] In August the frigate *Endymion* took the new Bordeaux schooner *Général Moreau* armed with 16 guns and a crew of 85 when she was six days out in 48°30'N, and before she had made any prizes.[85] Other patrols captured the La Rochelle ship *Hasard* in December 1797 and the 480 ton Bordeaux ship *Diane* when she was setting off for the Île de France. The evidence of this naval activity serves to show how a system of coastal patrols which was initially intended to check the flow of naval stores into Brest and paralyse the main battle squadron also limited the activity of corsairs. It was also a system which was readily extended during the Napoleonic War into a system of coastal blockade to prevent commerce from entering or leaving, whether in French or neutral - principally American - ships.

There was also an attempt to patrol the north coast of Brittany, but this was less successful than off the Atlantic coast. There were many difficulties navigating off the north coast of Brittany. The coast was lined with hidden dangers: submerged rocks lay off the shore, there were complex local currents and it was difficult to know the strength and speed of the tidal flow; local knowledge was essential, much as it was off the coast of Cornwall and South Devon. Naval officers, unlike the captains of privateers, did not possess this knowledge and it was bound to hamper their activities, for it was one thing to prepare charts of the coastline but another to learn the exact nature of the coastal currents. In spite of this an effort had to be made to prevent small coastal convoys from slipping along the shore under cover of darkness or the limited visibility of the winter days. The British policy was not to try and maintain a constant patrol of the coast, this was too dangerous, but to station a vessel off the Île de Batz. This was the most northerly point on the Breton coast and ships following the coastline had to run clear of the point. Six corsairs were taken in this way, three from Saint Malo, one from Paimpol one from Morlaix and another from Cherbourg.[86] This navel patrol also helped to check the movement of corsairs from Saint Malo and occasionally frigates ventured as far east as Cap Fréhel and Saint Brieuc, though it was unwise to maintain a blockade off Saint Malo on account of the coastal dangers.[87]

In spite of these perils every effort had to be made to limit the danger from the Saint Malo privateers, whose reputation was virtually the same as that of Dunkirk. By blocking the route along the coast to the west the corsairs were forced to sail north, past the Channel Islands. This had its dangers for the corsairs because the islands were traditionally the principal base for attacking French coastal shipping. The regular trade between Saint Malo and these islands provided the Channel Islanders with the local knowledge which was denied the naval officers and gave them every opportunity to prey on French shipping. Although the English corsairs, like their French counterparts, seldom risked battle with another privateer, they did try to capture the prizes which the French tried to send back to port, and this was a problem which concerned the Granville privateer as well. This was bound to influence French attitudes towards commerce raiding. When the coastal blockade and the effectiveness of the Channel Islands raiders was seen, there were fewer merchants willing to venture their capital in privateering ventures and it was more difficult to find crews. It also meant that captains were less willing to send prizes back to Saint Malo and either sent them to other ports which were not so effectively blockaded or ransomed their prizes. When they took this bond, and a hostage to encourage prompt payment, fewer men were needed on the corsairs because there was less need for prize crews. This reduced the cost of the voyages. On the other hand, it failed to bring any goods into Saint Malo which might have been sold to meet local needs or provide profit from sales to shareholders or on an open market. In practice however it seems as if the shareholders, managing owner and captain did not consider the venture in this analytical manner and were more concerned with the practical issues of financial support, the availability of able, young seamen and skilled craftsmen, ships and a generally held view of the chances of making money. The most that can be said is that everyone involved in commerce raiding at Saint Malo under these conditions used his own experience as the basis for his actions.

The threat to Saint Malo and Granville privateers did not end with the Channel Islands privateers; naval vessels were also based on the islands. Fifteen corsairs were taken by them near Guernsey, two off Jersey, two more off the Casquet Rocks, two near Alderney and one off the Seven Islands, probably the Îles Chausey.[88] One of these was the interesting case of the 17 ton *Ajax* of Saint Malo, captured by the privateer *Hasard* in July 1800. The managing owner realised that his vessel was small and frail and could be captured very easily. With this in mind the real captain, Joseph Boutrouche, was shown in the list of crew as the surgeon and another man, Jean Denis, as the captain. Denis did not serve as an officer but wanted to be paroled if the ship was captured. In this way he would have excaped imprisonment in one of the prison hulks or the new prison on Dartmoor and have led a comparatively free life at the expense of the British government in one of the small towns in Wales, central or northern England of the lowlands of Scotland to which officers were sent.[89] Whatever the reason it seems to have failed, since the ruse was detected. Small boats such as the *Ajax* did not always give up without a fight. The 36 ton *Pauline* was only taken by an armed English merchant ship after an eight hour struggle. Of the others, the 15 ton *Zéphir* of Saint Malo, also captured by a privateer, the *Rover* of Jersey and the others returning to port were the prizes of a variety of sloops, cutters and frigates. Their captains, who also lacked the local knowledge so important to avoid the perils of navigating in these dangerous waters, used local pilots and these probably also helped to guide the small raiding parties such as the armed lugger *Royalist* which took the *Sophie* in Cancale Bay in January 1797.[90] Nothing is known of the *Sophie* and it seems likely that she was a small coaster whose crew took to their boat and escaped when the *Royalist* approached. It would be wrong to assume from the above that the combined efforts of the Channel Islands privateers and a variety of naval vessels proved an effective blockade for the Saint Malo boats; many continued to sail and to return to port and there is one example of a Saint Malo boat, the *Coursier*, capturing the 100 ton brig *Belle Anne* in 1810 bound from Jersey to Madeira with a cargo of dry cod, brandy and apples.[91]

Naval patrols off the Channel Islands also served to check the progress of privateers from ports to the east when they tried to sail westwards towards the Channel Soundings. Boats from, Cherbourg were taken near Alderney and the Casquet Rocks: the 28 ton *Sans Souci* from Saint Vaast-la-Hougue, the 40 ton *Custine* and 65 ton *Rayon* from Cherbourg.[92] The area was an excellent cruising ground for British naval vessels because the French captains were forced to pass near the islands or sail along the southern coast of England, which was equally perilous. These captains relied on local knowledge but this was based on a knowledge of landmarks, currents and tides and provide routes which could be followed by men using the simplest navigational equipment. Few if any of the captains of these ships possessed charts and many in any case were likely to be illiterate. Their method of navigating was to follow the coastline, using their experience until they reached a landmark from which they followed a compass bearing to another familiar landmark. Those who possessed a map followed exactly the same procedure, and the maps were covered by an elaborate pattern of lines which radiated from focal points so that the mariner could easily make and follow his compass bearings. These rhumb lines thus reflected customary practice and it became comparatively easy for the British naval craft to base their cruise on such a focal point, in the certain knowledge that privateers would pass near by. It was in this way that 80 ton New England built *Hirondelle* from Dunkirk fell into British hands off Alderney in March 1793.[93]

Whenever possible naval patrols were mounted off ports from which corsairs were likely to leave. British vessels captured ten French corsairs in the vicinity of Cherbourg and another three off Cape Barfleur. Only three of these were from Cherbourg: the 18 ton English-built *Bonne Espérance*, the 21 ton *Crocodile* and the 13 ton sloop *Sans Peur.*[94] This accurately represents the nature of commerce raiding at Cherbourg; the port never possessed the wealth or experience to engage in privateering on any great scale. One feature of Cherbourg's commerce raiding which was typical of the experience of the smaller ports was the part played by the captain as an investor. Auguste Chosel, captain of the *Crocodile* had a 500 *livres* share in the boat which was a large sum for a provincial port, and François Lion was joint owner of the *Bonne Espérance.* The other vessels captured in these areas were all from other ports : Le Havre, Dieppe, Saint Valéry-sur-Somme and Boulogne, though there was one, the 42 ton *Avantageux* which was returning to Saint Malo from its second cruise in the eastern half of the English Channel.[95] By extending their patrols to the east the British warships were able to trap a variety of small craft which were attempting to evade the patrols by following the French coast. Eight were taken off prominent landmarks: five off Cap Barleur and three of Cap La Hogue.[96]

The task of patrolling the French coast to watch for privateers and small coasters was a tedious job for a naval officer and his crew. The men appointed to command the sloops and cutters were men of sufficient ability to rise from midshipman to lieutenant by way of the qualifying examination, but many of them lacked the family connexions which ensure their continued rise through the ranks of officers. There were exceptions; the fictional character Hornblower, immortalised in the series of novels by C.S. Forester and with a mock biography by C.N.Parkinson, passed through this stage on the way to fame and high rank, but there were not many like him.[97] Hornblower, like many other young lieutenants, spent many dreary weeks cruising off the north coast of France and saw little beyond a generally low and featureless coastline. It was to dispel boredom that patrols ranged far and wide in the hope of sighting and capturing a French ship. This is why the frigate *Niobe* entered the bay of Caen in 1810. There was little prospect of taking a ship of any considerable size there but the *Niobe* did find the 27 ton *Hirondelle* owned by a Caen merchant Hervieu Duclos, and fitted out at the tiny port of Saint Vaast-la-Hougue.[98] Much more promising for British naval ships was the approach to Le Havre, which had become by the end of the eighteenth century the entrepot for the prosperous cotton textile industry centred on Elbeuf and which was supplied by neutral shipping. During the wars there were some privateers fitted out at Le Havre and it was from there that the 50 ton *Custine* had sailed.[99]

From the mouth of the Seine at Le Havre to Dunkirk lay a number of small fishing harbours which occasionally sent privateers to sea. In all the ports there were experienced seamen who had sailed with the fishing boats to Newfoundland, off the Irish coast or in the English Channel and North Sea as well as on trading voyages to other European ports and the West Indies. Many had gained experience during the growth of commerce throughout France during the 1780's. The English response to this threat was to patrol the headlands along the coast, on the grounds that navigation there was less hazardous, naval ships could watch them with less danger than directly off the rest of the shore, and ships could not avoid them. All the headlands yielded their tally of prizes: the 55 ton *Hirondelle* of Calais between Dieppe and Fécamp, three more off Saint Valéry including one from that port, three off Dieppe, one near Tréport, one from Cap Gris Nez, one off Calais and two near Dunkirk.[100]

In some ways this was the weakest part of the British system of commerce defence, for so few ships were captured in these French coastal waters by comparison with the numbers that set sail from there. In some ways this was inevitable; captains of privateers did not sail until they knew that the British ships had been blown off their station. They also possessed local knowledge of tides and currents which the British seldom had and were able to evade blockading forces on their return, much as Jean Bart had done over a century earlier. On the other hand, the relative success of the British ships in the English coastal waters and in defending convoys shows that the Admiralty were right to place most of the emphasis on that, where they possessed the advantage. Convoys in any case tended to attract privateers and this made it much easier to defend trade and capture the raiders than endless patrols off a hostile and largely unknown coast. A further point is that these patrols off the north coast of France were not introduced as a permanent feature until 1806 and the figures show that of the thirteen captured, eight were taken between 1806 and 1813, three in 1793 as part of the initial mopping up of hostile ships and the last two in 1798 and 1799. It is significant that in the year of greatest activity, 1797, none were taken; the British naval force was occupied elsewhere.

Dunkirk, Boulogne and, to a lesser extent, Calais formed the pivot for raids on British commerce in the North Sea. Many of their privateers were captured off the coast of the Austrian Netherlands; Ostend and the island of Texel which were the most popular cruising grounds and where ships could anchor safely on a bank called the Broad Fourteens and ride out any storm.[101] A few corsairs were taken off the Austrian Netherlands - occupied by French forces before 1793 - the 40 ton *Patriote* of Calais and 62 ton *Jéna* from Dunkirk off Nieuport in 1793 and 1806; six off Ostend, four Dunkirkers and one each from Le Havre and Ostend (though owned by a Dunkirk merchant) and one captured while beached at Blankenberge.[102] The captors of these vessels, as in the English Channel were the smaller naval craft: cutters, sloops and brigs which were comparatively shallow draught and could sail close inshore. British naval vessels were active at the Island of Texel because this was where ships waited for high tide to carry them into the Zuider ZeeZuider Zee and on to Amsterdam. The larger ships had to offload some of their cargo to lighten the ship and there was always a number of lighters to carry goods. The continued importance of Amsterdam even during the French occupation of the Netherlands acted as a magnet to French corsairs. To reach the Texel they generally followed the coast and naval patrols captured several : two at the mouth of the Wester Schelde, the waterway leading to Antwerp, which was opened by the French after the occupation of the Austrian Netherlands. The 57 ton *Huit Frères* of Boulogne was taken off Westkapelle and the 52 ton *Furet* of Boulogne off Vlissingen.[103] Off the Maas, the waterway leading to Rotterdam, the frigate *Lizard* captured the 30 ton *Trois Amis* in 1793.[104] The 80 ton *Dragon* of Calais fell into British hands off the fort at Egmont and no fewer than eleven were taken off the Island of Texel, including the 200 ton *Jason* of Nantes and three others from 70 to 100 tons.[105] Some privateers ventured further: two were captured off the Island of Borkum and off the Danish coast in Jutland in 1797.[106] Another was taken in the same area by one of the Russian warships which assisted the British fleet.[107] During the Napoleonic War there were many British merchants who tried to evade the Continental System by shipping goods via the Island of Heligoland, and this attracted the *Cerf Volant* which was captured.[108]

Not all French ships cruised on the southern shore of the North Sea; many more were taken off the east coast of England, where they attacked the coasting trade and the convoys which escorted merchant ships from Hull to the Baltic and Norway. The smallest corsairs patrolled the low lying, deeply indented coast of Essex; here they could take refuge in one of the shallow creeks and lie in wait for small coasters, especially for the ships carrying woollens and corn from the East Anglian ports. Their captains needed local knowledge for the many sandbanks made navigation extremely hazardous. The English built 16 ton *Grâces* of Dunkirk was taken in the Swallet in July 1797 where her appearance and build made her appear English. The even smaller 10 ton *Espoir* from the same port was seized near the Naze Tower, one of the few landmarks on that coast, in June of the same year.[109] In both cases the captor was the same vessel, the revenue cutter *Viper*, which shows that on the east as well as the south coast these small craft played an important part in commerce defence. Packet boats sailed from Harwich to Holland but the channel leading to this harbour was narrow and was guarded by a fort on the Suffolk shore. This also helped to defend the important Ipswich corn trade, which attracted privateers when corn prices reached famine levels in northern France. Other corsairs were captured between Harwich and Orfordness: the 26 ton *Sans Peur*, the English-built *Maraudeur* and 126 ton *Contre Amiral Magon*, all from Dunkirk.[110] The *Sans Peur* had an American, Job Bunker, as first captain and the *Contre Amiral Magon* was commanded by the famous Jean Blanckmann, who was subsequently appointed Chevalier of the of the Legion of Honour in recognition of his success in the commercial war.

On this eastern coast, as off the south and south west of England, corsairs tended to, lie in wait to the lee of headlands which gave them some protection and where they could remain hidden from their intended victims. Orfordness was one, and two corsairs were captured there; two more were taken off Aldeburgh and another in the immediate vicinity.[111] One was commanded by a lieutenant in the French navy, Joseph Dorp and another by a Dutchman, Franciscus Leeuw, who had been born at Middelburg on the Island of Walcheren and had lived at Boulogne for seven years before his capture. His crew was a mixture of Dutch, Danes, Prussians, Swedes and French and this reflects his own cosmopolitan background. It would be wrong to assume that it was only Dunkirk, Boulogne and Calais ships which cruised off the east coast of England; the *Hardi Mendiant,* an English prize of 24 tons, had been fitted out at Cherbourg on behalf of a group of Morlaix merchants. All the captains of these ships possessed, or believed they possessed, the essential local knowledge, but it should be emphasised that large areas of the east coast were low lying and featureless. Jean Deville, captain of the 70 ton Ostend *Victoire* had no idea where he was when he was captured in May 1801 and there were others like him.[112]

Captains of privateers also possessed considerable knowledge of the pattern of trade of the east coast ports. Yarmouth, Boston, Lynn, Newcastle and Hull all engaged in extensive commerce in ship building materials with Norway and the Baltic and the trade already mentioned in corn and woollen cloth with northern Europe. There was also the extensive coal trade from the north east centred on Sunderland and Newcastle, though these colliers were manned by crews with a formidable reputation. Their cargoes were less attractive to Frenchmen than the other commodities. There was also whaling from Hull, though again the crews were regarded as tough and determined men and privateers made little attempt to interfere with them. The biggest prizes were the large ships from the north east of England, where specially built ships were used in the timber trade. Further south, Yarmouth was the centre of an important herring fishery which attracted boats from as far as Scarborough. An annual fair was held each Michaelmas and the famous smoked Yarmouth herrings were sent as far as Spain, Portugal and Italy. Yarmouth was one of the few east coast ports off which privateers could lie safely, for Boston and Lynn were protected by the elaborate sandbanks and channels of the Wash, where there was a constant danger of being driven ashore by strong north easterly winds. This helps to explain why so many French ships congregated off Yarmouth and the Dogger Bank and where the Admiralty had provided protection for the Yarmouth herring fishery in 1793.[113] Even Yarmouth held its perils for the unwary; ships were occasionally caught by a north east or easterly gale and driven ashore and all ships leaving Yarmouth for the north had first to weather Winterton Ness. To emphasise the dangers no fewer than four light houses were constructed between CaisterCaister and Cromer, and so dangerous were the Cromer Rocks that Cromer Bay was known to generations of mariners as the Devil's Throat.[114] In spite of these perils French ships cruised off Yarmouth and between 1797 and 1807 twelve were taken, five in November and early December when the Baltic trade returned and the remainder in January, February and mid-summer.[115]

The pitch, hemp and timber carried by the ships from Norway and the Baltic was particularly valuable prize, because trade between French ports and the Baltic was cut in wartime and it became difficult to obtain supplies through neutrals because of British naval patrols. Local supplies of timber were adequate, but hemp and pitch were very difficult to obtain. The local timber, from the forests of Flanders and northern France, was not of the same quality as the oak baulks and deals from Danzig and elsewhere in the Baltic, and this limited the shipbuilding to the construction and repair of relatively small ships which were not expected to have a long working life. So important was this Baltic trade for the French that corsairs lay off the Dogger, Well and Brown Banks to try and intercept English commerce though these areas must have been more perilous.[116]

Hull was the centre of this trade and received special protection. It was especially important because it acted as the entrepot for much of the commerce of the East Midlands and Yorkshire through the inland navigation of the rivers draining into the Humber. Lead from Derbyshire and Nottinghamshire, woollen cloth from Leeds, Wakefield and Halifax, butter from the East and North Riding of Yorkshire, cheese from the West Midlands and Cheshire, together with large quantities of wheat, were a great attraction for the French commerce raiders. So too were the Baltic items which formed the bulk of the return cargoes but iron, copper, potash, flax and canvas were also of importance. As an entrepot for the East Midlands, Hull shipping also traded in wine, oil and fruit from the Mediterranean, and from Hamburg came colonial produce, Bordeaux wines -when the trade was permitted - and produce from the East Indies. The distribution of this varied commerce posed serious difficulties in wartime, for the coastal trade could not easily be protected by convoys since it did not always fit into a clear pattern and the Admiralty did not possess sufficient ships. So Frenchmen familiar with this trade considered that there would be many small ships that would make valuable prizes. The captains of corsairs were unwilling to sail too far from their home port along the east coast and few cruised off Spurn Head, which in theory provided an excellent point from which to attack Hull shipping. Only two were captured there, one in December 1797 and two approximately a year later and another two at sea between Spurn Head and the Norfolk coast.[117] There were also problems of navigation off Spurn Head because it was continually changing its shape as sand from coastal erosion was deposited at the point. Flamborough Head was another suitable headland, and raiders could seek protection nearby in Bridlington Bay; Frenchmen used this as a base from which to attack the shipping which sailed directly north from Spurn Head before bearing north east from Flamborough Head for the Skagerrak. Winter cruising was usually restricted to the inshore waters, where the ships rolled less and shipped less water. This was important because damage to hulls and rigging was expensive to repair and captains could not afford to disable their ships.[118] Only four corsairs were taken off Flamborough Head, another four in 54°N and 55°N and one in Robin Hood's Bay.[119] The most interesting was the *Victorieux* taken in Robin Hood's Bay in February 1797, for this English-built, 27 ton vessel was commanded by an American, Thomas Huston, who had been born in Philadelphia. Huston had been commanding French ships for two years and had sailed under American colours, though the ships had been French owned. Though an American citizen, Huston had lived in many French ports and had fianally settled at Dunkirk when the *Victorieux* had been fitted out.

Few corsairs ventured beyond Flamborough Head and only four were captured there during the whole period. The prospects for commerce raiding were not as good as further south, for apart from the colliers already mentioned there were fewer than to the south; the north east and Scotland had a smaller population and lower standard of living. It is significant that the ships which were captured fell into British hands in 1798-1801 and 1807, years in which captains were searching for new areas for commerce raiding where the trade was less carefully defended. Scottish trade was seldom worth attacking; the Admiralty sent the 30 year old *Childers* brig to escort ships from Leith to Gothenburg in 1808, but the merchants recognised that she was unseaworthy and refused to sail under her escsort.[120] The few voyages which corsairs made to probe the defences were revealed by the place of capture: the 37 ton *Merveilleux* off Sunderland in April 1798, the 70 ton *Antichrist* off Shields in April 1801, the 60 ton *Courageux* off St Abbs Head in July 1799 and the 99 ton *Passe Partout* off Ronaldsay in May 1808.[121] The last is an interesting example of how French captains tried to obtain information about shipping movements; the Orkneys were the traditional centre for ships sailing north about to take on stores or refresh their men and the same is true of the Hudson's Bay Company ships, which took men on board there if they were needing extra hands. There were also traditional links with Norway, and the more adventurous captains such as Charles Torris of the Ostend *Passe Partout* could use the Orkneys as a fruitful cruising ground. He was unlucky; he was taken by an excise yacht, the *Royal George*, whose captain was probably expecting to catch smugglers rather than privateers.

From the Orkneys it was a comparatively easy run to the Norwegian coast - Orkney fishermen were frequently blown almost to the Norwegian coast by strong westerly winds. Bergen attracted corsairs because it was the second Norwegian port, the centre of a flourishing trade with England in peace time and was a port where prizes could be sold, new stores bought and ships refitted. There was also the risk that the English crew might recapture their ship. The *Anacréon* lost a prize in this way.[122] Nearby fjords were also used by French captains as bases for raiding English trade and it was to try and counter this that the Admiralty sent the 28 gun frigate *Hind* to cruise between the Orkneys and Norway early in the Revolutionary War. It was also hoped that the *Hind* would intercept a French convoy.[123] Some French captains, aware of the risks of using Bergen, occasionally used another, smaller port but this seldom proved satisfactory. There were no effective defences and it was comparatively easy for a British naval crew to capture a French ship even within the limits of the port. The 100 ton *Vrai Patriote* was captured in Stavanger after taking a Dutch prize there in 1793, the 36 ton *Sirène* was seized near the Naze of Norway, the 22 ton *Hirondelle* near Arendal and two, the 120 ton *Vengeur* and 75 ton *Rusé* at Christiansand.[124] All were from Dunkirk. The action of British naval crews boarding and capturing French ships and their prizes in neutral waters brought strong protests which were seldom of any effect. The need to defend the Baltic trade overrode other considerations. The Skagerrak offered prospects to French corsairs because very large English convoys passed through there in the spring and autumn. The 60 ton Le Havre *Auguste* recruited men in 1796 to replace deserters before cruising in the Skagerrak. This marks the furthest extent of French commerce raiding from northern Europe and it was left to merchants at Danzig, principally Pierre Andriel and Adolph Wolff, to equip privateers there during the period of the Continental System-Continental System when France and Prussia were at war. Three of their boats, the *Petit Diable*, *Tilsit* and *Général Rapp* were captured and it is likely these were more of an annoyance than a serious threat to English trade. In any case, there was an elaborate system of convoys to protect shipping within the Baltic from the time the merchant ships arrived to when they were ready to depart. The Danzig corsairs may in any case had been more concerned with taking Prussian ships than British.

The extensive commercial war which has been the subject of this chapter thus turns out to be an attempt by a great many experienced captains to take their ships to seas where they had local knowledge and experience of the organisation of trade and of the navigational features. To try and check them the navy used a range of vessels which were often rather larger but which were used to patrol the headlands and bays where corsairs were likely to wait. It thus became an elaborate cat and mouse game, in which both the English and French tried to outwit the other, the French cruising off the English coast and sometimes the smallest British naval vessels attempting to blockade the ports of the north coast of France and lie in wait off headlands, much as their enemy did across the English Channel. Thus on close examination the threat to British trade turns out to be far less organised and much more diverse than British merchants imagined, and more dependent on attitudes held by French merchants on the likely success of ventures. This in turn was often dependent on the availability of experienced seamen and suitable ships and the rise and fall of commerce raiding is thus dependent on a variety of factors which reflect conditions in France just as much as the number of British ships at sea. The rise and subsequent decline, a feature of both wars, is thus a reflection of the slow growth of optimism followed by doubts and uncertainty as the losses to British warships mounted. In the short run patriotism was less important than commercial considerations.

NOTES

1 Marcus, *Naval history of England, vol.2,* p 363.
2 For more information see W.E. May, *A history of marine navigation* (Hen-

ley-on-Thames, 1979), pp 32-5.

3 The 65 ton *Vengeur* of Boulogne was captured a few miles south east of the Downs in 1805; H.C.A.34/64; Archives de la Marine, Cherbourg 10P4/7.

4 H.C.A.32/983, 1005, 1089, 646, 818.

5 H.C.A.32/800, 843; Archives de la Marine, Cherbourg 4P3/17.

6 H.C.A.32/607, 520.

7 H.C.A.32/607, 520.

8 *Gayant, Hasard, Maraudeur, Providence, François et Furet No 2,* H.C.A.32/1004, 1057, 1104, 1152, 1035, 1268.

9 H.C.A.32/1058, 824, 829.

10 H.C.A.32/512, 511

11 H.C.A.32/806.

12 H.C.A.32/509.

13 *Sans Peur, Mandrin, Jeune Germaine, Cotentin, Prend Tout, Grand Diable, Hasard, Pensée, Thurot, Poisson Volant, Furet, Enfant de la Patrie, Fontaine, Justine, Unité, Aurore, Gabrielle, Grand Rodeur, Racrocheuse, Hasard,* H.C.A.32/832, 745, 686, 555, 799, 659, 671, 808, 866, 815, 627, 593, 620, 697, 958, 1036, 1045, 1161, 1049; Archives départementales du Pas-de-Calais, 9U21, Archives du tribunaux de commerce, Boulogne; Archives navales, Cherbourg, 4P3/17.

14 H.C.A.32/620.

15 Archives du Ministère des Affaires Etrangères, Correspondance Consulaire et Commerciale, Bergen, 2, 1793-1819, no pagination. Report on the *Fantaisie*'s prize, March 1793.

16 H.C.A.32/627; Archives départementales d'Ille-et-Vilaine, 15 R1/5.

17 H.C.A.32/807, 886.

18 H.C.A.32/494.

19 H.C.A.32/494.

20 H.C.A.32/1164, 1109.

21 H.C.A.32/494.

22 H.C.A.32/819, 823, 845, 937, 1044; Archives de la Marine, FF2/13.

23 H.C.A.32/609.

24 H.C.A.32/835.

25 Daniel Defoe, *A tour through the whole of the island of Great Britain* (2 vols, 1966 ed.), i,213.

26 H.C.A.32/696.

27 H.C.A.32/514, 610; Archives de la Marine, Brest, 2P6/31.

28 Defoe, *Tour through England*, i, 227.

29 Earl of Dundonald, *Autobiography of a seaman* (1860), pp 166-7.

30 H.C.A.32/807, 1153; Archives de la Marine, FF2/13; Archives de la Marine, Cherbourg, 9P6/1.

31 H.C.A.32/578, 1083, 744, 806, 1277, *Didon, Auguste, Indomptable, Marie Anne, Prends garde à lui, Incomparable.*

32 C.N. Parkinson, *Edward Pellew, Viscount Exmouth, Admiral of the Red*

(1934), p 100.

33 H.C.A.32/1028, 698, 1232, 745, 597, 1045, 1028, 1103, *Inconcevable, Venus, Milan, Delphine, Grand Argus, Friedland, Marsouin.*

34 H.C.A.32/807, 1093, 1207, 607, 725, 745, 845, 807, 828, 697, 641, *Petite Hélène, Magdelaine, Téméraire, Entreprise, Flibustier, Laborieux, Musette, Sophie, Papillon, Resolu, Incroyable, Coureur.*

35 Archives de la Marine, Brest, 2Q64.

36 H.C.A.32/867, 835, 844.

37 H.C.A.32/682, 1290, 886, 725, 650, 627, 686, 552, 866, 967, 990, 1073, 1012, 888, *Heureux Courier, Furet, Vengeur, Liberté, Guidelon, Fantaisie, Jean Bart, Calvados, Terrible, Bohémienne, Clarisse, Intrépide, Vengeur, Eliza*

38 H.C.A.32/62.

39 H.C.A.32/1286; Archives départementales d'Ille-et-Vilaine, 15 Rj/25; Archives de la Marine FF2/13.

40 H.C.A.32/512, 610.

41 H.C.A.32/609, 867, 844, 511, 513, 579, 658, 672, *Eclaire, Triton, Surveillant, Amis de Bordeaux, Adour, Duguay Trouin, Achéron, Grand Indien, Hardi, Invincible Napoléon*; Archives départementales du Morbihan, Lz 1598, *Sans Culottes,* ibid, Lz 939, *Hardi.*

42 H.C.A.32/844.

43 H.C.A.32/607. There was also an important provision trade between Nantes, La Rochelle, Bordeaux and Ireland, though this was carried in Irish ships.

44 Dundonald, *Autobiography,* p 184.

45 A. Friendly, *Beaufort of the Admiralty; the life of Sir Francis Beaufort, 1744-1858* (1977), pp 148-9.

46 J. Leyland (ed), *Papers relating to the blockade of Brest, Vol.1* (1906), p 83.

47 Ibid, p 53.

48 H.C.A.32/744, 825, *Mouche, Renard.*

49 H.C.A.32/579, 1077, 1277, 611.

51 H.C.A.32/1095, 611, 564, 702, 538, 556, 782, 679, *Minerve, Epervier, Coureur, Julie, Baalgad, Castor, Nantais, Télégraphe, Heureux.*

52 Archives de la Marine, Cherbourg, Corsaires et prises de l'An XI à 1814; Archives départementales du Morbihan, Lz 939.

53 H.C.A.32/593; Archives départementales d'Ille-et-Vilaine, 15 Rl/5.

54 H.C.A.32/535, 745.

55 Archives départementales d'Ille-et-Vilaine, 15 Rj/21.

56 H.C.A.32/965.

57 H.C.A.32/1049; Archives de la Marine, FF2/12.

58 H.C.A.32/867, 892, 888.

59 H.C.A.32/855; the *Endymion* was fairly new; it had been launched in 1797, T.D. Manning and C.F. Walker, *British warship names* (1959), p 183.

60 H.C.A.32/1144, 557, 832, 536.

61 H.C.A.32/1090.

62 Leyland (ed), *Blockade of Brest*, i, 357.

63 H.C.A.32/950, 897, 746, 819, 890, 823, 828, 1075, 1079, 892, 674, 753, 769, *Alerte, Vengeur, Minerve, Robert, Valeur, Revanche, Rusé, Jéna, Intrépide, Vigie, Henri, Mouche, Nouvelle Eugénie, Cerbère, Alerte, Coureur, Archus, Guepe, Rhuiter, Affamé, Aventure, Intrépide, Espiègle, Eagle, Espérance, Utile, Général Bernadotte, Légère, Troisième Ferrailleur, Cantabre.*

64 Leyland (ed), *Blockade of Brest*, i, 138.

65 Ibid, i, 301, ii, 252.

66 H.C.A.32/515, 566.

67 H.C.A.32/557, 914, 535.

68 H.C.A.32/897.

69 Archives départementales du Morbihan, Lz 1598.

70 Ibid.

71 H.C.A.32/834.

72 H.C.A.32/825.

73 Archives de la Marine, Toulon, 13 P3/4.

74 Dundonald, *Autobiography*, pp 173-4.

75 Leyland (ed), *Blockade of Brest*, i, 529.

76 H.C.A.32/516, 497, 950, 552, 1002, 593, 629, 620, 1041, 673, 697, 717, 1092, 750, 1130, 806, 825, 823, 841, 850, *Ami des Planteurs, Amiral Décrès, Coureur, Deux Frères, Espoir, Franklin, Glaneur, Heureuse Nouvelle, Incroyable, Juste, Mercure, Napoléon le Grand, Phénix, Ressource, Revanche, Sans Peur, Succès.*

77 H.C.A.32/620.

78 H.C.A.32/1139, 824, 887, 578, *Pélagie, Recovery, Vatout, Difficile.*

79 Dundonald, *Autobiography*, p 187.

80 Leyland (ed), *Blockade of Brest*, ii, 150-1.

81 H.C.A.32/914, 1005, 1061.

82 H.C.A.32/683, 574, 677, *Heureux, Didon, Heureux Hasard.*

83 Leyland (ed), *Blockade of Brest*, i, 54.

84 Ibid, i, 25.

85 Ibid, i,123.

86 H.C.A.32/743, 806, 847, 1090, 714, 633, *Morgan, Patriote, Souffleur, Lezard, Joséphine, Furet.*

87 H.C.A.32/564, 734; the 30 ton *Chasseur* and 10 ton *Malouin*, both of Saint Malo, were captured by the sloops *Brilliant* and *Seaflower* in March 1800 and April 1793.

88 H.C.A.32/522, 1240, 1157, 516, 568, 514, 521, 630, 746, 946, 956, 1324, 1109, 1157, 512, 664, 541, 558, 1174, 679, *Ajax, Zéphir, Pauline, Aimable Victoire, Courageux, Aventurier, Aventure, Furet, Marie, Amiral Ganteaume, Argus, Inconnu, Maître de Danse, Pommereul, Amitié, Hirondelle, Custine, Dorade, Sorcière, Heureux Speculateur.*

89 The details of prisoners of war are shown in Adm 98/107-326, Out Letters of the Medical Department, Adm 103 passim, Register of prisoners of war,

Adm 105/44-6, 59-66, Medical Department, Miscellaneous.

90 H.C.A.32/844.

91 Archives de Marine, Brest, 2Q/76.

92 H.C.A.32/664, 847, 725.

93 H.C.A.32/664.

94 H.C.A.32/531, 557, 844.

95 H.C.A.32/1041, 1232, 992, 521, 1310, 1193, 1018, *Espiègle, Vengeur, Cami, Avantageux, Duc de Tarante, Surcouf, Espérance.*

96 H.C.A.32/985, 1044, 511, 578, 593, 679, 672, 729, *Courier, Gouverneur Férino, Aventure, Daphne, Alisabeth, Heureux Societé, Hardi, Liberté.*

97 C.N. Parkinson, *The life and times of Horatio Hornblower* (1973).

98 H.C.A.32/1061.

99 H.C.A.32/541, 578, *Custine, Chauvelin, Diable Volant.*

100 H.C.A.32/678, 1325, 1075, 610, 961, 1044, 494, 1001, 1023, 1144, 621, 686, *Hirondelle, Emilie, Impromptu, Aimable Nélie, Général Candaux, Aimable Marie, Deux Frères, Entreprenant, Prospère, Furet, Jean Bart.*

101 Sir William Dillon, *A narrative of my professonal advantures (1790-1839)* (2 vols, 1955, 1956), ii, 154.

102 H.C.A.32/799, 1075, 640, 668, 754, 874, 824, 967, *Patriote, Jéna, Flibustier, Hasard, Jeune Marie, Masséna, Sans Pareil, Revanche, Brave.*

103 H.C.A.32/679, 1032.

104 H.C.A.32/863.

105 H.C.A.32/582, 705, 538, 541, 611, 841, 866, 825, 699, 751, 534, 832, *Dragon, Jason, Barras, Custine, Emouchet, Suffisiante, Vaillant, Custine, Revanche, Jupiter, Marsouin, Buonaparte, Sans Culottes.*

106 H.C.A.32/888, 807, *Victoire, Petit Furet.*

107 60 ton *Augustine* of Le Havre, H.C.A.32/509.

108 H.C.A.32/556.

109 H.C.A.32/654.

110 H.C.A.32/856, 744, 979.

111 H.C.A.32/729, 671, 541, 538, *Liberté, Hardi Mendiant, Custine, Bienvenue.*

112 H.C.A.32/902.

113 Marcus, *Naval history of England, vol.2,* p 23.

114 Defoe, *Tour through Great Britain,* p 70.

115 H.C.A.32/1218, 1028, 949, 659, 640, 558, 630, 901, 807, 938, 1024, 1076, *Vigilant, Friedland, Actif, Guerrier, Fantaisie, Chasseur, Flibustier, Voyageur, Poisson Volant, Chasseur, Furet, Jéna.*

116 H.C.A.32/896, 806, 807, 825, 991, 1083, 823, 943, *Virginie, Petit Pérou, Prospère, Renommé, Comtesse d'Huneburg, Impératrice, Riboteur, Alerte.*

117 H.C.A.32/888, 1290, 812, 520, *Victoire, Général d'Orsenne, Mercure, Perseverant, Anacréon.*

118 Sir William Dillon, while a lieutenant commanding the brig *Childers* had put into Berwick Bay to reset his rigging and replace a topmast in February 1808 while sailing from Sheerness to Leith; Dillon, *Narrative*, ii, 86.

119 H.C.A.32/581, 730, 798, 1014, 1205, 807, 675, 1002, 887, *Deux Frères, Légère, Optimiste, Eglé, Trente et Quarante, Voltigeur, Prodige, Husard, Décidé, Victorieux.*
120 Dillon, *Narrative,* i, 69.
121 H.C.A.32/747, 524, 561, 1157.
122 Archives du Ministère des Affaires Etrangères, Cossespondance Consulaire et Commerciale, Bergen, 2, 1793-1819, no pagination.
123 Dundonald, *Autobiography,* i, 55.
124 H.C.A.32/877, 846, 678, 891, 828.

4 The privateering record: managing owners

At the heart of the French war on commerce stands a group of men known collectively as *armateurs* or managing owners. These were the men who took the initial decision to fit out a ship and send it to sea, who then raised the capital by selling shares, bought a ship or had one constructed, hired the captain and crew and organised the venture until the ship and any prizes were finally sold, prepared the accounts and distributed the proceeds among the shareholders. At each stage they charged a commission for their work and were among the few people who consistently made a profit from these ventures. These managing owners were by no means a homogeneous group within French commercial society. Some were managing owners or captains who had been wealthy and influential before the war. The others were the owners of small coasters who had played a minor part in the economic life of the port. Many of these who emerge as organisers of commerce raiding ventures are thus new men, whose background is hidden in the minutiae of commercial life, but who in these wars occasionally became rich and famous from privateering. One reason for this remarkable shift in emphasis, at least in the major ports, is the heavy penalties exected from the rich in the form of revolutionary taxes and levies. At the same time the public hatred of wealth at a time of hardship made the rich merchants keep out of the public view as much as possible, and it was only with the passing of time that a few ventured to organised privateering voyages.

Pressure on the leading merchants began to rise in 1790, and an examination of the events at Dunkirk reveals the process. In 1789 a number of merchants had managed to avoid being included in the tax rolls, but this was quickly corrected by more zealous revolutionary officials. The total tax receipts for Dunkirk in 1789 had amounted to 27,349 *livres*.[1] The next year the total was raised to 36,237 *livres*, not by levying taxes at a higher rate - the average was lower - but because the tax rolls were more complete. This was followed by a series of measures which laid heavier financial demands on the population. The basis of this taxation was the income and property value submitted by the merchant, but the demand came at a period of acute financial crisis when it was extremely difficult to raise loans when the income had fallen. Property values were also to some extent irrelevant, since merchants could not realise the full values of houses and ships in the depressed market. Merchants did manage to continue trading until the outbreak of war with Austria in 1792, but they did so under increasingly uncertain conditions; the *assignats* were not valid as a medium of international exchange and bills of exchange could not easily be created in the absence of a stable currency. Commercial paper became increasingly expensive and difficult to obtain and coin very rare. In 1792 many merchants in Dunkirk, St Malo and throughout France were facing bankruptcy. The figures for tax revenues from St Malo and St Servan reinforce this impression:

Tax income from St Malo and St Servan[2]

	1790 *livres*	1791 *livres*	1792 *livres*
St Malo	153,365	121,171	13,306
St Servan	15,051	13,695	13,036
			2,798 Supplement

These figures reveal the distress of one of the leading ports, but they only provide part of the picture, for the merchants were unable to pay the sums demanded. Of the total of 319,185 *livres* that was due in these years, 75,778 *livres* were unpaid in 1792. The main burden of the taxation bore heavily on the wealthy. In Dunkirk the 268 wholesale merchants paid one fifth of the total and the 32 richest paid almost one third of that.[3] If this had been paid on the pre-Revolutionary income it might not have been an unjust burden, but in the financial crisis it was another matter. A merchant taxed on his earlier income could not easily raise money from his capital assets - house, ships and stock - when coin was scarce and *assignats* not worth having. At the same time wealthy merchants could not defy the government and refuse to pay, for they were widely regarded as social parasites who were exploiting the misery of the poor by manipulating the commodity markets. In some cases this was undoubtedly true; it was normal commercial practice to speculate in commodities. The majority however were more likely to try and find ways of raising the taxes demanded.

ST MALO

St Malo provides a detailed picture of this decline in the fortunes of the leading merchants. In the 1780's it had been flourishing, and merchants participated in a variety of trades. The details can be seen in the records of the *Inscription Maritime* which show how each of the inscribed seamen were employed through the crew lists or *rôles d'equipage*. The leading family in the 1780's and the years before the outbreak of war with Britain in 1793 were the Dubois. Benjamin Dubois, the head of the family, was managing owner for 11 ships in 1790. His eldest son was managing owner of another 5 and his youngest son, Dubois le Jeune des Corbières, another 2.[4] Benjamin Dubois' largest ship was the 500 ton *Royal Louis* which sailed to the Île de France. The next was the 334 ton *Général Washington* which was sent to New York via Lorient, and the 280 ton *Picardie* was used in general European commerce. Dubois was also managing owner of two ships of at least two hundred tons: the 160 ton *Sophie* and the 100 ton *Franklin*; the first sailed to New England and the latter to New York via Lorient, probably accompanying the *Général Washington*. The remaining ships consisted of the 90 ton *Suffren* which sailed to New York, the 80 ton *Jean Jacques*, which went to the Grand Banks fisheries off Newfoundland and four coasters: the 80 ton *Télémaque*, 45 ton *Va et Vien*; 35 ton *Elizabeth* and 22 ton *Sophie*. Dubois' eldest son used five ships to fish off the islands of St Pierre and Miquelon South of Newfoundland: the 110 ton *Succès*, 100 ton *Elizabeth*, 90 ton *Baron d'Espérance*, 70 ton *Marguérite* and 50 ton *Susquavie* (?). Dubois' younger son was managing owner of two ships: the 100 ton *Bon Patriote* and 85 ton *Duchesse de la Châtre* and used them in short distance coastal trade. Collectively this formed a large group with far ranging interests, each of which complemented the rest.

The moderate sized boats used in the fishery off St Pierre and Miquelon supplied salted fish to markets in Spain, Portugal and the Mediterranean as well as to the north eastern states of America. The ships to Île de France and North America formed the basis of a valuable trade in French and European exports, which were gathered at Lorient and St Malo by the smaller coasters and these also acted as a link between St Malo and the southern and western coasts of France. It was a pattern of trade which largely guaranteed success, for each part balanced and complemented the rest. The family of Dupuy Fromy et fils managed the largest fishing fleet at St Malo; 14 of the 16 ships sailed to the Newfoundland fisheries, two of them the 70 ton *St Rémy* and 70 ton *Marie Anne* to the Grand Banks, one ship sailed to Cadiz, the 180 ton *St Joseph*, and the 120 ton *St Christophe* was employed in the general European trade. Some of the fishing vessels were very large: the *Grand St Pierre* was 400 tons, the *Neptune* 350 tons and there were three others between 200 and 250 tons: the *Pêcheur, Louis Auguste* and *Françoise*. The family also managed another four over 100 tons and the other two were the 90 ton *St Charles* and 60 ton *Ste Emilie*. Many of these were large partly because they were designed to carry a heavy catch but also because the shore based fisheries required many extra men to erect the drying stages and prepare the fish. In terms of the total tonnage Dupuy Fromy et fils managed a larger fleet than Benjamin Dubois and his sons: 2,820 tons against 2,667 tons, but the Dubois fleet was more varied and potentially more profitable because of this.

Another important family was Grandclos Meslé which managed 9 ships in 1790 and had interests in the slave trade, the West Indies, Newfoundland fisheries and the European and short distance coasting trade. Their largest ship was the 540 ton *Mesny*, which went to Guinea in 1790 and the 300 ton *Père de Famille* complemented this through trade with the West Indies via Cadiz. Another 300 ton ship, the *Américain*, was used in the general European commerce and there were also two fishing boats, the 200 ton *Stanislas* and 90 ton *Postillon*. The remaining three ships were all small; the 60 ton *Pauline*, 40 ton *Pierre* and 30 ton *Eléonore*. Others who managed more than one ship included Desjardin Fichet, whose four ships sailed to different fisheries off Newfoundland: the 325 ton *Désire* and 180 ton *Gentille* went to the Petit NordPetit Nord, the 50 ton *Marie* to Trois Îles and the 190 ton *Favori* was destined 'to Newfoundland'. Guibert père and Pottier de la Houssaye each managed three ships; the former sent his, ranging from 100 to 350 tons, to the Petit Nord, the latter sent his 110 and 60 ton ships to the fisheries off St Pierre and Miquelon and his 45 ton vessel was employed in the local coasting trade. Pottier de la Housseye may also have had two others, the 150 ton *Six Frères* and 175 ton *Véritable* which sailed the following year to the West Indies and Gold Coast.[5] Another managing owner of several ships was Pierre Héron, whose three ships, *Marie Jeanne* 75 tons, *Jeune Reine* 70 tons and *Hyacinthe*, 90 tons, were all employed in the short distance coasting trade but he also shared in the New England commerce with Gonidec and Amicolon by partnership in the 180 ton *Alouette*. Another merchant who also had wide ranging commercial interests was Jallobert, who managed the 110 ton coaster *Héros*, the 80 ton *Sylvain* with his son and the 200 ton *Titus*, which sailed to Newfoundland, was managed jointly with Herbert de la Forte Barre. Menain Robert Menain Robert frères frères managed the 250 ton *Ste Anne* and 260 ton *St André* and another ten 70 and 80 ton vessels were managed by Canneva aîné, le Couffle and Chenu Piednoir, five of them by Canneva aîné. All these were fishing vessels that sailed to St Pierre and Miquelon and the Grand Banks. There remain a number of ships managed by a variety of merchants; many of the ships were around 80 tons and were used in the Newfoundland fisheries, the remainder stayed in the waters off northern and western Europe.

The picture remains essentially the same for the next two years, 1791 and

1792; though the number of ships declined, the ratio in each trade remained about the same. When war was declared in 1793 the government was anxious to utilise the maritime resources at St Malo and elsewhere and attack enemy trade, and passed a number of measures which tried to make commerce raiding an attractive proposition; at the end of January men were released from the *Inscription Maritime* to serve on corsairs and in February the government renounced all claims to a share in the sales of prizes.[6] The response of the Malouin merchants is interesting. Few of the men who had dominated the port's trade in the previous decade took an active part in privateering. Many fell victim to the Terror or fled. This left a comparatively small number of experienced men. Dupuy Fromy, who managed sixteen ships in 1790 and had sent thirteen to sea in 1791 fitted out a single privateer in February.[7] The 60 ton *Jeune Emilie* was a brigantine, which had been built in New England in 1783 and before the outbreak of war had gone regularly to the Newfoundland fisheries. Dupuis Fromy appointed Jacques, probably his son, as captain to ensure a proper control of the ship and the voyage proved a financial success. A Dutch ship, the *Liberté* of Saardam, was captured and the ship and cargo were sold for 1,014,000 *livres*.[8] There were several unusual features of this voyage of the *Jeune Emilie*. The first is that as a ten-year-old ship she was probably the oldest to be used as a privateer from St Malo in either war, though she had been launched in the last year of the previous Anglo-French-American conflict and must have been designed to sail fast. Another advantage to the owners was that because the *Jeune Emilie* had been built in North America she probably possessed certain characteristics in her appearance which made her appear slightly different from the usual French ship, and when flying a United States flag was able to pass for an American ship. With one or two members of the crew able to speak English the *Jeune Emilie* could sail relatively freely in the English Channel. The only risk of capture was to meet a British naval ship commanded by a vigilant captain. But he had to be careful before carrying out a detailed search or even boarding her, for the Americans resented the right of British naval officers to enter their ships to search for deserters. Thus the *Jeune Emilie* had the perfect disguise.

Another family which had been important before the war and which engaged in commerce raiding in 1793 was the Dubois family. Alexis Dubois the youngest son, who lived in St Servan, fitted out the 250 ton *Guidelon* jointly with a St Malo merchant Fichet, who had been a part managing owner of a Newfoundland fishing vessel, as well as three with Dujardin, another Newfoundland merchant.[9] The ship was apparently managed by Nicholas Guidelon who was appointed captain, although at 61 he was comparatively old, though in excellent health.[10] The *Guidelon* was a new ship and cannot have been designed for speed. She was captured South of the Scilly Isles during the summer and the voyage was a complete failure; no prizes taken.[11] In the absence of other leading families from commerce raiding the responsibilities fell on lesser men. The first letter of marque was given to Robert Menais frères, who before the war had sent a 260 ton ship, the *St André*, to Newfoundland. The new brigantine which they fitted out as a corsair was the 60 ton *Républicain* and they chose as captain a man who was experienced in the Newfoundland fisheries, René Raffy. Raffy had been captain of the *Marie Joseph* in 1786 and had taken her to the fisheries off St Pierre and Miquelon. In the following two years he had commanded the same ship, which was transferred in 1789 to the *Michel Joseph*, commanded the *Maria Sophie* in 1790 and the *Pourvoyeuse* in the last two years before the outbreak of war in 1793.[12] Raffy proved an excellent choice for he took the 203 ton *Peggy* of Greenwich which was sold with her cargo for 379,000.[13]

The largest corsair in this year of the war was the 450 ton *Duguay Trouin*, fitted out by two St Malo merchants, Guillemaut and Bodinier, who managed the 50 ton coaster *Pierre* as well. Each had experience in other ventures; Guillemaut as joint owner of the 60 ton *Auguste* which had sailed to Martinique in 1791 and Bodinier in the 250 ton *Maréchal de Castries* that had fished on the Petit Nord in Newfoundland.[14] The two men put their experience to good use in this unusual venture. The ship-rigged *Duguay Trouin* was very large and expensive to fit out and raising sufficient capital was a major problem. The choice of captain added considerable prestige to the venture, for Dufresne Le Gué was a St Malo man, born in 1761, who sailed to the Guinea coast in large ships every year from 1786 to 1790. Moreover, the *Duguay Trouin*, like the *Jeune Emilie*, had been built in 1783 and was fast for her size. In this ship Le Gué captured two prizes, the *Bonne Espérance* and the 520 ton *Albemarle* of London, which produced a total of 1,501,848 *livres*.[15] The other large ship which was used as a privateer was the 235 ton *Tigre*, fitted out by Delastelle. Nothing is known of this man; he did not manage any ships before the war and was probably an experienced officer who decided to try his luck as a managing owner when he saw a number of prize ships arrive in St Malo. His *Tigre* was given a letter of marque in May, three months after the outbreak of war, and was one of the last to be sent to sea before all privateering was halted by an embargo. The voyage proved a success; the Danish ship *Neptune* was seized and sold with her cargo for 398,902 *livres*.[16]

The next most successful venture was the *Malouin*. This was a tiny 10 ton vessel, which carried five two pounder guns and was given a letter of marque in February 1793.[17] The managing owners were Canneva and Leyritz, the first of whom had appeared in the shipping records as managing owners of Newfoundland fishing vessels. In 1790 he had sent the 80 ton *Anne* and *Marie Anne* to the Grand Banks and the 80 ton *Angélique*, 55 ton *Dauphine* and 86 ton *Marguérite* to St Pierre and Miquelon. The Newfoundland fisheries had given him the experience of choosing small vessels that were light and manoeuvrable in the inshore fisheries and he was able to use this experience in selecting the *Malouin*. Its shallow draught made it an ideal vessel to cruise in the English coastal waters and it was under these conditions that the *Elizabeth* was captured, later sold for 559,000 *livres*.[18] Towards the end of April the boat was taken by the

Brilliant off St Brieuc as it was working along the coast. The success of the *Malouin* encouraged Canneva and Leyritz to send another ship to sea in May. This was the 45 ton Boston built brigantine *Malouin*, which captured the *Ruby*, later sold for 134,800 *livres*.[19] The *Malouine* returned safely to port at the end of August, no doubt partly helped by its American appearance.

Gautier le jeune and Foucher represent another aspect of the St Malo trade. The former had appeared in the shipping records as the owner of a 39 ton sloop the *Louis Henry*, which he employed in the local coasting trade. In 1793 the two men fitted out a 25 ton lugger, the *Hirondelle*, which carried three small cannon and six swivel guns.[20] Their choice of a small vessel with fore and aft rig showed that they wanted a vessel which could sail quickly under variable conditions when the wind was likely to veer; much time could be lost on a square rigged ship in changing the set of the sails, but a sloop, schooner or lugger could do this more quickly. The choice proved a good one and the *Hirondelle* captured the 290 ton *Marie Anne* of Greenock which was sold later for 502,794 *livres*.[21] Another merchant with a similar background and greater success was Marion fils, who in 1790 was the part owner of two coasters, the 9 ton sloop *Suzanne* and the 60 ton brigantine *Ste Anne*. In 1793 he fitted out the *Furet* (tonnage unknown) which in the course of the cruise captured three ships, the *Dame Elizabeth* of Hamburg, the *Amitié* and the Bremen ship *Felix*.[22] These were sold for a total of 1,556,037 *livres*, which was the largest amount raised from a single voyage at St Malo in this year. None of the other ventures in 1793 were successful. Pierre Héron had been managing owner of three brigantines in 1790: the 70 ton *Jeune Reine*, 75 ton *Marie Jeanne* and 90 ton *Hyacinthe* which he used in the coasting trade, and a part share in the 180 ton brigantine *Alouette* which was employed in the New England trade. In April 1793 he fitted out the 25 ton *Laborieux* with a member of the Peltier family, who were the managing owners of a small coaster and fishing boat. The *Laborieux* was captured 10 miles South of the Lizard at the end of April and Pierre Héron's later venture, the 25 ton lugger *Suprême*, fitted out in May was managed by Gilles Rouillard, who was appointed captain. This was also captured.[23] Aimable Clairault, the managing owner of the 7 ton coasting lugger *Aimable Liberté* before the war, fitted out the 6 ton *Coureur*, built in 1790 and commanded it himself. Charles Lemoine, who in 1790 had had been managing owner of the 70 ton brigantine *Marie Françoise*, fitted out the 9 ton English built *Custine* jointly with Prunet, but their boat also fell into British hands. The captain, Pierre Kerpoisson, born in 1767 the son of a farm worker, had commanded a number of small coasters before the war.[24]

The fame of St Malo as a centre for commerce raiding also encouraged a Rouen company Pontevé et Cie. to participate. In March and April two vessels were given letters of marque; both had been built at St Pierre or Miquelon for the cod fishery. The first to set sail was the 60 ton *Liberté*, built in 1789 and commanded by a Granville man, Luc le Redde, who had commanded Dupuy Fromy et fils' 70 ton *Marie Anne* on a voyage to Newfoundland in 1790. This did not save the *Liberté*, which fell into British hands in April South West of the Scilly Isles after taking the *Juno* of Bremen in 49°30'N 10°W of Paris.[25] Pontevé et Cie had no more luck with their other ship, the 60 ton *Egalité*, built in 1787. This was captured later the same month in 49°21'N; both ships cruised in the same area, both were seized by the frigate *Hind*.[26] One of the most successful voyages was managed by two men, one of whom had been the captain of a small coaster in 1790 and had risen to be part owner of a larger vessel in 1791; the other is unknown. Captain Duchesne had been master of the 45 ton *Chasse Marée Neptune* in 1790 when it had sailed to Jersey with cider; in 1791 he became the part owner, with Consorti, of the 80 ton barque *Marguérite*, which they used in the local coasting trade.[27] Duchesne was thus in a good position to choose a suitable craft for commerce raiding and knew many of the captains. The 70 ton *Ambitieux* was commanded by his partner's son, Jacques Pintedevin and before its capture had taken the *Industry*, *Active* and *Union*, which were later sold for 245,967 *livres*, 1,433,000 *livres* and 193,000 *livres* respectively. The *Ambitieux* also captured the 280 ton American ship *Andrew* bound from Charleston to Amsterdam in 49°N 18'N, 10°W of Paris and a Danish ship bound from Malaga to Stettin with wine and oranges in 50°N 11°W of Paris before being captured.[28]

There followed a lull in commerce raiding at St Malo. The government placed an embargo on it to try and provide sufficient sailors for the navy and although the embargo was raised on 23 Thermidor Year III (15 August 1795) commerce raiding at St Malo only began again in 1796. Only nine ships were fitted out in this year, and six were captured. Joseph Fichet, who had enjoyed spectacular success with Alexandre Dubois and the *Guidelon* in 1793, fitted out the 85 ton Irish built brig *Coureur* in Ventôse Year IV (February 1796) but the ship was captured by the sloop *Porcupine* and revenue cutter *Fox* north of Ushant.[29] Fichet joined another merchant, Guibert of St Servan, a newcomer to privateering, in fitting out the 30 ton lugger *Providence*, but that was captured off Lands End in November by the armed cutter *Dover*.[30] The next year, undeterred, they fitted out the new 130 ton brig *Triton* but it only took a single prize. This raised only 3,503 *livres* - less than the crew's advance (6,953 *livres*) and the *Triton* was captured in 40°N in February 1798 by the *Melpomene*.[31] Their other venture, the 30 ton English built cutter *Expédition* took no prizes and was not used again. This did not completely destroy the resolve of the partners, for in the last year of the war they fitted out the 56 ton *Providence*.[32] Lauriole, Lemoine et Cie., whose *Custine* had been taken in 1793, ventured the new 11 ton lugger *Entreprise*, commanded by Joseph Lauriole, but it was taken by the revenue cutter *Duke of York* near the Isle of Wight in August.[33] The largest vessel which sailed from St Malo this year was the 100 ton *Pichegru*, fitted out by Duchesne and Pintedevin.[34] This partnership had been very successful in 1793 but the new venture failed to make any profits and the ship was fitted out in March the following year by a merchant at Brest, Cowell and was captured off Portland by the brigantine *Resolution*. Duchesne and Pintedevin also fitted out a 100 ton Baltimore ship the *Morgan* at Lorient in March and appointed an American, John Coffin Whitney as captain, but it was captured NW of the Île de Batz by the *Suffisante*.[35] The other three vessels were equally small and were all fitted out by managing owners who were otherwise unknown. Claude Martin of St Servan prepared the 12 ton *Patriote* but this fell to the sloop *Suffisante* off the Île de Batz in June.[36]

As confidence gradually began to return in the winter of 1796-7, some merchants decided to make a second attempt at making money and fulfilling their patriotic duty. Benjamin Dubois, who had been so wealthy and influential before the war and who had participated in commerce raiding through his two sons in 1793 fitted out the tiny 6 ton *Téméraire*.[37] Nothing is known of the captain, L'hôtelier, or the voyage except that the vessel was wrecked and neither Benjamin nor his two sons fitted out another vessel this year. Dupuy Fromy et fils had also been successful with their *Jeune Emilie* and sent her to sea again under a new captain Jean le Bedel. Le Bedel was very experienced; he was 48 years old, had been appointed captain in April 1787 and provisional *lieutenant de vaisseau* in Nivôse Year II. In 1793 he had been appointed second captain of the *Jeune Emilie* and assumed full command when Captain Fromy fell ill.[38] Under le Bedel's command the corsair took two prizes, *Bataillon* and *Comet* which were later sold for 93,249 *livres* and 2,998 *livres*, before being captured in her turn in 49°10'N 12°24'W in February 1797.[39] Dupuy Fromy et fils' other venture, the 153 ton *César* had been built in 1772. However, it only took one prize, a Prussian vessel, which produced 4,198 *livres* and was probably less than the cost of preparing the *César* for her voyage. In March the privateer was taken in 44°17'N 17°W by the *Cambria*.[40] Duchesne and Pintedevin followed their ventures of 1796 with the 97 ton *Favori*, built in New England in 1778, but whose disguise as an American vessel did not survive a meeting with John Bazeley, whose frigate *Hind*, one of Lord Bridport's fleet, captured her in 49°40'N 15°4'W of Paris in January 1797.[41] However, this did not deter the partners from fitting out a second ship, the new 36 ton *Audacieux*, built at St Servan, which seized the *Young Mary* before being taken by the revenue cutter *Diligence* in June 1797.[42] The prize was sold for 33,000 *livres*, and encouraged Duchesne and Pintedevin to fit out a third vessel, the new 53 ton lugger *Courageux*, which captured the *Hope* and *Vengeur*, later sold for 13,249 *livres* and 324 *livres*.[43]

During this year the greatest success came to another new man, Fantan, who had not been the managing owner of any ships before the war. He fitted out the three-masted ship *Minerve* of 260 tons which had been built at La Ciotat in 1785.[44] The ship made five captures, two over 100 tons, and another was ransomed. The total proceeds amounted to 230,107 *livres*; his son, Fantan jeune Thomas aîné fitted the ship out for its second voyage the following year. The two men also bought a 22 ton cutter which had already made one successful cruise under the management of another new man, Sainton, in 1796. During the first cruise the *Espérance* had sent in prizes to a total value of 187,238 *livres*.

Under Fantan jeune and Thomas aîné the *Espérance* was given a letter of marque in November 1796 but was captured in the middle of the English Channel in April 1797 by the cutter *Grand Falconer*, after sending in the *Juliana*.[45] This proved a very valuable prize; it was later sold for 442,634 *livres*. Fantan le jeune also gained experience in preparing vessels for commerce raiding by equipping the 18 ton lugger *Jean Bart* for the Dunkirk merchant Dauchy. The *Jean Bart* had been built at Dunkirk in 1780 during the War of American Independence and still possessed the qualities of speed and manoeuvrability which had been needed earlier. No details survive of the cruise, but the lugger made another and was captured by the cutter *Telemachus* off Start Point in November after taking the *Fly*, which was sold for 185,806 *livres*.[46]

Canneva and Leyritz followed the successful first voyage of the *Malouin* and *Malouine* in 1793 by a new venture in 1797. Canneva joined Martin and Santerre in the 85 ton American schooner *Laure*. The first cruise produced two prizes worth 293,040 *livres* and this compensated Santerre for his other venture with another man, Autier, whose 70 ton Boston built brigantine *Malouine* ended her cruise at Lorient without taking any prizes.[47] Lemoine, a merchant who had been managing owner of a coaster before the war had had two unsuccessful ventures in 1793 with two different partners, made another two attempts in 1793 by himself. The first was an English built vessel, the 8 ton *Audacieux* and the second was another 8 ton vessel, the new lugger *Surprise*.[48] There is no record of captures by either and although both returned safely to St Malo, neither made another voyage.

Despecher frères, whose *Bons Amis* had been the only successful venture from St Malo in 1796, sent her to sea again in 1797 under the same captain, but in partnership with Dupuy Fromy, who had been so successful in 1793. There is no record of any prizes from this venture and this small, Fowey-built vessel was taken by the frigate *Spitfire*.[49] Delpeux frères had better luck, though they lost their ship. The seven year old, 60 ton Boston-built schooner *Amitié* captured the American ship *John*, later sold for 146,992 *livres*, but was herself taken by the English privateer lugger *Plymouth* West of Guernsey.[50] Of the remaining managing owners, Lememe and Gautier, whose younger son had enjoyed some success with the lugger *Hirondelle* in 1793, fitted out the 50 ton Spanish-built brig *Flibustier*, but this was captured by the sloop *Spider* off the Lizard in May.[51] Several of the other managing owners were new men, who had not owned ships at St Malo before the war: Michel Delastelle, with a 29 ton English-built cutter *Marie*, Jean Ravaleux et Cie of St Servan with the new 32 ton cutter *Buonaparte*, captured in March; Thomazeau et Cie with the 21 ton *Incroyable* which was seized NNW of Ushant in September and Julien Capel who fitted out the tiny 2 ton tartan *Aventurier*.[52]

Many of the men who ventured ships in these hazardous voyages in 1797 were experienced ship owners, though there were a number whose experience was probably in the wholesale trade and as officers of merchant ships. The success of some of these voyages, especially that of Fantan and Thomas' *Minerve* encouraged others because there was always an interval between the arrival of a prize and its sale in which rumours of the value circulated and expectations were raised of enormous profits. This helped to encourage others to organise privateering ventures and one consequence was the emergence from recent obscurity of some of the more famous pre-war managing owners and merchants. There were others for whom the early ventures formed an apprenticeship. The results of the first years reveals that a man needed more than luck to make a profit; he had to be able to choose a ship that was fast and manoeuvrable and could remain at sea in all weathers; the captain had to be fully experienced in handling the type of ship employed and he had to be able to maintain discipline and morale among his, often multinational, crew. The first years of privateering are a test of ability in all these fields and the unsuccessful were eliminated. Those who survived include Benjamin Dubois, who gradually and very cautiously re-entered the privateering world.

In the autumn of 1797 Dubois fitted out the 128 ton *Bougainville*, which had been constructed locally at Mont Morin. Its first prize was the *Frédéric le Grand*, taken in December and later sold for 1,185,555 *livres*. Later in the same cruise two smaller vessels were also captured, the *Hope*, and*Harmony* which were sold for 2,471 *livres* and 1,908 *livres*. The *Bougainville* proved a lucky ship for Dubois for under a succession of captains it captured many more prizes: the Liverpool in February 1798 on the second cruise and sold for 521,476 *livres*, three more on the third cruise for a total of 220,359 *livres* and finally another seven ships on a fourth cruise before falling to the *Amazon*, probably off SW Ireland.[53] The third and final cruises returned prizes to a total of 793,858 *livres*, making a total for the four voyages of 2,735,627 *livres*.[54] Of these four the first was the most profitable but the continued success served to encourage Dubois to send privateers to sea. In the spring of 1798 he fitted out the 96 ton brig *Tartare*, which captured three ships to a total of 662,270 *livres* before in turn falling victim to the *Cleopatra* in 47°50'N in May.[55] Thereafter, apart from the voyages of the *Bougainville* already mentioned, the last of which was carried out in the name of one of his sons -Dubois fils et Cie - the Dubois family only directed one more venture, that of the new 143 ton *Heureux* which was captured by the *Amelia* off the mouth of the River Loire in May 1801 before she had taken any prizes.[56] By then the Dubois family luck had run out, or the steady loss of the best captains had made it difficult to recruit experienced men to command their ships.

Another important partnership in these years, Duchesne and Pintedevin, has been built on their extensive knowledge of the coasting trade and had gained some early successes in the commercial war. In 1797 they again used similar ships. In the spring they fitted out the 8 ton *Surprise*, built in St Servan the previous year. They hired as captain the experienced Charles Rogerie and paid him the large advance of 400 *livres* which he soon justified; he took the *Friends Increase* which was sold for 14,862 *livres*.[57] Later the *Surprise* made a second voyage under a different captain, Auguste Langlois, but after an unsuccessful cruise which ended at Cherbourg the ship was not used again. In 1798 Duchesne and Pintedevin sent the *Courageux* on a second voyage and hired an experienced man as captain and paid him 400 *livres* advance as well. This was also unsuccessful and brought income of 453,659 *livres*, of which the largest amount came from the sale of the *Fanny* and *Betsy* for 273,998 *livres.*[58] Later in 1798 the *Courageux* made another cruise, but this produced no prizes and the voyages in 1799 and 1800 were equally unsuccessful, though under different captains. In 1798, flushed by the success of the second voyage of the *Courageux*, Duchesne and Pintedevin fitted out the 72 ton cutter *Quinola*. This had been built in England the previous year and under the command of Michel Pagelet captured five ships to a total value of 207,745 *livres.*[59] In 1799 they acquired another ship of the same name, also built in England though of 40 tons. Their first was renamed *Grand Quinola* and the second *Petit Quinola* the former cruised under Thomas le Blanc, who also received an advance of 400 *livres* and took two ships worth 351,903 *livres*. The *Petit Quinola* under Jean-Baptiste Pinal took two ships which were sold for 285,9345 *livres.*[60] In 1800 the *Grand Quinola* sailed again and made a fourth cruise in 1801; the *Petit Quinola* also cruised in these years and neither took any more ships. The other two ventures by Duchesne and Pintedevin were equally disastrous. The 35 ton cutter *Sophie* set in the early spring of 1798 and fell into British hands off Start Point.[61] Their other ventures in 1798, the new 48 ton *Aventageux* failed to take any vessels in its first cruise and was seized by the *Ajax* off Cherbourg in January 1800 on its second.[62] Their last venture was equally unprofitable; the new 17 ton *Ajax* took no prizes and was sold to another St Malo merchant, Thomazeau. Under him the *Ajax* was commanded by Joseph Boutrouche but took no prizes before being taken by the English privateer *Hazard* off Guernsey in July.

Gautier, whose younger son had joined Foucher in fitting out the *Hirondelle* in 1793, had cooperated with Duchesne in the coasting trade before the war. In 1797 Guislard fils, previously unknown, joined Gautier et Cie in fitting out the new 50 ton lugger *Zélie.*[63] They hired Gonidec le jeune for 400 *livres* and before the ship was captured South of Start Point in January Gonidec had taken five prizes worth 85,583 *livres.*[64] This encouraged Gautier le jeune and Guislard to fit out another cutter, the new 86 ton *Milan*, but this fell into British hands when captured by the *Boadicia* South East of the Lizard in February 1799.[65] This marked the end of their ventures. Another partnership which, like the two others, had been based on experience in the coasting trade and earlier commerce raiding was that of Amiel and Lemoine. Their new 35 ton cutter *Delphine* took two prizes which were sold for 31,193 *livres* but the corsair was captured by the frigate *Niger* South of the Lizard on Christmas Day 1797.[66] Amiel and Lemoine fitted out no more ships; they cannot have made much profit on the voyages. Another managing owner, Fortin aîné, whose father had traded with the Mediterranean before the war, fitted out the new 95 ton brig *Juste* in 1798 which took the *Superb* and a Prussian vessel *Dame Gertrude* and the *Wilding*, the last jointly with the *Patriote* of Brest. The combined total came to 662, 177 *livres*, though 269,416 *livres* had to be shared with the *Patriote*.[67] This voyage was followed by a second in 1799 which produced the *Adventure*, sold for 188,775 *livres*; a third voyage in 1800 which ended at Lorient produced 459,275 *livres*. Fortin aîné then appointed Sauchau, a Lorient merchant, to prepare the *Juste* for her third voyage and during this the *Juste* was captured by the *Amelia* South West of Ushant in February 1801.[68] After his early success Fortin joined Bertrand Lemême in fitting out the 150 ton *Hirondelle*, but it made no captures. Apart from sharing the third voyage of the *Juste*, the two men did not fit out any more ships together.

Fantan and Thomas aîné, whose *Minerve* had been successful in 1797 and was captured in 1798, prepared the new 49 ton lugger *Heureuse Espérance* late in 1799. They chose Alexis Basset as captain and on his second voyage he captured the valuable *Juliana* and three other prizes, which were sold for a total of 211,293 *livres*. The *Heureuse Espéance* fell into British hands South South East of the Start in December.[69] Encouraged by this success they decided to try their luck with the two-year-old, 50 ton *Providence*, which Sainton had sent to sea for two voyages without any success. The partners appointed René Rosse as captain and paid him an advance of 600 *livres* but he was unsuccessful. Fantan and Thomas made a final attempt with a new 50 ton cutter *Quatre Frères* in 1800 and in this final venture captured the *Ann* which was sold for 166,863 *livres*.[70] The only other managing owners to make a substantial profit in 1798 were Canneva, Santerre and Martin whose *Laure*, on her second voyage in March captured a Danish ship, the *Superb*, which was later sold for 331,560 *livres*.[71] After this the partnership was dissolved and the *Laure* made her last voyages under the control of Thomas and Martin.[72]

The largest ship to be sent commerce raiding was the *Duguay Trouin*, which had been sent to sea in the first year of the war by Guillemaut and Bodinier and had captured shipping valued at over one million *livres*. This huge 500 ton ship, formerly called the *Baron Bender*, had been used in the African slave trade and was probably fast for her tonnage - slaves had to be carried quickly to their destination - and was theoretically the ideal corsair. When she made her second voyage in the winter of 1797 she carried a crew of 172 and 24 cannon, though many were of small calibre.[73] On her first voyage the *Duguay Trouin* had been able to overawe all but the largest naval escort and from a distance her armament, which presumably included a number of dummy cannon, appeared far greater than it really was. In February 1798 her captain, Nicolas Legué, met the frigate *Shannon* off Cape Clear. The *Shannon* was a new ship, launched in 1797 and more than a match for the privateer.[74] Guillemaut did not fit out any more ships during this war.

None of the other managing owners took any prizes. Michel Delastelle, whose *Tigre* had been successful in 1793, fitted out the 29 ton, English-built cutter *Marie*, but this fell to the hired cutter *Penelope* North North West of Guernsey in November.[75] Michel Delastelle followed this in 1798 with the new 200 ton *Mercure* and appointed a relative, Charles Delastelle, as captain. He took no prizes and the *Mercure* made a second cruise the following winter under Jacques Fromy, who had successfully commanded the *Jeune Emilie* in 1793. As a recognition of this experience he was paid the large advance of 600 *livres* and justified it by taking two prizes worth 29,704 *livres*. However the crew alone had received 21,460 *livres* and the additional cost of provisions and sundry stores and repairs probably used up the balance. To make matters worse the *Mercure* was captured by the *Melampus* West South West of Ushant in February 1799. Another unsuccessful partnership was that of Marion Frères and a Nantes merchant, Duguen. They probably hoped to emulate the success of Marion fils in 1973, when his *Furet* captured prizes worth over 1.5 million *livres*. This new partnership fitted out the 280 ton *Belliqueuse* and hired Benoît Giron who had been captain of the *Furet*, but it was captured in January 1798 by the frigate *Melampus* in 48°30'N.[76] While the *Belliqueuse* was at sea the partners also fitted out the new 160 ton *Furet*, which had been built at Nantes. This was also unsuccessful.[77] They made a final attempt with another Nantes merchant Bernard jeune and the *Furet* in February 1800 but in March this too was captured in 42°30'N by the *Minerve*.[78]

One of the smallest vessels to be used as a privateer was the 12 ton *Vengeur*, which was fitted out by Cosson. He was probably a member of the wealthy Cosson family of which Pierre, a rich wholesale merchant, paid 3,908 *livres* in taxes and forced loan and a further 390 *livres* in Messidor Year II.[79] Cosson was not a managing owner of ships before the Revolution and it appears that his knowledge of ships and captains was inadequate for successful commerce raiding. The *Vengeur* took no prizes; it returned to port but was not used again. The partnership of Nicol aîné and Lesnard's new 160 ton ship *Baalgade* was equally unsuccessful. It failed to take any prizes in either its first or second cruise. In February 1800 it was captured in 50°N 18°W.[80] Nicol aîné and Lesnard made no more ventures.

The success of a handful of managing owners in 1797 and 1798 showed that commerce raiding could offer success to a few. Many chanced their luck in 1797 and in many ways privateering from then until the end of the war appears more as a test of economic survival, which only the most experienced could pass. In 1799 there was a modest revival because, as many in Britain expected that the war would end and the financial burden of maintaining French prisoners became more severe when the French government suspended payment for their maintenance, many were released and returned to France.[81] Even if they did not go to sea they formed a pool of experienced seamen, many of whom had been successful before their capture, who could offer advice on the best prospects for commerce raiding. In consequence some new partnerships were formed. Erusset and Maucron fitted out the new 50 ton cutter *Hasard* and hired Dutemple, the successful captain of Cosson's ship *Vengeur* at the relatively generous advance of 480 *livres*. This time Dutemple was more successful; he took two ships worth 182,647 *livres*, but was then captured.[82] Encouraged by this success the partners fitted out the 50 ton schooner and former English vessel *Adventure* but in December 1799 this was captured West of Guernsey by the *Aristocrate* without making any prizes.[83] Their final attempt was with the 119 ton *Aventurier* in 1801 but this too failed to take any ships before peace was signed.

Another newcomer to commerce raiding in 1799 was Ethéart, who fitted out the 31 ton lugger *Marsouin* paid his captain Julien Marestier the large advance of 600 *livres*. Marestier failed to take any prizes and the ship did not put to sea again. However, Ethèart appointed Marestier to the command of the 46 ton lugger *Renard* in 1801, though he again failed to take any prizes, and on the second voyage was replaced by Joseph Prader Niquet, who captured the English *Williams and Smith* that was later sold for 31,638 *livres*.[84] Another unsuccessful partner-ship earlier in the war had been that of Nicol aîné and Lesnard. In 1800 Lesnard joined Duhamel to form another partnership to fit out the 256 ton *Jeune Bougainville*, a venture in which Duhamel invested 50,000 *livres*. Fortunately for him the cruise proved a success; six ships were captured and were sold for 319,535 *Livres*.[85] During this voyage the *Jeune Bougainville* called at Lorient and a month later was taken in 46°55'N 9°50'W.[86] After that Duhamel was in a British prison and Lesnard fitted out another large ship, the 376 ton *Petit* or *Premier Consul* but this was unsuccessful. It was captured in March by the *Dryad* in 51°10'N 14°10'W.[87] In another partnership between Bourdas, a relative of Julien Bourdas, wholesale merchant and former Conseilleur Secretaire de Roi and Boutruche, the 12 ton lugger *Rusé*, a former English vessel, was fitted out.[88] Boutruche's son was appointed captain at the high advance of 900 *livres* - the current rate at the time was 600 *livres*.[89] Another merchant who made a late attempt at privateering was Pierre Havard, whose 1793 venture had ended with the capture of his ship. In 1800 he fitted out the 12 ton pinnace *Bons Amis* and another 12 ton vessel *Décidé*. Neither was a success and in the case of the *Bons Amis*, the captain Julien Bilheu was only paid 200 *livres*. This was only one third the rate for that year and the captain of the 25 ton lugger *Furie* received 600 *livres*.[90] Another small privateer in 1800 was the new 11 ton lugger *Furie*, fitted out by Caroule of St Servan and Chavet.[91] One prize was captured and was sold for 7,816 *livres*; the *Vengeur* then passed to Thomas Rouxel but was captured by the cutter *Swan* West of Start Point during the summer.[92] The last newcomer to fit out a privateer at St Malo during the Revolutionary War was François Beauche, whose 15 ton *Courageux* sailed in the spring of 1801 and was captured North East of Guernsey in April.

The Napoleonic War, like the war which preceded it, began with an attack on commerce, though in 1803 the effort was more muted than in 1783; 10 ships in 1803 compared with 22 ten years earlier, and seven of the ten were captured. Some of the managing owners were familiar figures in privateering from the previous war; Thomazeau had fitted out a number of ships and in 1803 he sent his 92 ton *Malouin* to sea. This had cruised twice at the end of the previous war with considerable success, but was captured by the privateer *Speedwell* in 44°30'N 15°W in July without taking any prizes.[93] This marks the end of commerce raiding for Thomazeau for eight years and it was not until 1811 that he again organised a privateering venture with the new 15 ton *Malouin.* This was little more successful for it only took a single vessel. Thomazeau followed this with the 136 ton sloop *Junon* under the command of the experienced Thomas Prader Miquet in the winter of 1811-12 and Thomazeau made a final venture with the *Timon*, for which two prizes are recorded.[94]

Another experienced partnership was that of Lemême and Gautier, who fitted out the *Espoir* and the 45 ton *Sorcière*. The first was captured but on the first voyage the *Sorcière* captured prizes worth over 84,000 *francs* and the ship continued to sail each year, under different captains, until her capture by the privateer *Mayflower* west of Jersey in April 1806.[95] By then she had seized at least seven English ships which were sold for 437,969 *francs.*[96] Lemême and Gautier also used the *Courier de la Manche* but in 1806 this was fitted out by Canneva and made an unsuccessful cruise - two of the prizes were returned to their owners and the privateer fell to the frigate *Alcmene* in 49°30'N 10°30'W of Paris in January 1807.[97] This marks the end of commerce raiding for Lemême and Gautier by the partnership re-formed in 1806 as Gautier le jeune et fils. Their first venture was disastrous: the *Voltigeur* was captured before taking any prizes. The second, the 70 ton *Confiance* built the previous year at St Malo, took prizes worth 25,881 *francs* during the winter of 1806-7.[98] The next year the *Confiance* was sent on an armed trading voyage to Martinique with a letter of marque *en guerre et marchandise* and was used again as a privateer from 1809 to 1811, taking prizes which were sold for 526,164 *francs.*[99] The ship was then replaced by a smaller vessel, a new 90 ton sloop which bore the same name but was captured by the sloop *Dasher* in 49°48'N 11°13'W of Paris in January 1812.[100] The only other ventures by Gautier jeune et fils were an ill-fated voyage to Martinque planned for the *Hirondelle en guerre et marchandise* which never which materialised and the new 35 ton sloop *Maâtre de Danse* which captured a prize worth 32,500 *francs*. The sloop was herself captured in June 1810 after a month at sea by the *Bonne Citoyenne* North of Guernsey.[101] Another relative, Angloise Gautier, fitted out the *Deux Fanny* in 1813 which took a single ship.[102]

This sense of continuity from year to year and war to war can be seen in several other voyages in the first year of the Napoleonic War. Guibert fils, who had entered the partnership of Guibert Fichet in 1796 and continued to send ships to sea until the end of the war, fitted out the 137 ton *Courier de Terre Neuve* in 1803, but it was captured by the *Plantagenet* in July in 48°57'N 15°30'W of Paris.[103] That was his last privateering venture. Two other merchants who had enjoyed success in the previous war, Martin and Duchesne, formed a new partnership to prepare the 46 ton *Magdelaine*, but it was taken without making any prizes West of the Lizard by two Guernsey privateers in July.[104] This marks the end of their partnership and it was not until 1811 that the old partnership of Duchesne and Pintedevin emerged from obscurity to fit out a new vessel, the 20 ton *Courageux*, which cruised intermittantly between

June 1811 and June 1812, took prizes on its first voyage worth 41,628 *francs* and was captured by the frigate *Rhin*.[105]

Ravaleux, a St Servan merchant, had been unsuccessful in 1797 with the *Buonaparte* but made a second attempt with the *Dinanais* in 1803, which took one prize worth 37,824 *francs* and ended the voyage at Vigo.[106] Jean Ravaleux et Cie sent no more ships to sea in this war. The other managing owners in 1803 were all new men. Kerpoisson, who fitted out the *Fanny* was a former captain who had commanded the *Baalgade.* He was unsuccessful as a managing owner; the *Fanny* was captured. So too were Lecouturier's *Eléonore* and Gilbert frère's *Espiégle*; only Michel Pagelet's 21 ton *Fantaisie* returned safely to Bayonne and made a second voyage from there.[107] In the late autumn Pagelet returned to sea as captain of Marion frère's 225 ton foreign built *Brave*. He took two ships, the *Magnet* from Poole to Quebec with planks and the *Marquis* from Poole, one of which was ransomed. The total income was only 5,036 *francs* however and the *Brave* was captured by the *Loire* in 49°30'N 14°30'W of Paris early in 1804.[108] This marked the end of Marion frère's ventures; their earlier efforts had also been unprofitable.

After these initial failures in the opening months of the year, the career of Robert Surcouf opens a new stage in commerce raiding. Surcouf was no ordinary managing owner but one of the most daring and experienced of all privateer commanders.[109] He had achieved fame in 1796 as the captain of the *Emilie* in the Indian Ocean and used the Île de France as a base. Early in the year, when it was considered dangerous for large ships to be off the east coast because of the prevailing monsoon, he appeared off the mouth of the Hoogli. He achieved complete surprise and captured two merchant ships and a pilot brig. The latter was the perfect disguise for a privateer, because all shipping bound for Calcutta needed the help of a pilot to navigate the constantly changing waterways of the Sandheads. The *Triton* East Indiaman was captured on 29 January by Surcouf and sixteen men, though the British ship carried a crew of 150 men. In 1799 Surcouf cruised in another ship, the *Clarisse* in the Bay of Bengal where he took many more prizes and practically blockaded Calcutta. When he had to take the *Clarisse* to the Île de France to refit he was offered the *Confiance*. In this Surcouf was able to outsail all the British warships which came within sight and also captured over a dozen merchant ships. Surcouf remained in the Indian Ocean for the rest of the Revolutionary War and returned to St Malo in 1802, where he was appointed colonel in the National Guard.

During the Napoleonic War Surcouf's initial venture was the *Caroline* which was fitted out, like his earlier ventures, in the Île de France.[110] Then he returned to St Malo. This was followed in January 1805 by the 70 ton sloop *Confiance* which had been built in St Malo two years earlier.[111] The first cruise made a loss; only the 111 ton *Betsy* was taken in 50°30'N 9°30'N, bound from Falmouth to Cork with coal for the British army.[112] The new ventures based on his home port were less profitable than his earlier voyages in the Indian Ocean. The *Confiance* continued at sea until early in 1806, but her prizes, one

Swedish and an English, did not meet the cost of fitting out and the *Confiance* ended its voyage at Sables d'Olonne.[113] Surcouf's next venture, the 55 ton *Marsouin*, which began her voyage late in 1805, was at first no more successful. But under François Brebel, appointed captain in November 1806, Surcouf's luck changed. In January 1807 two English ships were captured which produced 280,384 *francs* - a substantial profit.[114] The third cruise, under the command of Jean Bottrelle, produced two prizes, one Portuguese and one Hamburg ship, but there is no record of the proceeds of this cruise and the prizes were probably returned to their owners. The *Marsouin* was captured by the frigate *Iris* South of the Lizard in January 1808.[115] By this time Surcouf had returned to the Indian Ocean as the commander of a privateer. It was widely believed that he had made six or seven million *francs* from his privateering, though this was presumably from his ventures in the Indian Ocean during the Revolutionary War.[116] Surcouf sailed from St Malo in March on the 18 gun *Revenant*, which had been built as a corsair and was extremely fast. He evaded the British blockade off Île Bourbon and entered Port Louis on 10 June. He then harried the rice trade between Bengal and Madras to provide food for the population of Île de France and cruised off the Sandheads with the frigate *Piémontaise*. Surcouf was able to remain there for some time because the *Revenant* was faster than the ships of the British squadron but in 1809, after a two year cruise, he returned to St Malo. In October Surcouf sent the 111 ton brig *Revanche* to sea but in a month it was captured by in 49°N 14°W of Paris.[117] For his next venture Surcouf hired Jean Bottrelle to command a new 12 ton cutter *Biscayenne*.[118] Bottrelle had been on the *Marsouin* when it was captured in 1808 and had been released subsequently, but he failed to take any prizes. Surcouf continued to fit out ships: his next was the new 30 ton sloop *Dorade*, but this was only at sea for a week in May before being captured by the sloop *Favourite* in 49°50'N 6°W of Paris.[119] In August Surcouf sent another ship to sea, the 150 ton *Auguste*, which was sent to the Grand Banks. This too was captured, by the frigate *Rhin* in 48°39'N 10°W of Paris in September.[120] In spite of these setbacks Surcouf persisted and in August 1811 fitted out a new 50 ton lugger, *Edouard*. This proved more successful; it took the *Sarah*, sold for 63,000 *francs* but on the second cruise was taken off the Lizard by the gun brig *Derwent* and sunk.[121] Surcouf's final venture was also unsuccessful; the new 70 ton cutter *Renard* made two cruises between May 1813 and April 1814 and made a loss on each.[122]

Surcouf's career is important for a number of reasons. In the first place was far more successful as the captain of a privateer in the Indian Ocean than he was as the managing owner of ships at St Malo. But that does not necessarily mean that his St Malo ventures are less important. As the captain of the *Emilie* in 1796 he was fortunate in capturing the perfect vessel for commerce raiding, the pilot brig *Cartier*. But he exploited this with a daring and imagination that few of his contemporaries possessed. His other commands, which were specially built, were exceptionally fast by comparison with British warships and he was able to outsail his opponents. The success of these early ventures, when he was a young man in his twenties, made him a rich man. When he tried to repeat his earlier success in European waters he was less successful, but there were formidable difficulties facing the captains of privateers in European waters, which were patrolled by a variety of naval vessels, some of which were extremely fast. But his success in the Indian Ocean, complemented by his charm, courtesy and good humour made him appear as a gentleman in an age in which the old fashioned courtesies were being abandoned. It was this, and his earlier success in the Indian Ocean, which enabled him to persuade people to invest in his European ventures which were far less profitable.

Another managing owner with experience in the earlier war was Thomas aîné, who had joined Fantan jeune and Martin. In 1804 he fitted out the new 160 ton *Général Perignon*, which was to prove a lucky ship. In the first voyage it made captures worth 83,407 *francs* and 475,504 *francs* on the second after refitting at Lorient.[123] The *Général Perignon* continued to cruise from St Malo from 1806 to 1808, when she ended her voyage at Rivados. For the next two years she was based in South West France and continued to take a succession of prizes; in 1810 she was fitted out for Thomas by Basterrèche frères et Cie, but was finally captured in 46°N 6°W of Paris by the frigate *Amazon*.[124] Thomas' next ship, the *Duguay Trouin*, was wrecked at Audierne and made a loss; this was followed in November 1805 by a 50 ton cutter, the *Constance*, built in 1803. This was another lucky venture and was commanded by the experienced François Blanchard, who had been successful in the Revolutionary War as captain of Thomazeau's *Malouin*. On his first voyage Blanchard captured at least six ships worth 99,447 *francs*; the *Constance* made two more successful voyages in 1806 and 1807 and was then replaced by another 40 ton vessel, built in 1805.[125] In the early summer of 1808 Thomas fitted out the 140 ton *San Josepho* and appointed François Blanchard as captain. The success of this venture was more modest and in February 1809, during the second voyage the ship was captured by the frigate *Undaunted* in 49°30'N 9°30'W of Paris.[126] Shortly afterwards Thomas fitted out the 100 ton sloop *San Joseph* commanded by Joseph Wittevrongel, who in 1803 had paid 600 dollars to be a burgher of Bergen. Whereas most of the St Malo captains took their ships to the North and West, Wittevrongel's experience lay in the North Sea and he cruised eastwards along the English Channel as well as in the Soundings. His richest prize was the English *Jane*, which entered Granville as prize in January 1809 with a cargo of fish, oil and furs and was sold for 94,599 *francs*.[127] In September 1810 the *San Joseph* was finally taken in 40°N 8°W of Paris by the frigate *Rhin*; she had on board a list of telegraphic signals which had been issued in Brest in November 1807 and were used by the chain of telegraph stations on the islands along the coast.[128] Thomas' last two ventures can be described briefly; late in 1809 he fitted out the 80 ton *Comte d'Hunebourg* which was taken in February 1810 in 49°25'N 8°30'W of Paris by the sloop *Pheasant* and made a loss. His final venture was the 20 ton *Petit Charles* in 1811. In the previous year it had been fitted out by Le Tellier but had made a loss; Thomas appointed Jean Didaboure as captain. The captain's name is Basque and the intention was presumably to send the *Petit Charles* to the more fruitful hunting ground off the Iberian coast. But it seems that this venture was unsuccessful as well.

Louis Blaize et fils tried to emulate the earlier success of Robert Surcouf. After their initial venture in 1797 they fitted out the *Napoléon* in 1804 and sent it on a two year cruise in the Indian Ocean. It took three prizes and, like Surcouf, used the Île de France as a base; in 1806 it was trapped in Hood Bay near the Cape of Good Hope by two British frigates.[129] In March 1807 the 300 ton *Revenant* was fitted out and Robert Surcouf was appointed captain; this ship cruised twice in the Indian Ocean and then was requisitioned by the state.[130] The *Gazelle* was also in the Indian Ocean at the same time with a letter of marque *en guerre et marchandise;* she returned safely to St Malo in 1808.[131] The following year another of their ships, the *Général Junot*, was captured while on a similar voyage, as was the *Fantôme*, a joint venture with Robert Surcouf.[132] In 1810 the *Gazelle* made another voyage, her last. The company's final venture was in the winter of 1811-12 with a new 160 ton ship, also named the *Gazelle*, which was taken by the frigate *Leonidas* in 40°54'N 8°W of Paris.[133]

Canneva was also a merchant who had acted with a partner in the previous war but decided to be indepent in the Napoleonic War. His first ship was the 70 ton *Courier de la Manche*, which he fitted out for Le Même and Gautier in 1805. During the initial cruise one of the prizes was retaken and another had to be returned to its owners, but the voyage was still profitable.[134] It made its second voyage in 1806 and in January 1807 was captured by the frigate *Alcmene* in 49°30'N 10°30'W of Paris.[135] Alexandre Dubois also returned to commerce raiding in 1806. This important pre-revolutionary merchant played a comparatively small part in commerce raiding in either the Revolutionary or the Napoleonic Wars, but in 1806 he fitted out the 150 ton *Bougainville*, which on its first cruise captured the slaver *Mary & Ann*, which was sold for 61,434 *francs*.[136] It made a second cruise in mid-summer and a third at the end of 1806 and was taken by the sloop *Scorpion* in February 1807 in 50°N 9°W of Paris.[137] Of the three the first and third seem to have been the most successful; Captain Jacques Debon took the *Mary and Hannah* on the first cruise and the *Commerce* of Bristol on the third, laden with wine from Oporto to London and the *Rebecca*.[138] Dubois' success with the *Bougainville* encouraged him to fit out the new 50 ton lugger *Speculateur*. The first cruise made a loss but Dubois persevered and in 1807 in a second voyage the ship took prizes worth 50,814 *francs*. In 1808 it was sent was taken on its first voyage in 1807 and the new 50 ton *Général Junot* was taken by the sloop *Raleigh* South of the Lizard in January 1809 while on a voyage *en guerre et marchandise* to Martinique.[140]

The other managing owners remain shadowy figures. Some enjoyed a moderate success. Magon Vieuville's new 150 ton *Glaneuse* made 172,590 *francs* from the sale of its prizes on its first cruise in 1806 and 47,554 *francs* on the second but was captured in November 1807 by the sloop *Scorpion* in 49°N

12°W of Paris.[141] Magon also sent the new 100 ton *Glaneur* to sea in 1807 but this was captured in December by the same sloop 24 miles North North West of Ushant.[142] His final attempt was in 1810 with a new 120 ton lugger, the *Glaneuse*, but this was taken by the *Northumberland* in 49°20'N 6°W of Paris at the end of November.[143] Another attempt at commerce raiding was that by Alexandre Protet et Cie, who sent a number of small vessels to sea, but they had even less success. The first, the three year old lugger *Bohémienne* took two vessels off the English coast and two more in 1807 before it fell into British hands North of the Scilly Isles in October.[144] Protet et Cie. made a second attempt with the new 150 ton *Zéphir* in 1808, but this was captured by the Jersey privateer *Rover* in March.[145] Two years later Protet made a third and final attempt with the new 50 ton *Alexandre* but this too fell into British hands South of the Lizard in September 1810.[146]

A number of men fitted a single ship and continued to send it to sea until it fell into British hands. Jallobert frères sent their new 90 ton ship in December 1807 and it remained at sea, with a refit at Lorient in 1809, until it was taken by the *Plover* sloop off the island of Batz in November 1811.[147] Finally St Malo acted as a magnet not only for seamen from other ports seeking work but also for merchants trying to take advantage of the supposed success of St Malo's privateering. In 1808 the firm of wholesale merchants at Caen, Gast et Cie, fitted out the 48 ton lugger *Harpalos*, which made two brief cruises in February and April, without taking any ships. The letter of marque was then withdrawn when a number of deserters were discovered on board. The boat was sold to the more experienced Duchesne and Pintedevin and Gast et Cie retired from organising commerce raiding.[148]

It will be evident from this account of privatering at St Malo during the two wars that the period witnessed a major economic shift from the pre-Revolutionary commercial elite to a diverse group of newcomers. These were the managing owners of small coasters, comparatively modest participants in the Newfoundland fisheries or experienced captains and other officers. Under normal conditions some of them could have expected to rise to prominence through luck or marriage, or like Surcouf, by using his fame as a privateer captain in the Indian Ocean to command a succession of privateers. The most interesting feature of privateering is the was in which captains where chosen and ships built specifically for commerce raiding. Many of these managing owners appeared briefly on the commercial scence; they made a single venture and when that was unprofitable they lost the confidence of their backers. Only Robert Surcouf, backed by the earlier reputation and considerable personal charm, was able to continue to send ships to sea when many were unprofitable. It was in his favour that accounts took some time to settle; this provided a breathing space in which he could capitalise on the prizes which had been captured and persuade waverers that the next voyage would be a still greater success.

There was inevitably a delay between the end of the voyage and the presentation of accounts. This was partly because the accounts could not be completed until all prize ships and their cargoes had been declared fair prizes and sold and partly because when the managing owner decided not to send the ship to sea again the corsair had to be sold and the money added to any profit. There was also an incentive for a managing owner to delay payment to shareholders and crew because he could earn some interest on money paid to him. The accounts were always approved by a court, for the statement of profit or loss had to have the approval of an independent body. Up to the Revolution this was the Admiralty Court, when this was abolished it was replaced by a *tribunal de commerce*, a body established in all ports and composed of locally elected members.[149] The law of February 14, 1793 gave the tribunal jurisdiction over prize cases and this was confirmed by the laws of 3 and 18 Brumaire Year II, (24 October and 8 November 1793). The law of 3 Brumaire also stated that 6 *deniers* of each *livre* profit should be paid to the Invalides for the support of widows and orphans of sailors and crippled seamen.[150] On 1 Thermidor Year V the payment to the Invalides was reduced to 1 *denier* per*livre*.

In addition to approving the final accounts of voyages the tribunal also adjudicated in disputes concerning the charges for ship repair, non payment of crew members and the relative shares of two or more privateers in the case of joint capture. On 25 Ventôse Year VII (15 March 1799) a law gave the tribunal de commerce complete jurisdiction over privateering and on 2 Prairial Year XI (21 May 1803) an order divided the accounts into two stages; *liquidation particulier* and *liquidation générale et définitive*.[151] The first stage established the nett value of the sale of each prize; the second was the final settlement of all accounts which established the shares of all participants. There were four main parts to the *liquidation particulier*: instruction, judgement, sale and the division of shares. The crew list, which formed part of the documents of the *Inscription Maritime*, stated the share that each member of the crew was entitled to and the division of the proceeds from any prizes was established first by the captain and two or three officers and a *juge de paix* or a representative of the *commissiare de la marine*. Articles 91 and 92 of the law of 2 Prairial Year XI divided the proceeds: one third to the crew of the privateer, one fifth to the crew of a merchant ship sailing *en guerre et marchandise*. This was not a radical change; there had occasionally been local variations and the aim of the law, as in so much of revolutionary legislation, was to establish conformity. The law also fixed the maximum number of shares that a crew member could have. This ranged from 12 shares for the captain, 10 for the second captain and 8 for the first lieutenant down to one and a half for the sailors, 1 or half for soldiers, half or three quarters for untrained boys and a quarter or half for cabin boys. The purpose of this was to restrict the number of shares that could be held by the officers as a whole and gave considerable latitude to private bargins between the managing owners and individual crew members.

The *Liquidation généale* was the final form of the accounts and was approved by the tribunal de commerce and the *Préfet maritime*.[152] It discussed any disputes that had arisen between the shareholders or crew and managing owner, the prizes and profits from each voyage and the final accounts of crew, shareholders and Invalides de la Marine. Under the law of 2 Prairial Year XI the captain also received an additional two and a half to five per cent of the nett profit. This was intended to compensate for his loss of the right to seize the sea chests of captains of captured ships, known as the *chapeau de capitaine*. The Invalides account was credited with 1 *sou*per *franc* (replacing the earlier 1 *sou*per *livre*) on each item in the accounts: commissions, shares of each prize, crew's advance payments, as well as 5 per cent on the total profit. In some cases 10 per cent was deducted for the maintenance of prisoners of war following an order by the Directory of 14 Brumaire Year VIII (4 November 1799) and confirmed by an order of the Consuls of 7 Fructidor Year VIII (24 August 1800). The deduction, which had been levied when the cost of maintaining the growing number of prisoners of war in Britain had become an acute financial burden, was stopped when the burden was transferred to Britain.[153] There were also certain legal charges to be met: the cost of registering documents was 2 per cent, customs dues were levied on prize goods and the managing owner received a commission - usually 2 per cent - and officials who had performed work associated with the tribunal also had to be paid. Occasionally, in spite of the efforts of the tribunal to resolve all disputes and agree the final form of the accounts, disputes could occur later. In this case - usually when the value of the shares of a prize shared between the crews of two or more corsairs was disputed and the case was taken to the appeal court, a supplement was issued to the *liquidation générale*.

DUNKIRK

St Malo is the only French port where much evidence has survived for this period of the financial returns on these voyages. At Dunkirk, St Malo's great rival as a privateering centre, it is impossible to make an accurate assessment of profits and losses. However, Christian Pfister's study of the port's seventeenth and eighteenth century commerce reveals the identity of many of the men who became managing owners of corsairs.[154] The 1794 census of shipping at Dunkirk reveals that 54 merchants were the managing owners of shipping totalling 13,500 tons and that 8 men controlled almost half. But these were not the same men that dominated the commercial war against Britain and France's other enemies.[155]

In the Icelandic and Newfoundland fisheries for example the pre-Revolutionary leaders had been Gillodts, Grimonpré, Morel and Casteleyn.[156] Of these, only Morel fitted out corsairs in either the Revolutionary or Napoleonic wars. In 1793 Morel frères fitted out the 60 ton *Vaillant Custine* in 1793 but this was captured North North West of the Texel in March. Their other joint ventures were with Renier, a tobacco merchant, in 1799 when they fitted out the 93 ton *Marsouin* which was also captured off the Texel.[157] This was a remarkable collapse of fortunes for a family which between 1763 and 1789 had organised eighty-eight voyages to the Icelandic and Newfoundland cod fisheries and the whale fishery.[158] One reason for the family's lack of enterprise is probably the desire to keep out of the public eye, for in the new, egalitarian society it was a disadvantage for Dominique Pierre Morel to have held the titles of Echevin Conseiller de la Chambre de Commerce de Dunkerque before the Revolution.[159] Of those in the second rank of merchants in the whale and cod fisheries: Aget-Liébart, L'Hermitte, Lorthioy, Salomez and Pol only Aget-Liébart emerged during these wars as a managing owner. In 1794 Aget managed 484 tons of shipping, but he did not fit out a corsair until Year VI(1798) and his 98 ton *Reconnée* was captured off the Dogger Bank.[160]

After the fisheries, the colonial trade also occupied an important position, though it was never as important. Each year before the Revolution two or three ships had sailed to the West Indies, and the peak had been reached in 1785 when thirteen had sailed. Five commercial houses had dominated this trade: Emmery-Vanhée, Peychiers frères, Carpeau, Coppens and Archdeacon-Gamba. These five had sent one quarter of the ships between 1763 and 1788.[161] Jean-Marie-Joseph Emmery was a member of one of the leading commercial families at Dunkirk. His father, Frédéric François-Joseph Emmery, also a wholesale merchant, had held the post of Swedish consul at Dunkirk and had been appointed Chevalier de l'Ordre de Vasa. He had married Cathérine Françoise Vanhée, daughter of a Flushing merchant in 1754. His son Jean Marie-Joseph was in his turn Swedish consul, Colonel of the National Guard and member of the Legislative Council.[162] When war broke out with England in 1798 the partners Emmery and Vanhée took no part in commerce raiding, although in 1794 they were credited with managing 1,071 tons of shipping and were the second commercial house in Dunkirk behind Debaecque frères. It was not until Year VII (1798) that they fitted out their first corsair, the 70 ton *Barras* which had been built in Ostend. The ship cruised in 1799 and was finally captured in November by the frigate *Driver* north of Texel.[163] Emmery and Vanhée took no further part in privateering until 1804, when they fitted out the *Amiral Bruix*.[164] That set sail in October and in the course of the first cruise took nine prizes, six of them in the North Sea, and were sent to Flushing and Amsterdam. Then the captain moved to the coastal waters off the Iberian Peninsula, where he captured three more ships, one of which he ransomed and the other two were sent into Spanish ports. The cruise ended there and during the following three years the ship sailed under the command of the Dieppe captain Jean-Jacques Seille in the North Sea. His success encouraged Emmery and Vanhée to persevere with commerce raiding and ine 1807 they fitted out the 70 ton *Tilsitt*. The ship continued to cruise in the North Sea in 1803 and 1809 and captured a variety of shipping, including a number flying the flag of the tiny state of Papenbourg during 1809. But it is significant that prizes were not sent back to Dunkirk, where there were British naval patrols, but to Amsterdam, Rotterdam, Hoetziel and Bergen and the *Tilsitt* was refitted at

Amsterdam in 1809. This evidence suggests that the venture was a success and it is likely that the *Tilsitt* which cruised from Dunkirk is the same vessel.[165] The success also helps to explain why Emmery and Vanhée fitted out the 95 ton *Furet* at Calais in 1809 and at Dunkirk the following year.[166] The voyage follows the familiar pattern; prizes were sent to Amsterdam and other ports outside France and in 1811 Vanhée moved to Bussum in Holland, presumably to be closer to the new centre of business in Amsterdam. The final venture of Emmery and Vanhée were the *Général Durosnel* and 55 ton *Pourvoyeur.*[167] The *Pourvoyeur* was the first to set sail, in October 1811, and in the first cruise took two Swedish and one English ship and sent them to Amsterdam and Ostend. During the second another five were captured - two Danish, two Swedish and a Prussian - and were sent to Arendal and Christiansand, the modern Oslo. Here the *Pourvoyeur* was refitted in November and made a final cruise under the command of Joseph-Michel Bart, a distant relative of the famous Jean Bart. The other ship, the *Général Durosnel*, made one voyage and sent a single prize to Viborg. The remarkable feature of these ventures is that none of the privateers was captured by British naval vessels. This must have been partly due to luck but also to the judgement of Emmery and Vanhée in choosing successful and experienced captains. They possessed one advantage in this respect. As colonial merchants they had sent ships to a number of ports in the North Sea to distribute the West India produce and the captains they had employed knew the North Sea well. Their captains also concentrated on shipping that did not usually sail with the large British convoys, and they did not fit out more than one ship at a time until the final stage of the Napoleonic War. Vanhée's links with Dutch ports also provided the means of supervising the sal o prize an fittin ou on o th ship whe th Britis blockad of Dunkirk made it dangerous to return there. Another West India firm that showed a passing interest in managing ventures of this kind was Peychiers, whose *Zéphir* cruised in 1810-11.[168] Peychiers frères had sent ships on fourteen voyages to the West Indies between 1763 and 1788; in 1790 the brothers paid 25,000 *livres* into the voluntary loan; the *Zéphir* is a modest venture compared with their previous commercial activity.

An important aspect of Dunkirk's commerce before the Revolution had been the cod and herring fisheries of the Dogger Bank and Shetlands. These had earlier been dominated by seven companies: Gillodts frères, Grimonpré fils, Delbaere, Casteleyn frères, Ryngaert, Nottebaert and Mazurier, though war with Britain had by 1793 brought disaster to several. Mazurier had become bankrupt in 1779, Ryngaert in 1780 and Gromonpré in 1783. Only one name appears in the lists of managing owners of privateers during the Revolutionary and Napoleonic wars: Mazurier le jeune. But his venture was not a success; his 29 ton *Pensé*, built at Honfleur in Year VI (1796), put to sea the following year and was captured North North East of Beachy Head by the sloop *Racoon* in January 1798.[169] Mazurier le jeune fitted out no more ships. Of the others who occasionally sent ships to the fisheries, only Froy fitted out a corsair; his 58 ton *Eglé* was at sea during the winter of 1807-8 and captured four ships which were taken to Amsterdam, Groningen and Delft, but the *Eglé* was herself taken off Flamborough Head by the revenue brig *Royal George* in January 1808.[170]

The other managing owners came from a variety of backgrounds. Peter Allard, who fitted out the 21 ton *Lyonnais* in 1803, which was taken by the gun brig *Vixen* off the North Foreland in December, was one of the richest men in Dunkirk according to the records of personal wealth on which the voluntary loan was based.[171] Unlike the others already described, this man was not a shipowner but a wholesale merchant. Altazin, or Haltazin as he is sometimes named, was the managing owner of the 60 ton *Custine* and 43 ton *Furet* in 1793, and both were captured. He came from a family of merchant seamen; his father had been captain of the *Duc de Penthièvre* which had sailed to the West Indies in 1753 and the son had moved from Boulogne to Flushing in 1779 to escape the war with Britain.[172] Another managing owner from a seafaring background was Debaillon, whose 15 ton *Liberté*, commanded by a lieutenant in the French navy, François Dorp, was captured after a short cruise in 1797 off Orfordness.[173] Chevalier, a newcomer to the Icelandic cod fishery between 1778 and 1792, fitted out the 59 ton *Espérance* in 1796 and the 90 ton *Perséverant* in 1799. Both fell into British hands, the first off the French coast and the second in 53°N in the North Sea.[174] Another newcomer to the Icelandic fishery was Jean Declerck, a comparatively wealthy man who paid 37,000 *livres* into the voluntary loan in 1790 and a further 30,283 *livres* in the forced loan of 1793.[175] Declerck fitted out one corsair in 1809. He had more success; his *Comtesse Dorsenne* captured six prizes, five of them Hanoverian, before falling into the hands of a British warship.[176]

Other merchants whose background was in commerce and industry in Dunkirk was Stival and Varlet. Pierre-Joseph Stival, a *Maître en pharmacie,* had married the daughter of a tobacco merchant and in 1775 tried to establish a distillery and smuggle Dutch gin into England.[177] François Varlet was a sugar refiner.[178] These two men fitted out the new 54 ton *Jéna* in 1806 which captured two prizes before being seized North of Nieuport by the sloop *Cruizer*.[179] The tobacco merchant, Vercoustre, fitted out the *Revanche* late in 1806, which captured three prizes and returned safely to Dunkirk.[180] Of the other managing owners, nothing is known beyond their names, and most fitted out no more than one ship. Occasionally a man from comparatively humble beginnings, with no recognisable status in Dunkirk, made a success of commerce raiding. Dauchy, a wholesale merchant who does not appear in Pfister's comprehensive study, fitted out his first privateer, the English built 58 ton *Flibustier* in 1796, when interest in commerce raiding began to develop. This was captured in February off Yarmouth but by then he had another vessel at sea, the 70 ton *Aventure*.[181] As a result of his revolutionary activity, helped perhaps by this venture, he achieved local fame and went to Paris as a member of the Committee of Five Hundred, the lower house of the Revolutionary Assembly under the constitution of the Year III. This prestige helped to win him support for more privateering ventures. Although the *Aventure* was captured, he was given a letter of marque for another corsair in Fructidor Year V (September 1797). This was thè 12 ton *Epervier*, commanded by a Honfleur man, Hammon, GeorgeGeorge Hammon or Hammond, and the ship continued to cruise until it was taken in turn off the French coast late in 1798.[182] While this ship was at sea Dauchy fitted out another, the 66 ton *Chasseur*, at Honfleur. This was captured off Yarmouth in mid-summer.[183] Later in the same year he sent the 112 ton *Boulonnais* to sea. This was his largest ship, but after capturing the *Patience* of Workington and the *Neptune* of Greenwich - later re- taken - the *Chasseur* was itself captured.[184] The same year Dauchy's 61 ton *Husard* was fitted out at Honfleur but was captured in September in 54°31'N.[185] Because of these losses Dauchy shifted his attention to other ports and his last two ventures were the 50 ton *Flibustier*, fitted out at Ostend in 1799 and the 20 ton *Vengeance* which sailed from La Rochelle in 1800. Both were captured: the first off the Texel in March 1800; the second in 42°10'N 9°48'W in April the same year.[186] Dauchy did not fit out any privateers in the Napoleonic War. His ventures may have been profitable for his shareholders but all appear to have been taken and he was probably the only person to benefit. His fees gave him an income even when the shareholders made a loss. The only other men to fit out more than one or two vessels were Reanz de Vries and Pierre Boulon. Like Dauchy, they came from comparatively humble backgrounds and are otherwise unknown. The first man fitted out eight ships between 1803 and the end of the Napoleonic War, of which five were captured.[187] Pierre Boulon sent five ships to sea, one jointly with Emmery, the colleague of Vanhée between 1808 and 1813 and only lost one, the 81 ton *Furet* which was wrecked.[188]

BORDEAUX

St Malo and Dunkirk were both ports with a distinguished record of privateering in the wars of the late seventeenth and early eighteenth centuries, and although both were relatively quiet during the mid-eighteenth century it is hardly surprising that interest should have been rekindled during the Revolutionary and Napoleonic wars. Bordeaux is a different case. It did not have a history of large scale privateering but there was considerable interest in commerce raiding during these two wars. The reason for this will be dealt with elsewhere, but the pattern of organisation which emerges is broadly similar to that already seen at St Malo and Dunkirk. During the 1780's Bordeaux had become the richest port in France, with an extensive trade in colonial goods and also in items that were grown or manufactured for the colonial population in the port's hinterland along the tributaries of the Gironde. One consequence of this unparalleled wealth was that after the Revolution the government regarded Bordeaux as one of the principal sources of capital and was anxious to use this wealth and its commercial relations with northern Europe to obtain the commodities which the country desperately needed. This alone would have removed much of Bordeaux' wealth and reduced the opportunities for the richer merchants to lead the privateering attack against the enemies of France. But the shortage of money became acute through punitive taxation as well as the collapse of the *assignat*. What made matters worse for the commercial aristocracy of the port was that Bordeaux became embroiled in a political struggle within the National Assembly and the defeat of the Girondins brought heavy penalties on the leading citizens. The cumulative effect of this was to drive most of the wealthier merchants from public view. Some, as Butel has shown, were able to engage in privateering by buying shares in ventures; a practice open to merchants in all ports.[189] In Bordeaux before the Revolution most ships were fitted out by members of the same family or commercial partnership.[190] This arrangement did not change fundamentally after 1793.[191] The same groups continued to raise money among themselves partly, one suspects, from habit and partly because it ensured that any profits would remain in their own hands. But this gradually changed as it became more difficult to raise money and was recognised as an activity in which it was better to share the risks. But it remained the practice to try and raise the money from among Bordeaux merchants and their associates. On 15 Messidor Yr V (3 July 1797) the Bordeaux merchant Cambon, who had originally lived at Cap François published a prospectus for the corsair *Décidé*. All the 145,000 livre shares were subscribed originally by Bordeaux men, but one of the principal shareholders, Destanques, tried to sell his shares in Paris through another associate, Nairac, who was staying there.

But it was not always easy to raise capital at Bordeaux: on 22 July 1808 the Bordeaux merchant Jacques Conte fitted out the *Phénix* for a voyage *en guerre et marchandise* for Cayenne. Shares to the value of 10,000 fr. in the venture were sold in Paris, to Gourbilion et Cie; 11,000 fr. were raised at Amiens from Roussel, 1,000 fr. at Colmar from Busman, 2,000 fr. at Altona from Wild. This was at a time when the financial reserves of Bordeaux merchants were becoming strained. In Thermidor Year V (July 1797) Destangues was unable to raise 180,000 *livres* in Bordeaux to build a privateer.[192] But this was probably because of the losses of privateers, which had made many merchants wary of investing in them. At other times there were merchants who continued to invest in privateering and sometimes bought shares in ventures at other ports: in Year VI Destanques invested 2,000 livres in the *Heureuse Nouville* of Brest and the same amount in the *Providence* of St. Malo.[193] The evidence thus shows that whereas before the Revolution finance was raised within families, after 1793 money was raised among groups of business associates and shares were only sold outside Bordeaux when it proved impossible to sell them in the customary way.

One of the richer pre-Revolutionary men had been Martin Arnauld, who had paid 675,468 *livres* for a Treasury contract; Arnauld fils joined Buisson - otherwise unknown - to fit out the 250 ton *Diable à Quatre* in Year VI and 300 ton *Sophie* two years later.[194] Both were captured, the *Diable à Quatre* in 45°30'N

3°44'W by the frigate *Thames* in October 1800 and the *Sophie* in 45°20'N 13°W of Paris in August 1798.[195] Another important firm in pre-Revolutionary Bordeaux had been Feger, Gramont et Cie, which had interests in the West Indies and the Île de France. One of the largest ventures had been the *Maréchal de Mouchy*, insured for a West India voyage for 550,000 *livres*, representing interests in Basel, Paris and Bilbao.[196] In 1798 Gramont fitted out the 400 ton *Flore* at Brest; this ended its cruise at Bordeaux in May.[197] For his other ventures Gramont joined a partnership which sent a number of ships with letters of marque *en guerre et marchandise* on commercial voyages - a feature of Bordeaux' commercial activities during the war but one which was seldom practiced at other ports. In June 1801 Gramont et Cie., Chariot et Garaigne sent the *Blonde* to sea. The ship was away until August 1803, probably in the Indian Ocean, and returned having captured ten ships.[198] Gramont's other venture, with Arregnaudeau, Chegaray and Garaigne was to send the *Joséphine* from Rochefort to Cayenne and the Île de France in September 1808.[199] It returned to Arcachon and the following year made a similar voyage before returning to Bordeaux.

Protestant merchants formed an important commercial group within Bordeaux' commercial society. Many had originated in the Cévennes: Bonnaffé, Sens, Nairac, Baour and Barthes. Balguerie was from the Agenais, Pellet from the Rouergue and others were from Bordeaux: Laffon, Sageron and Gautier.[200] Of these Gautier Jeune played an important part in commerce raiding and voyages *en guerre et marchandise*. His first venture was in Year V, when his 400 ton *Hyène* was fitted out at Bayonne by Labrouche, a St Jean-de-Luz merchant. The *Hyène* was later refitted at the same port but was captured in 38°30'N 18°30'W by the frigate *Indefatigable* in October.[201] In 1800 Balguerie jeune arranged for the 600 ton *Psyché* to be fitted out at Nantes by Chaurand and the ship ended her voyage at Passagès in the following spring. During the early autumn of 1801 the *Psyché* was sent by Balguerie jeune and Bergeret to Île de France and was there when war broke out again. She remained in the Indian Ocean until her capture early in 1805.[202] Soon after the beginning of the Napoleonic War Balguerie jeune and Jean Nourguibie (otherwise unknown) fitted out the 180 ton *Aventure*, formerly the *Eclair*. Of the three prizes, one reached Santander and the others were recaptured; the *Aventure* fell into the hands of the British in 48°N 20°W of Paris in October.[203] In 1808 he joined a number of merchants in a flurry of activity. Early in the spring he joined Briolle and Olanyer aîné in sending the *Hyène* to Martinique and the following year sent the ship to Île de France, where it was captured.[204] In June Balguerie jeune, Olanyer aîné and Vernier had the *Impératrice bien aimée* fitted out at Rochefort for a voyage to Guadeloupe.[205] Balguerie jeune, Lequesne and a Havre merchant Foache had the *Cornélia* fitted out at Rochefort for a similar voyage but it was captured by the frigate *Amazon* in November on its return.[206] Balguerie, Dandiron and David cadet sent another vessel to Martinique in the autumn of 1808, the 291 ton *Bonne Louise*, but this was also captured. In November Balguerie, Lugnol and Olanyer sent the patriotically name *Napoléon le Grand* from Rochefort to Martinique, but this also fell into British hands on its return voyage. Balguerie joined another consortium in the new 193 ton *Aventure* which was fitted out by Duguesne and Chicon Bourbon, but his was captured by the frigate *Fortunée.*[207] The final joint venture was in November with Plassiard and the Protestant merchants Baour frères in the *Charles* for a voyage to Senegal. After the ship returned, it was fitted out by Plassiard, Baour frères and Chegaray for a second voyage in the late autumn of 1809 and took at least one prize.[208] In 1809 Balguerie jeune was the sole managing owner of the 64 ton *Agile* which was fitted out at Lorient for a voyage to Senegal but was captured by the frigate *Phoenix* in May and his final venture was the 265 ton *Comète* which sailed from Bordeaux in 1814 and was captured by the *Andromache* in 45°45'N in March.[209] The example of Balguerie jeune, partly in commercial voyages and partly in commerce raiding shows that he was prepared to take a variety of risks. His early privateering ventures were probably unprofitable because they were few and far between, but he was caught up in the speculation of 1808 and joined a number of other merchants to share the risks. Most of the men were probably from the Protestant community, though few of them are important enough to feature in the history of the port. Another Protestant company which was well known before the Revolution but which made only one privateering voyage was Nairac et fils, whose family had originally come from Castres in 1660. Nairac's 200 ton *Argus* was captured off Vigo in April by the *Pomone*.[210]

The Pellet family provides one of the few contrasts; a family that was rich before the Revolution but which participated in privateering on a fairly large scale. Jean Pellet had been one of the most famous colonial merchants and a member of the Protestant community.[211] When he died in 1772 he was also one of the principal landowners and drew a considerable income from rents. The Pellet's willingness to stand up for regional rights against centralised government made the family popular and helped them to weather the revolutionary storm.[212] The record of privateering at Bordeaux shows that the Pellets joined the Le Fort family in a number of ventures.

In Year V (1797) they fitted out two ships, another two years later and a fourth at the end of the Revolutionary War. The First two were the 120 ton *Epervier* and 80 ton *Chasseur.* Nairac, another Protestant merchant, was also a shareholder and the ship captured a prize that was later sold for over a million *livres*.[213] But against this gain must be set the value of the corsair, for the *Epervier* was herself captured in 50°N 24°W in November 1797.[214] The other corsair was also lost; in September she was captured by the frigate *Unity* in 45°20'N 5°W.[215] Encouraged by the success of the *Epervier* the partners fitted out the 400 ton *Determiné* but this was also captured in July 1799 in 45°40'N 20°W of Paris.[216] Their final venture was the 250 ton *Guepe*, but this was taken in Vigo harbour in August 1800.[217] This was their last venture.

Daniel Lacombe was one of the principal managing owners of corsairs. He was personally responsible for seven ships and had a joint interest with Pierre Lucadoux in an eighth. He was not one of the best known merchants before the war and seems to have owed this success in commerce raiding to a family connexion with the important revolutionary figure Jean-Baptiste-Marie Lacombe, who was President of the Military Commission.[218] Daniel Lacombe's first ships were the 200 ton *Gironde* and 180 ton *Pont de Lody*, both of which were granted letters of marque in 1798. The latter was however captured in March in 44°N 14°W by the *Cambria*; the *Gironde* survived for two years but was in turn captured in July 1800, though it made a profit on the second, third and eighth cruises.[219] In November 1798 Lacombe was given a letter of marque for the 80 ton *Vigie* but in May the following year it was captured off Cape Finisterre by the *Resolution*.[220] The same year Lacombe sent the 150 ton *Friponne* with a cargo of wine, flour, spirits and dry goods to Saint Domingue, but the ship was captured in the Bay of Biscay in May.[221] It is an indication of the poor financial return on these corsairs that Lacombe formed a partnership with Pierre Lucadoux (otherwise unknown) for the *Représaille*. This made two cruises off the Iberian coast and captured five ships. Lacombe, encouraged by this, was again the sole managing owner of the 300 ton *Vénus* in 1803, but it was captured by the *Thunderer* in July in 46°N 15°W of Paris.[222] His next venture was two years later, when the *Brave* cruised from Santander under the command of the experienced Captain Quoniam. This was followed by a lull and it was not until 1809 that Lacombe fitted out a former English prize, the 243 ton *Rôdeur.* Details of Lacombe's instructions to his captain Pierre Marrauld in January 1809 have survived and they show that Lacombe did not specify the area in which the ship was to cruise. The captain was instructed to use his judgment and experience of the pattern of trade flow to decide where he should cruise to intercept British convoys. However, Lacombe was more specific about another aspect of the voyage; the ship was to cruise for the first two months in the track of returning convoys and send prizes to French or Spanish ports as appropriate. Then, as the days began to lengthen in early summer and British naval patrols were extended, the captain was to leave this station and sail for Cayenne. On the way he was to try and intercept ships returning from Brazil towards Madeira, take them to Cayenne and sell them there. With the proceeds the captain was to purchase colonial goods for the return voyage.[223] The *Rôdeur* completed her first voyage, presumably sailing to Cayenne but was captured in October in 44°N 7°W of Paris by the frigate *Seine*.[224] The *Rôdeur* seems to have been a lucky ship for Lacombe; in December 1810 he fitted out the *Rôdeur No 2* and this made two voyages in 1811.[225]

Jacques Conte was considered by contemporaries to have made his fortune from privateering.[226] His career demonstrates however that his luck came from one ship and that in general he was far from lucky. His first ship was the 500 ton *Général Dumouriez*, which was one of the largest ships that ever cruised as a privateer. It took a Spanish ship, the *San Jago Apostel* returning from South America, but this prize and the *Général Dumouriez* were both taken.[227]

Conte fitted out his next ship in 1796, the 150 ton *Eclair*, which was a much smaller vessel. This was taken off Cape Clear the following January.[228] Later in 1797 his 60 ton *Eagle* cruised off the Portuguese coast and was captured off Lisbon in November.[229] The small 30 ton *Flibustier* which had sailed from St Jean-de-Luz fell to the frigate *Diana* in 43°40'N 10°W in September.[230] Conte's efforts continued with the 180 ton *Heureux*, which was taken off Bayonne in August 1798.[231] The same year he was given a letter of marque for the 250 ton *Vengeance*, which cruised for two years before being captured in 45°50'N 7°40'W in January 1800.[232] In 1798 he had joined Taudin (otherwise unknown) in sending the *Confiance* to Île de France.[233] This is the ship that was commanded by the famous Robert Surcouf and which was responsible for making Conte's fortune. The first voyage appears to have been relatively unimportant but it was on the second, after Surcouf had been appointed to the command, that the *Confiance* captured the 820 ton Indiaman *Kent*.

The *Kent* was outward bound for Bengal, and Surcouf attacked her in Balasore Roads near the delta of the Ganges. The East Indiaman was well defended by a crew of ninety or a hundred men and carried forty one passengers, many of whom were able to join in the defence. Surcouf led the attack, dressed as a seaman to preserve his anonymity and only succeeded in capturing the *Kent* after a struggle in which the *Kent's* captain and twenty one men were killed and another thirty five were wounded. The East Indiaman was a magnificent prize, very large and carrying species and trade goods. With his share of the proceeds and his reputation as a daring and successful captain Surcouf was able to establish himself later as the managing owner of privateers at St Malo.[234] However, for the managing owner of the *Confiance*, Conte, this was only one of a number of ventures, though it was probably the most successful and established his fortune. In 1801 he had joined Audibert Frères in fitting out the *Bellonne*, which under the command of Jacques Perraud took three prizes in the Indian Ocean.[235] When the Napoleonic War broke out the *Bellonne* again put to sea under the command of Perraud. But her first cruise was off South West Ireland and on 14 August Perraud took the *Lord Nelson* East Indiaman off Cape Clear.[236] It took Perraud an hour and a half to subdue the ship and her crew did not surrender until the captain and six others had been killed, another twenty seven had been wounded, the mizon mast had been destroyed and the ship disabled. Then Perraud's luck changed. While he was escorting the *Lord Nelson* to Corunna he was chased by H.M. brig *Seagull* and an action began which lasted from five in the afternoon to half past eight. Then the *Colossus*, 74, arrived and the *Bellone* was forced to abandon her prize. The corsair later put into Passagès and took a new crew on board.[237] This demonstrated the risks of commerce raiding in the seas off Western Europe and the *Bellone* returned to the Indian Ocean where there were fewer warships. During the following two years Perraud continued to cruise there. He was feared by merchants of the East India Company for the *Bellone* was fast and well handled and Perraud continued to take prizes. The *Bellone* was finally captured off the coast of Ceylon by the *Powerful* 74, and *Rattlesnake* sloop, much to the satisfaction of the Commander-in-Chief.[238] However this was not the Conte family's final venture. In 1807 Conte fils joined Limousin and Pierre Guirons in fitting out the new 120 ton *Phénix* at Rochefort for a voyage *en guerre et marchandise* to Cayenne.[239] It returned safely to Bordeaux and in the autumn of 1809 made a second voyage, cruising off the Iberian coast. At least one ship was captured, the Portuguese ship *Santa Anna* formerly the *Chatham* of New York, which was sent to Fayol and was sold in March 1810.[240] Then the *Phénix* was refitted and put under the command of Jacques Perraud, who had been released from prison in Britain. However, in September the *Phénix* was captured by the frigate *Aigle* in 45°N 32°W of Paris.[241]

Of the other merchants who fitted out privateers during these wars, only Seignoret and Ségur appear to have been important. Seignoret, who joined Corerreau (otherwise unknown) in fitting out the 140 ton former American ship *Auguste* in 1799, was of comparatively humble origin. But in 1784 his daughter had married into the wealthy Rinchon family, to the great astonishment of the merchant community.[242] This gave him access to considerable wealth. The *Auguste* which Seignoret and Corerreau fitted out was sent on a voyage *en guerre et marchandise* with a general cargo but was captured in 40°41'N 20°54W by the *Melpomene* in June after a sixty hour chase.[243] This was the last ship that these partners sent to sea during the war.

Before the outbreak of the Revolution Jacques de Ségur had been one of the richest Bordeaux merchants. During the wars which followed as Jacques Ségur - he dropped the aristocratic de - he fitted out three ships.[244] The *Brune* and *Brunette* were fitted out in 1797 and were captured, the first in 44°N 14°W and the second off the Ile D'Yeu.[245] The following year Ségur sent the 420 ton *Courageux* to the West Indies and it returned safely to Bayonne. In 1799, after a refit at Bordeaux the *Courageux* set sail again, but was taken by the *Alcmene* off the Portuguese coast.[246] Ségur did not fit out any more ships. Of the other merchants, Lefebvre managing owner of the 300 ton *Flore* in 1798, had invested 300,000 *Livres* in ships in 1789.[247] The *Flore* was captured and Lefebvre did not fit outanymore ships.[248] Nogé, a Bordeaux shipbuilder, joined Guillot, Fange and Rogerie jeune in the equally unsuccessful *Diane* that was taken soon after leaving the Gironde on a voyage to the Ile de France.[249] Of the large German community in Bordeaux only the names of Schildt and Jude appear among the managing owners. They joined Muratel in the equally ill-fated 217 ton *Général Mathieu*, which was captured in 1808 on a voyage to Martinique.[250] Nothing is known of the other managing owners, most of whom lost their ships.

NANTES

In 1792, on the eve of the Revolutionary War, Nantes ranked third among

French ports in terms of the total tonnage behind Bordeaux and Marseilles.[251] But in terms of average tonnage Nantes was the more important: 384 tons against 340 for Bordeaux and 220 for Marseilles. Only the East India ships, based at Lorient, were larger at 478 tons.[252] Lorient had lost its monopoly of this trade but all East India goods had to be imported into France at Lorient. The basis of Nantes' prosperity was the slave trade. In the 1780's Nantes controlled 40 per cent of the French total and it provided a market for a variety of goods which were exported, mainly to the Congo and Guinea, with a smaller quantity to Mozambique and Senegal, though this had been under British control between 1763 and 1783. Goods exported included fire arms, copper basins, cowrie shells, rope, knives, Breton and Cholet linens, brandy, bar iron, pipes and wine.[253] The proceeds of the sale of these slaves, principally in Saint-Domingue - Guadeloupe and Martinique took comparatively few - was invested in raw sugar, cocoa, coffee, cotton, indigo, pepper and rice.[254] Of these muscovado sugar was the most important and the bulk was sent to Orléans, the capital of sugar refining in eighteenth century France, though smaller quantities were sent to Angers, Saumur and Tours.[255] Orleans was also the focal point for much of French internal trade, for the town lay on the principal North-South axis which linked the Mediterranean with the North and the East-West line along which was carried the colonial goods imported at Nantes.[256] In the first half of the eighteenth century Nantes had been the leading sugar importer but after the Seven Years War it had been overtaken by Bordeaux. After the War of American Independence the slave trade expanded and imports of raw sugar had risen again, though Nantes never recovered her early dominance.[257] Merchants engaged in the slave trade began to use larger ships and the average tonnage rose from 170 to 218. Before the War of American Independence only 26 ships had been over 250 tons; after 1783 there were 178 - over half - and 42 were over 500 tons.[258] One reason for this growth was the wartime profit, which had created a new generation of managing owners.

After 1783 many voyages were organised by independent newcomers, many of whom formed temporary partnerships. By 1789 this new form of commercial organisation had largely replaced the older, long established companies which had traded on a regular basis. In 1789 the slave trade reached its peak but then began to collapse as the market was glutted. In 1790 and 1791 84 ships left Nantes for West Africa - the peak had been 92 in 1789 - but prices in Saint-Domingue were lower than formerly and profits fell. In 1792 the trade received its *coup de grace* from the slave revolt and fall in coffee prices.[259] At the same time Nantes' commerce with the Loire towns was damaged by the collapse of the internal economy and declined from 25,709 tons (the 1792 total) to 6,019 tons and from 41,572 tons to 10,408 tons for the colonial imports.[260] The only increase was in American imports, from 1,170 tons to 3,679 tons. The uprising in the Vendée destroyed the network of internal commerce for a number of years. Nantes did not fall into the hands of the *chouans* - the attack was beaten off - but the town was the scene of savage trials and the mass execution of captured rebels. The port did not have a background of privateering on any considerable scale, and only a small number of corsairs had put to sea from Nantes during the mid-eighteenth century wars. But in 1793 there was sufficient enthusiasm for ten ships to sail, of which six were seized. For the next four years the port was quiet; the Vendée revolt continued spasmodically, and although it had little direct effect on Nantes, it destroyed the prospects for commerce in the hinterland and made it difficult and dangerous to transport goods to a wider market. Benoît Bourcard, a Swiss merchant from Basel who had settled at Nantes before the Revolution, acted as a commission agent during the Revolutionary and Napoleonic wars, but did little business between 1794 and 1796.[261]

There was no shortage of ships at Nantes for commerce raiding. Some were giants: the *Comt d'angivilliers* and *Breton* belonging to Pelletier, Michaud et Cie were each over 1,000 tons, but were unsuitable for privateering because they did not carry a heavy armament and were probably fairly slow. But apart from the 200-400 ton slavers there were other, much smaller vessels: *Petit Duc* 37 tons, *Maure* 20 tons, *Parfaite Union* 27 tons and *Passe Partout* 45 tons were all used in the 1780's either as escorts to larger ships or had sailed independently. All could be used in the North Atlantic. There was thus a wide range of shipping available. The ships chosen in 1793 however were comparatively large: three were of 300 tons, one of 200 and two of 160 and 100 tons and four whose tonnage is unknown.[262] After the first unsuccessful year in which six of the ten vessels were captured, privateering gradually recovered: one sailed in 1795 and four the following year, all of which were fitted out by Félix Cossin, except the 150 ton *Furet*, which was managed by the partnership Marion Frères and Duguen. It was not until 1797 that privateering at Nantes expanded dramatically to 57 ships. This included a number of small vessels - two of 12 tons, the *Poisson Volant* and *Reine D'Angleterre* - which were pressed into service.[263] But the absence of the established merchants from the list of *armateurs* is striking and reflects the same changes in society that have already been noted at the other ports. One looks in vain for Pelletier, Michaud et Cie, Owners of the huge *Comte d'Angevilliers* and *Breton* already mentioned. Similarly Arnous et fils and Perrotin et fils who had engaged in the slave trade between 1783 and 1792 - nine and seven voyages respectively - are absent from the list of privateering *armateurs*.[264] This is not to say that they did not invest in commerce raiding, but that they no longer occupied an important position in it in either the Revolutionary or the Napoleonic wars.

One of the most successful Nantes managing owners was Félix Cossin, who sent privateers to sea during the Revolutionary War but not in the Napoleonic. In 1793 he was responsible for the 200 ton *Espérance* and *Intrépide*. The first was captured in 47°N 15°W by the frigate *Druid* in May. The other returned safely to port; in 1794 it was first hired by the state and then sold.[265] Cossin's next venture was the 250 ton *Eugénie*, which was at sea from December 1795 to March 1797, when it was captured by the *Cleopatra* in 41°30'N 14°W of

Paris.[266] Only three other Nantes corsairs were at sea in 1796 and two, the 300 ton *Musette* and 80 ton *Actif* were Cossin's. The *Musette* captured two prizes, the *Industrious Abeille* from Newfoundland laden with cod, fish oil and furs and the *Alerte*, though in December she was captured by the *Hazard* in 49°30'N.[267] The *Actif* was at sea from October 1796 to January 1797 apart from a short refit at Bordeaux during her second cruise, but she fell into British hands in 48°N 12°W of Paris.[268] Cossin's determined efforts helped to encourage others and some of his ventures were profitable: Bourcard's investment of 1,000 *livres* in the *Intrépide* brought him a return of over 2,000.[269] By 1797 the troubles in the Vendée had been brought under control and it looked as if Nantes might become an entrepot for imported and captured goods which could be distributed by land and via the Loire to markets as far away as Switzerland. This encouraged men to invest in privateering. No fewer than fifty-seven were at sea from Nantes during 1797, and ten of them were Cossin's. The first to sail was the 300 ton *Confiance*, which left Nantes in January and remained at sea until the following March.[270] The next was the 300 ton *Nouvelle Eugénie*, which left in March and took the 200 ton *Spencer* of London laden with coffee, sugar and cotton before being captured off Cape Finisterre in May.[271] The 120 ton *Félicité* set sail in the autumn and captured the *Kelly* which, with her cargo was sold for 55,782 *livres*.[272] The last three were fitted out at the end of the year: the 120 ton *Julie*, 200 ton *Caroline* and 500 ton *Volage*. All three were seized the following year and the shareholders made a loss on at least two, the *Julie* and *Caroline*.[273] Enthusiasm for commerce raiding began to wane the following year, partly because profits were not as high as anticipated and partly because merchants were unable to dispose of prize goods once the initial demand had been met. But Cossin persisted; in 1798 he fitted out the *Clarisse* and 250 ton *Papillon*; of the two the latter was captured in April 1799 in 49°30'N 17°W.[274] Cossin's last venture was the *Elizabeth*, which put to sea in Year IX; nothing is known of this beyond the name and it probably failed to take any prizes.[275] This marks the end of his ventures which seem to have been less profitable as the years passed. This would explain why he failed to send any more corsairs to sea during the Napoleonic War.

Other active managing owners were Desclos Lepeley et Perruchaud which established a branch at Paris in 1808 as Desclos Lepeley et Cie.[276] The company did not enter commerce raiding until 1807, when a letter of marque was given for the 130 ton brig *Malvina*. The ship sailed from Nantes in January, captured one prize and was then taken by the *Guerrier*. In 1808 the company established the branch in Paris and was given a letter of marque for the *Argos* to sail from Dunkirk.[277] From this point the two parts of the company fitted out ships independently; in September 1809 another vessel, the *Vautour*, sailed from Boulogne and after using this as a base for two voyages prepared her third and final cruise at Calais. In the course of three voyages the *Vautour* captured six ships.[278] Two years later the company fitted out two more ships: the 100 ton, one year old sloop *Milan* and the *Loup Garou*, took two prizes and returned safely to port.[279]

The only other managing owners to fit out more than one or two ships were Cyprien Laporte, Bertrand et Feydeau and Louis Levesque, all of whom are otherwise unknown. Laporte was responsible for four: the 100 ton *Poisson Volant* in 1793 which took three prizes and was captured in 1797, the *Jeune Adèle*, *Marianne* and 12 ton *Poisson Volant*, of which the last was captured near the Isle of Wight.[280] Bertrand was a man who tried his luck in commerce raiding at the beginning of the war, though he made complicated arrangements. The ship he managed, the 100 ton *Franklin*, was owned by the well known merchant Benjamin Dubois and Bertrand arranged for the ship to be fitted out by François Donjon of St Servan and begin its cruise at Port Louis. It was described in the letter of marque as a frigate but only carried twelve four pounders and four swivel guns. It was taken off Ushant in May.[281] In 1797 Bertrand joined in the general rush to fit out ships and sent the *Indien* to sea, apparently without success.[282]

Bertrand's final attempt in the Revolutionary War was made jointly with Feydeau and was the 90 ton brig *Vénus* which took the *Speedwell* of Guernsey and sold it at Tenerife.[283] The partnership appears again in the first year of the Napoleonic War when the men fitted out the *Vénus* which sent one prize to Tenerife and refitted at Santander.[284] There followed a lull until 1809 when the partners refitted the *Dame Ernouf* on behalf of Jean Goyen and Antoine Erffren at Point à Pitre.[285] Their final venture was in 1810 with the 191 ton *Duc de Danzig*, commanded by François Aregnaudeau, Member of the Legion of Honour. He captured two ships, the *Tottenham* and the *Jane* but the latter could not be sold in France and was sent to Charleston, where it was sold for the equivalent of 290,000 fr. The second cruise was made in the West Indies and off the coast of North America; it lasted nineteen months and one prize was sent to New York.[286] Louis Levesque, the last significant managing owner, was responsible for five corsairs. He did not enter commerce raiding until 1797 and his first ship, the new 40 ton *Marie*, was captured in November. His second was the 150 ton *Vigilant* which set sail in April 1798 and refitted at Bilbao. The following year two ships were fitted out by his son, the *Nouveau Vigilant* and 150 ton *Pégase*; the latter fell into British hands.[287] Levesque fils prepared his next ship in the autumn of 1809, the new 241 ton *Napoléon le Grand*, which took two prizes and was then captured off Ushant by the *Edouard* brig.[288]

LA ROCHELLE AND BAYONNE

Bordeaux and Nantes dominated the commerce of the French Atlantic coast, but some merchants at those ports also had links with La Rochelle, Bayonne and, further to the South, the small port of St Jean-de-Luz. Early in the eighteenth century the estuary of the River Nive, on which Bayonne was situated, began to silt up and after 1714 the trade had begun to decline. So too did the annual fairs and it was at this point that a number of merchants moved away from Bayonne. To some extent the decline was halted by successful commerce raiding during the eighteenth century wars, when privateering was relatively quiet elsewhere. It became popular again during the Revolutionary and Napoleonic wars.[289] La Rochelle on the other hand had not been able to grow during the eighteenth century to the same extent as Bordeaux, partly because the port lacked effective communications with the interior and partly because of navigational hazards which made it difficult to leave or enter the harbour under certain conditions. La Rochelle's economic hinterland extended to Fontenay to the north east, as far as Niort and Poitiers to the east and to the south east to the brandy country round Saint-Jean-d'Angély, Saintes and Cognac.[290] But the port was separated from this hinterland by miles of salt marshes and the oil of the countryside beyond was too poor to grow cereals. The produce which the region did produce: salt, poor quality wine and brandy could be exported to the West Indies but production of them fluctuated, producers and shippers were hampered by taxes and the trade in salt and brandies were damaged by competition. The only industry was some sugar refining, linked to the import trade in muscovado. To make matters worse, the entrance to the small harbour was often hazardous. Ships had to enter via a narrow channel in which navigation was further hindered by fierce tides and the channel, like that at Bayonne, was slowly silting up during the eighteenth century, ships above 150 tons could not enter. As a result ships often anchored in the outport between the foundation of the Dike de Richelieu and the two towers of St Nicolas and the Chain which guarded the entrance to the old port. There they unloaded part of their cargo into lighters before entering the harbour, where, owing to the restricted area, they had to moor side by side at right angles to the quay. No ships could enter or leave at low tide and when the weather was bad ships had to anchor in the relative safety of the lee of the Ile de Ré, where a lighthouse was erected. The result of these growing hazards to navigation is that by the end of the eighteenth century some merchants were no longer using La Rochelle directly and instead sent their ships to anchor in the mouth of the River Charente, near Rochefort or Marans at the mouth of the River Seudre, where they unloaded their cargoes on to small coasters which carried the goods to La Rochelle. Many of the other merchants who continued to use La Rochelle directly kept a watch for their ships from the ramparts between the Tower of the Four Sergeants and the Tower of the Chain so that they could send lighters to them.

Most of the ships which entered La Rochelle were returning from Saint Domingue, and approximately half were slavers which had sailed first to the West coast of Africa. In the decade 1780-92 116 ships were fitted out for Saint Domingue, another 4 for Guadeloupe, 15 for Martinique, 6 for Cayenne, 8 for the French West Indies, 118 for West Africa and the West Indies.[291] Thus of a total of 378 ships engaged in commerce, local fishing and the European coasting trade, 267 were employed in the colonial trade. La Rochelle, like Nantes and Bordeaux, had become dominated by this, partly because the colonial trade had grown during the eighteenth century and offered good prospects. But it was also because the trade with Canada which had also been important up to the Seven Years War - 133 ships had sailed there in the decade 1750-59 out of a total of 367 - had been lost when Quebec and Montreal fell into British hands. All that remained was a small number of vessels that went annually to the Newfoundland cod fishery. The figure of 133 for Canadian trade probably exaggerates the value of Canada for La Rochelle merchants, for the total for the previous decade had been much lower - 52 ships - but it is possible that the figure of 133 represents a growth in population and individual wealth in Canada as much as an increase in the shipment of strategic *Matériel* for the conflict with the British colonies. Either way, the loss of Canada was a severe blow and the subsequent increase in colonial trade after the American War of Independence did not fully compensate for this, because it was the major Atlantic ports, Bordeaux and Nantes, which took the greater part. Nor were efforts to develop trade with North America any more successful; early efforts failed when it was believed that the slave trade offered better prospects.

The only other trade which grew during this time was with the Ile de France in East India commodities, and slaves. Between 1769 and 1785 La Rochelle sent 26 vessels to the Indian Ocean, and they obtained slaves from East Africa, which had reached Ile de France via Madagascar, coffee from Ile Bourbon, (also known as Ile de Réunion), Indian cloths and Bengal silks from Pondicherry, Chinese porcelains and spices from the Dutch East Indies. The creation of a new East India Company in 1785 threatened this trade, but merchants at La Rochelle, Bordeaux, Nanates, Marseilles and St Malo continued to trade to Ile de France while they attacked the privileges of the new company. Indeed, the vigour with which they campaigned shows the importance of this trade, in spite of its high costs, and suggests that ports were beginning to turn from the West to the East Indies.[292] Apart from these overseas activities, La Rochelle merchants did not engage in the European coasting trade. The goods they imported, together with Malouin cargoes of fish from the Grand Banks which were also discharged at La Rochelle, were carried to markets in northern and southern markets by other merchants, principally the Dutch. The main reason was that they were able to use smaller crews than the French, whose manning levels were fixed by law and were often twice as high as the Dutch. The latter also had considerable experience in navigating in the Baltic, which was an important market for colonial goods. The consequence of these geographic disadvantages and sluggish commercial growth was that La Rochelle's share of French external trade fell from around 6 per cent in 1728-32 to between 2 and 3 per cent after the American War of Independence. La Rochelle's rivals: chiefly Bordeaux, Marseilles and Nantes all grew much faster and La Rochelle slowly declined. Even the majority of goods which were shipped for the slave trade originated elsewhere. The consequence of La Rochelle's failure either to develop a variety of trades or to manufacture the items exported was that many merchants moved elsewhere and by the eve of the Revolutionary war there remained only 27 managing owners.

One family which was established at La Rochelle and Bayonne were the Chégarays. Thomas became a managing owner in 1794 through his marriage to Marie Lanusse, whose father had bankrupted by the events in Saint Domingue. Thomas' father Michel was a lawyer and a deputy in the National Assembly in 1789. His mother Marie was the daughter of Lasserre, mayor of Bayonne and a wealthy merchant. Thomas left La Rochelle during the Terror and appears to have gone to Bayonne to join his younger brother Pierre-Antoine. The first sign of a partnership between the two was in 1796 when they were given a letter of marque for the *Rochelais*. This captured two prizes which were sent into Spanish ports but it was taken in September.[293] The following year the brothers fitted out the 170 ton Rochelle ship *Succès* at Bayonne on behalf of the Rochelle merchant Jean-Baptiste Noel.[294] The same year they fitted out the 150 ton *Mouche* at La Rochelle which took three prizes, one English and two Portuguese. These were later sold for a total of 1,415,366 *livres*.[295] During her second cruise the *Mouche* captured an American ship, the *John and Richard*, and the brothers subsequently became embroiled in a long legal battle over the justice of the seizure which resulted in the ship being returned to its owners and compensation being paid.[296] Soon after capturing the *John and Richard* the *Mouche* was herself taken by the frigate *Diana* in 51°N 20°W.[297] Before the case of the *John and Richard* had been brought to an end the Chégarary brothers acquired another ship, the former Spanish prize *Barra*, which they renamed the *Abeille*. Her first cruise began in November 1797, but of three prizes only one, the Portuguese *Mosquito*, reached San Sebastian and was sold for the equivalent of 22,570 fr., from which legal costs had to be deducted of 7,874 fr.. This was sufficient to encourage the brothers to send the *Abeille* to sea for a second cruise, in the course of which five ships were captured, two American, one English and two Portuguese. This produced a nett total, less commisions and legal costs, of 455,761 fr. and the *Abeille* made a third cruise in December 1799, in which one American and an English ship were taken. The final result was that although the sale of prizes had raised a total of 756,045 fr., the cost of fitting out amounted to 631,000 fr..[298]

One of the last ventures by the Chegaray brothers during the Revolutionary War was to use the former English prize, the lugger *Enfant du Carnaval*. This made one cruise to the South West and took the English ship *Greencastle*. Part of her cargo was sold at Tenerife and the remainder at La Rochelle, but the corsair was captured in September. However the cruise was profitable because the ship and cargo were sold for 101,070 fr. against 56,00 fr. for fitting the ship out for her voyage.[299] More important for the Chegaray brothers was their one per cent commission, which amounted to 3,100 fr. Their final venture during the Revolutionary War was made jointly with a Bordeaux merchant, J.B. Grammont. They sent the 300 ton *Oncle Thomas* - the *Abeille* renamed - to sea in November 1800 and in the first cruise this took two English ships, *Brittania* and *Leander*. The cruise proved very successful; each shareholder received 21,730 fr. for each 1,000 fr. share. By this time the younger brother had also fitted out a ship at Bayonne in 1798, the 76 ton *Colombe*, but this was captured by the frigate *Magnanime* in August in 44°22'N 11°50'W.[300]

Their success in the Revolutionary War encouraged the Chegaray brothers at La Rochelle to fit out more privateers early in the Napoleonic War. Their first was the 110 ton *Felix* which was managed jointly with Garesché (otherwise unknown), and which sailed in mid summer 1803. Its two prizes were recaptured and the *Felix* was seized by the *Amazon* in 46°N 13°W of Paris.[301] In the autumn the Chégaray brothers, with J.B.Grammont at Bordeaux fitted out the *Oncle Thomas* again and in the course of this second voyage took two more English ships, *Imperial* and *Venus*, which were sold in Cayenne. The result of the two voyages was a nett gain of 900,000 fr., which included the proceeds of the sale of the ship, against expenses of 60,000 fr.. The Chégaray brothers also gained 25,635 fr. in commission. Chégaray frères and Jean Larroulet also sent the 22 ton *Deux Amis* to sea from Bayonne early in the Napoleonic War, but there is no record of any prizes being captured.[302] Chégaray frères and Grammont also fitted out the 500 ton *Blonde* at Bayonne. This fought a number of actions, embarked more sailors to replace the wounded in November but was captured in August 1805.[303] Chégaray and Laroulet also sent the *Brilliant* to sea from Bayonne in mid-summer 1803; this took two prizes and ended its cruise at Vigo in April 1804.[304] Chégaray frères' final venture was in 1808 when, together with Grammont and Arregnaudeau, another Bordeaux merchant, sent the *Joséphine* to Cayenne and the Île de France.[305] This was one of the trading voyages prepared at Atlantic ports in 1808. The ship returned safely and ended her voyage at Arcachon because of the fear of a British naval blockade further north.[306]

The principal managing owners at Bayonne were Basterrèche frères, merchants and shipowners before the Revolution and who established a bank at Paris. Few Bayonne corsairs fell into British hands; many were small and could evade the larger British warships and Bayonne was situated in waters where British warships were unwilling to sail for fear of being caught on a dangerous lee shore. Thus Bayonne managing owners did not face the same risks in commerce raiding as men at other ports, but they still had to make a profit. It seems that Bayonne, as a relatively small and isolated port, escaped the full effect of the Revolution and Basterrèche frères were not seriously damaged by the financial crisis. Their first corsair was the 110 ton *Sana Souci*, which cruised between April and July in 1793.[307] This was followed, as at other ports, by a lull in commerce raiding which lasted until 1797, when in early summer they fitted out the 150 ton *Adour* which was captured off Cape Clear in June.[308] Other ships followed; in November Basterrèche frères were given a letter of marque for the 41 ton *Hirondelle*, but this was captured in December after a short cruise.[309] The loss of this ship did not deter Basterrèche frères, nor their supporters though their ship was much smaller, in February 1798 they were granted a letter of marque for the 10 ton *Aventure* which cruised until June, when it entered St Jean-de-Luz.[310] At the same time the brothers prepared the 70 ton *Impromptu* at St Jean-de-Luz.[311] In June the 150 ton *Impatient* was given a letter of marque and cruised until early in the following year. During the summer Basterrèche frères, fitted out the 40 ton *Araignée*, but this was taken in 44°41'N 8°6'W in September by the *Triton*.[312] The 250 ton *Husard* followed in November, and this sailed to the West Indies, probably with a letter of marque *en querre et marchandise*: it was captured in Surinam River.[313] The following spring the *Aventure* was at sea again and took a Portuguese prize that was later sold for 90,00 fr.[314] There followed a lull in the brothers' activities and they did not send their next ship to sea until the spring of 1807 when the 165 ton *Eve*, commanded by Etienne Pellet from Hendaye put to sea. Apart from a short stay at San Sebastian the *Eve* was at sea until June and captured two prizes.[315] In September 1808 the 170 ton *Prince de Neufchâtel* was at sea and sent a prize to Lorient.[316] At the end of that year Basterrèche frères et Cie prepared the 165 *Amiral Martin* for a voyage. This proved one of the most successful of all the ships fitted out, for it continued to cruise until March 1809, when it fell to the sloop *Plover* in 46°N 11°W of Paris. In 1810 Basterrèche frères replaced it with another ship of the same name of 210 tons which had been built at Bordeaux the previous year, and this was at sea until the autumn of 1811.[317] Three other corsairs were fitted out in the winter of 1809: the *Dauphin*, *Perignon* of St Malo and the new, Bayonne built *Navarrois*. The first sent one prize to Bilbao, the second returned safely and the third was captured by the frigate *Rhin* in 45°26'N 7°W of Paris in March 1810.[318] These were followed in January 1810 by the 28 ton *Général Darmagnac*, built at Bayonne in 1809, which took two prizes on its first voyage and continued to cruise until the early summer of 1812.[319] Late in 1810 the 210 ton *Vice Amiral Martin* sailed but took no prizes and was captured late in 1811.[320] The last venture of Basterrèche frères et Cie was the small *Beau Noir* which only carried a crew of ten. This sailed late in 1813.[321]

Basterrèche frères dominated Bayonne privateering. But a handful of other men also fitted out a number of ships and enjoyed a modest success. Dufourcq et fils began in 1793 with their 110 ton *Ami des Planteurs*, formerly the *St François*. The Dufourcq family's background was in the whale and Newfoundland fisheries; Pierre Dufourcq had commanded a Newfoundland ship in 1767, had bought the 70 ton brigantine *Minerve de St Jean de Luz* in 1786 and the 120 ton brigantine *Cap de Ray de Bayonne* in 1790. This does not place him in the same class as Dubois at St Malo, but it provided experience and modest capital.[322] The first privateering venture ended when the *Am des Planteurs* was captured by the *Lucan* Privateer West of Ushant in June after a fight lasting an hour and a half.[323] But Pierre Dufourcq was a popular republican; he was elected mayor and in Fructidor Year III (September 1794) he bought the *Bon Accord* for 100,000.[324] Dufourcq was able to use the safe position of Bayonne and the opportunities for trade with Spain to support his more risky privateering voyages. But after his experience with the first corsair, he restricted himself to small vessels which were cheap to fit out and which could evade British warships more easily. He thus abandoned his earlier attempt to use his experience in the fisheries to join the St Malo ships in the Soundings and concentrated instead on the comparatively close waters off northern Spain and Portugal. His 10 ton *Labourdin*, fitted out at St Jean-de-Luz, entered Santander in 1794 with two prizes, his 30 ton *Entreprise* sailed the following year and in 1798 and 1799 he had the 80 ton *Aigle* and 25 ton *Général Brune* at sea.[325]

Another Bayonne merchant who took some part in commerce raiding, though he did not enter until 1807, was Pierre Giron, who is known only as a wholesale merchant. His first vessel was the 32 ton *Jéna* which was captured South West of cape Finisterre and was destroyed at sea.[326] The following spring he sent another ship, the *Phénix*, but he shared the risk with another Bayonne merchant Laporte Duluc. It was a small boat with a crew of only 18 men and an armament of two swivel guns but its share of a prize ensured that the voyage would be profitable. Giron was encouraged by this and fitted out another vessel independently. This was the *Printemps*, which sailed from St Jean-de-Luz and made a profit of 15,897 fr. from its single prize.[327] This was also a small vessel, for it only cost 5,684 fr. to prepare and was sold for 2,160 fr. at the end of its voyage. For the final venture Giron decided on a different approach. His 52 ton *Jason* was larger than the others and cruised in a different area, but it was captured in 45°30'N 9°W of Paris in September.[328] Another merchant with a similar experience but who confined his ventures to the closing years of the Revolutionary War was Jean Baptiste Joanhau. He sent two small ships to sea in 1798 and early 1799, both confusingly called *Hasard*, one of which was a lugger and the other a small coaster. Auliacq who commanded one of them was appointed captain of the 24 ton *Tigre* in December 1798 and the *Phénix* in 1801. During the Napoleonic was Joanhau only fitted out one corsair, the 10 ton *Phénix* in 1808.[329] The experience of Labrouche, a St Jean-de-Luz merchant, was similar; at the beginning of the Revolutionary War he owned at least two ships. In 1798 the 80 ton *Rusé* and 108 ton *Cantabre* were fitted out by another merchant, Récur. Labrouche confined his efforts during this war to the 8 ton *Coro*, shared with Passement (otherwise unknown) which made a profitable voyage, the 49 ton *Retour*, 43 ton captured in 40°58'N 9°W and 20 ton *Hardi*.[330] Labrouche also prepared the 400 ton *Hyène* for the Bordeaux merchant Balguerie jeune.[331] During the Napoleonic War Labrouche fitted out another four; the 9 ton *Représaille* which captured two ships and shared in three others, the 225 ton *Intrépide* captured off Cape Finisterre in November 1809, the *Cupidon* in 1810 and the 12 ton *Constance* in 1813[332] Jean Larroulet was another Bayonne merchant with an interest in commerce raiding: three small ships in the Revolutionary War and three more in the Napoleonic: *Courageux*, 8 ton *Diligent*, 36 ton *Diligent*, *Auguste*, *Entreprenant*, *Auguste*. The only other merchants to show more than a passing interest in commerce raiding were Louis Pêche (11 ships, all in the Revolutionary War) and Récur, already mentioned in connexion with two of Labrouche's ships, and who also fitted out four other vessels during the Revolutionary War.

MARSEILLES

At the end of the eighteenth century Marseilles was the second most important French port behind Bordeaux. Her merchants traded with the Levant, the Barbary coast, Southern Spain and the West and East Indies, but Marseilles' merchants did not control the distribution of these goods throughout western France and northern Europe. This was in the hands of merchants from the French Atlantic ports and from Sweden, Denmark, Holland and Britain. In this respect Marseilles was no different from Bordeaux, whose imports were distributed to the important north European and Baltic markets by merchants from there. Like her commercial rivals, Marseilles also expanded her trade during the eighteenth century and especially during the period of striking growth between the end of the War of American Independence and the outbreak of the French Revolution. Like Bordeaux and Nantes and to a lesser extent the other leading French ports Marseilles owed some of her commercial growth in this period to a development of trade with the colonies of the West Indies. Her merchants also benefitted from the lifting of the monopoly of commerce with the East Indies, though only to the extent of being able to fit out ships for the long voyage east and reaping from the sales in Lorient, for the order forbidding sales of east India goods at any other port remained in force.

The main reason for Marseilles' success as a port was that it lay at the focal point of a number of important trade routes. The valley of the Rhône provided a means of access not only to the great industrial city of Lyons but also to the states of the Swiss Confederation and Southern Germany and there were occasionally tentative links as far afield as Vienna. Silk for the Lyons spinning and weaving industry was an iportant industry through the seventeenth century, though during the eighteenth it was gradually supplemented by cotton as the Swiss industry at St Gallen, Basel and Neuchatel prospered and influenced the development of the cotton industry in Alsace. Another important commodity imported at Marseilles was wheat, much of it from the Barbary states, though for a short time in the 1780's supplemented by significant imports from the Ukraine which had been carried from Black Sea ports. Wheat was needed to feed the population of southern France, for the narrow coastal strip, Alpes Maritimes and Massif Central could not produce sufficient to feed its population. Apart from a range of raw materials and food which passed through the port en route for northern markets Marseilles was also dependent on imported oil and soda for the manufacture of its soap, large quantities of which were also sent north via the Rhône valley[333] Marseilles' control of this land- and waterway lay in her geographical position close to the mouth of the Rhône and also to the fact that large ships could not enter the estuary, which was comparatively shallow. Goods destined for this trade route had to be unloaded first at Marseilles and then carried by comparatively shallow boat to Beaucaire. It was this that provided the basis for the great annual fair at Beaucaire which acted as the meeting point for commerce from the north and south and which relegated Marseilles to the highly profitable position of Mediterranean entrepot rather than the controller of trade with central and northern Europe. It was for this reason that Marseilles also became the centre of an important trade in Languedoc cloth and wine from southern France, and large quantities were exported via Marseilles to the Levant and Barbary coast.

During the course of the seventeenth and eighteenth centuries Marseilles merchants expanded this diverse and profitable trade to include ventures to the West and East Indies, though Marseilles merchants had already traded with the Spanish colonies for some time.[334] The growth of the West India colonies offered many prospects for trade in cloth, wine and Mediterranean produce as well as providing sugar, coffee, indigo and other commodities that could be sold in Mediterranean and European markets. From a comparatively low level in the early eighteenth century - two or three a year - Marseilles trade with the West Indies grew to around a hundred at the end of the 1780's and led to the development of a valuable sugar refining industry though Marseilles never seriously challenged Bordeaux and Nantes.[335] Merchants at Marseilles, as at other ports trading with the West Indies had found in the 1780's that profits were shrinking for the reasons already described. By this date commerce with the East Indies was appearing in a more favourable light. The first voyages had taken place early in the eighteenth century under the control of the French East India Company and it was not until the company's monopoly was abolished in 1769 that the same merchants sent ships independently.[336] Between 1771 and 1785 when the company was re-established and its privileges renewed Marseilles merchants organised 72 voyages to the East Indies. Then fierce argument raged between the new company and the Marseilles merchants who had established themselves in the trade. Marseilles merchants continued to send ships east of the Cape of Good Hope: 38 under French flag and 5 more as neutrals. In 1790 the company was abolished as part of the ending of privilege in the state, but by then French commerce was in decline.

Marseilles commerce on the eve of the French Revolution had developed to a remarkable degree. Its total commerce (55m. *livres*) - with the West Indies was equal in value to that with Italy and surpassed only by trade with Levant.[337] Marseilles had overtaken all French ports except Bordeaux and even in its sales of fish - mostly dried cod brought by Malouin fishermen from the Grand Banks - it had overtaken all the fishing ports of the English Channel. But in wartime this trade was often interrupted by British naval patrols and the Toulon squadron could not provide adequate protection. Even when the commerce was carried in neutral ships it had to run a British naval blockade and merchants invested in privateering partly to make good their losses and partly, as in the Revolutionary and Napoleonic Wars, as a means of gaining the goods they needed. From the War of the League of Augsburg Marseilles privateers were at sea, though in smaller number than in the English Channel and they tended to attack unprotected neutral shipping rather than the English vessels which were always defended by convoys. The situation changed in 1793 because the federalist revolt and repression, which reflected the general suspicion of rich merchants, had severely weakened the commercial class. The charge had been laid against them that they wanted revolution in order to monopolise public office.[338] The patriots emerged triumphant in the municipal elections of January-February 1790 and although there were many merchants among the new representatives, they were drawn from the second rank. They joined the public in regarding the richest merchants as a source of capital who should be prepared to support the state generously, as well as providing employment. As at other ports, there was a widespread belief that merchants were engaged in hoarding and speculation and when an armed force was raised to aid the Revolution merchants were forced to provide funds.[339] Some of the richer merchants had bought land in the sale of the *biens nationaux*, but in general they avoided the limelight. The outbreak of war with Britain in 1793 struck at the foundation of their business activities and it is not surprising, in view of the British naval presence in the Mediterranean and their treatment by Revolutionary bodies, Marseilles had a distinguished privateering record.[340] During the War of the Spanish Succession, a total of 75 commissions had been registered between 1705 and 1712, and although this was considerably less than at St Malo, they carried on average substantially larger crews. Little is known about commerce raiding from Marseilles during the mid-eighteenth century wars and the disorders which struck Marseilles after the Revolution limited the opportunities to engage in commerce raiding thereafter. In the first year of the war 43 letters of marque were granted, which compares very favourably with Dunkirk's 49 and St Malo's 25.[341] But this was the peak year; in 1794, in spite of the embargo there were apparently 2 corsairs at sea and in 1796 there were another five letters of marque granted. In 1797, which for many other ports was the peak year, Marseilles had only 20 ships, compared with the 43 in the first year of the war. In the same year 34 ships were at sea from Dunkirk, 33 from Le Havre, 57 from Nantes and 29 from St Malo. Although these 20 Marseilles boats recorded 64 prizes - a better average for each boat than in 1793, when 43 corsairs took 35 prizes, there was a decline in 1798 to 14 and in 1799 there were only 8. But privateering seems to have kept the special character noted by Bromley; the ships carried a large crew in proportion to their size and they ranged from one 7 ton vessel to a ship of 600 tons. There was another difference between the Marseilles privateers and others: the method of financing the voyage. The evidence of the Bourcard papers shows that at Nantes and elsewhere on the Atlantic and Breton coasts where Bourcard had interests managing owners raised money for ventures by issuing a prospectus and inviting colleagues and business associates elsewhere to buy shares, which were sold in units of 1,000 livres each or occasionally in half shares of 500 livres. Occasionally a subscriber might buy a number of shares in a venture and hold more than 1,000 livres in shares. At Marseilles however it seems that a group of business associates shared the cost of fitting the ship out equally among themselves and in consequence the value of shares varied considerably: there were 38 shares at 285 *livres* each for the *Epervier* in 1793 and shares in *Républicain* and the *République Française* cost 3,000 *livres* each.[342]

The outbreak of war with Britain in 1793 was followed by other commercial disasters. In 1793-4 there was a regime of repression which hunted down real or supposed enemies of the state. Many merchants suffered fines and imprisonment. Marseilles' trade collapsed with the closure of traditional Mediterranean, European and North American markets. However in March the demand for corn and other provisions was met by Genoa merchants who sent large numbers of small boats with rice, ham, cod and other commodities. In May alone 171 ships arrived and this trade continued to flourish until 1799.[343] A little trade survived with the east coast of Spain, Provence and Languedoc, but the total tonnage was no more than a small part of the pre-war trade. Under these harsh economic conditions some merchants abandoned commerce; their place was taken by a variety of newcomers, including a number of Italians from Genoa, who took this opportunity of developing commercial links with new parts of the French empire and used neutral flags to try and guarantee security. This commercial decline is also reflected in the handful of privateers which put to sea during the Revolutionary War: one in 1796, three in 1797, none in 1798 - years in which commerce raiding flourished elsewhere - one in 1799, none in 1800 and one vessel in the final year of the war. Only the commerce with Arles and Genoa appeared to flourish: 1,325 and 1,022 ships entered from these two ports respectively.[344] The Peace of Amiens provided a temporary respite and when war began again in 1803 there were again merchants who were prepared to risk their money in raiding commerce, though not on a scale comparable with other leading French ports. Benet was a merchants who had traded to the West Indies and Spain and sent his 101 ton *Concorde* to Cayenne on a voyage *en guerre et marchandise*. The ship made a successful return and the following year was sent to Martinique but was taken off the Azores in June.[345] The Benet family was one of the few that took an active interest in commerce raiding. Louis Benet and André Martin had fitted out the 380 ton, two year old *République Française* in 1793, but it was taken.[346] Their partners the Martins were merchants with trading interests in Arles, Languedoc, Italy, Nice, Odessa and northern France. Martin fils had also sent a ship to Quebec. Etienne, the father, who did not fit out any corsairs, had been one of the richest merchants in Marseilles and had become mayor.[347] Later, in 1808, Antoine Vincent Marie Martin was president of the Tribunal de Commerce.[348] The Benet family abandoned commerce raiding until 1803 when Jean François Xavier Benet sent the 101 ton *Concorde* to sea. His next venture was the *Fougeux*, which was given a letter of marque in the spring of 1804 and made a profit of

59,887 fr. from a single prize.[349] At the end of 1805 his next ship sailed. This was the *Etoile*. It took the *Lion* and sold it in Spain, as well as a Swedish ship, the *Gustave Adolphe,* which was sold in Tunis. This voyage was also profitable: 66,387 fr. were divided among the shareholders.[350] For the next four years he did not fit out any more corsairs and for a time was a partner in the firm Bénédec Saizac et Cie, which also included François Bénédec and Hipolite Saizac, both of whom were wholesale merchants in Marseilles. This partnership was dissolved in June 1809 soon after Benet had sent another privateer to sea.[351] This ship was the *Eole*, which was captured after taking a prize that was sold for 193,546 fr. However, the expenses of the voyage were considerable and when the accounts were finally agreed they showed a loss.[352] In 1810, after the unsuccessful voyage of the *Eole*, Jean Benet, who was living in the rue de Phare, was joined by Jacques Christopher Benet, a wholesale merchant at Toulon and François Benet, a retailer of La Ciotat who jointly formed a new company.[353] In 1811 Jean Benet sent his last privateer to sea. This was the *Payson la Tour*, which took one small vessel and the venture was unprofitable.[354]

Among the merchants who came to Marseilles to fill the commercial vacuum was Nicholas Dodero di Andrea.[355] In 1809 he was trading with Spain and Sardinia and also fitted out a privateer, the *Liqurie*. This proved a successful venture, for it took at least one valuable prize in two voyages and made a nett profit of 22,507 fr. on the first voyage and 47,527 fr. on the second.[356] The same year he sent the 307 ton *Belle Etoile* to the West Indies with a letter of marque *en guerre et marchandise*, but the ship returned in October to Bayonne to avoid the British naval blockade in the Mediterranean.[357] Dodero developed his business in 1810 by joining a group of merchants who formed an insurance society. The capital of 90,000 fr. was raised by selling fifteen 6,000 fr. shares and two half shares of 3,000 fr..[358] In the same year he joined Jacques Monbouché to form Jacques Monbouché et Cie, wine sellers and vinters. The company was to exist for four years and had capital of 48,000 fr., of which Dodero subscribed 32,000 fr. But his fortune began to change and 1812 proved disastrous. He lost 40,000 fr. on goods he owned in Spain which were captured by rebels, 53,690 fr. on two ships taken while carrying false papers - they were intended to show the vessels were Sardinian - 30,132 fr. lost on goods sold at Abd el Kerin and losses on a number of ships, one of which was the privateer *Charlemagne*. He invested heavily in overseas ventures: the *Belle Etoile* was sent to Guadeloupe, for which insurance cost 75,788 fr. and ships to the Levant cost him 42,700 fr.. Dodero was a merchant of some importance; he owned two houses in Marseilles in the rue Santé, two shops in the rue du Port, two houses in Genoa, 19,911 fr. in shipping and sundry other items which totalled 222,206 fr.. But because of his losses he had debts of 1,473, 344 fr. and in July 1812 was declared bankrupt. His privateering had formed a small part of his extensive business ventures and played an insignificant part of his collapse.

Another group with wide commercial interests was Auguste Durand et Cie, who traded with Spain, Italy and Languedoc until Year X and then with the Levant. Auguste was one of four brothers who shared control of the Durand Bank which had been founded in 1736.[359] Between the Directory and the Restoration Auguste sent fourteen ships to sea and hired three ships to the Bay of Tunis for the record price of 1,600,000 fr..[360] In Year XII, as recognition of his success he was appointed president of the Chamber of Commerce. But he only fitted out a single corsair, the *Intrépide*, in 1810. This proved a success and its prizes were sold for a total of 144,444 fr. although it was five years before legal disputes were finally settled and a profit of 20,593 fr. was declared.[361] Two well known Jewish merchants, Jacob Cohen and Bacri, traded to Tunis and Algeria but these men only fitted out one privateer, the *Ziza*.[362]

CORSICA

One of the unusual features of the privateering was the interest shown by merchants and ship owners in Corsica, principally in 1797 and 1798 when there was also considerable interest in commerce raiding elsewhere in France. Although no personal details of these managing owners have survived, it is evident that they used their vessels - mostly small craft under ten tons - against shipping which sailed without convoy protection: Italian, Spanish and Danish. Among the more ambitious managing owners were members of the Aréna family who sent seven corsairs to sea between Year IV and Year VI (1796 and 1798). The largest was the 14 ton *Dangereuse*, which sailed from Bastia in Year V (1797).[363] Two other managing owners were Antoine and Louis Cecconi, who fitted out seven between them between Year V (1797) and the end of the Revolutionary War; one of these was the comparatively large *Alerte* of 43 tons, which sailed in Year VI (1798) and captured two prizes, one Turkish and a Danish vessel.[364] Towards the end of the Revolutionary War Louis Cecconi fitted out the 4 ton *St Pierre* at Leghorn, which had been an important entrepot for British trade with the Italian peninsula.[365] Santelli and Berlingeri sent three ships to sea in Years V and VI and Santelli frères equipped another four in Years VI and VIII. All sailed from Bastia and most were very small; the 85 ton *Vengeur* which was at sea in Year VI was the exception.[366] One of the most successful corsairs was the 5 ton *Terreur* which cruised in Year VIII (1800) and captured an Austrian ship which was later sold for 18,753 fr. and a Danish prize for which 11,344 fr. was paid.[367] Jean Balthazar and Charles Sapey were responsible for another eleven vessels. The only other managing owners of any consequence were Antoine and Barthel Sisco, who sent five corsairs to sea in Year VII (1800).

NOTES

1 C. Pfister, 'Le port de Dunkerque sous l'Ancien Régime français (1662-

1789); étude économique' (Doctoral thesis, Univ.of Lille, III, 1981), p 367.

2 Archives départementales d'Ille-et-Vilaine, L654, Etat de situation de la contribution patriotique dans l'arrondissement du district de Saint-Malo...de 5 juillet 1792, An V.

3 Pfister, 'Dunkerque', p 369.

4 Archives départementales d'Ille-et-Vilaine, (hereafter referred to as A.d.Rennes), 9B 669, rôles d'armement, 1790. This forms the basis of the analysis which follows.

5 A.d.Rennes, 4S 36, rôles d'équipage; corsaires, grand pêche et cabotage.

6 The full details are in M. Maistre, 'Les corsaires de la Manche sous la Révolution et Empire' (Ecole de Guerre, 1929), no pagination.

7 L. Benaerts, *Le régime consulaire en Bretagne; le département d'Ille-et-Vilaine sous le Consiulat et l'Empire (1799-1894)* (Paris 1914), pp 46-7.

8 Ibid, p47. All the names of prizes have been given in the form shown by Benaerts where this is the only source, i.e. with a French spelling.

9 The 190 ton *Favori*, 50 ton *Marie Joseph* and 130 ton *Gentille.*

10 Although captured, he was released in Pluviôse Year II (February 1793) and subsequently served successively as captain of the transport *Grande Rivière*, of a gun boat, of the unarmed warship *Salamandre* and finally of Gun Boat No 5. He died on 27 Thermidor Year VIII; A.d.Rennes 4S 2, f 25.

11 Benaerts, *Régime consulaire*, pp 46-7.

12 A.d.Rennes, 4S 1, f 38, Capitaines et maîtres, 1785-1796; Benaerts, *Régime consulaire*, p 47.

13 A.d.Rennes, 4S 346.

14 A.d.Rennes, 4S 1, f 50.

15 Benaerts, *Régime consulaire, p 47.*

16 Ibid.

17 H.C.A.32/734.

18 Benaerts, *Régime consulaire,* p 47.

19 Ibid.

20 A.d.Rennes, 15 Rl/5.

21 Benaerts, *Régime consulaire*, p 47.

22 A.d.Rennes, 15 Rl/5, H.C.A.32/725,835.

23 Ibid.

24 A.d.Rennes, 4S/1.

25 A.d.Rennes, 15 Rl/5,Archives départementales du Morbihan, Lz 1598, H.C.A. 32/725.

26 H.C.A.32/593.

27 A.d.Rennes 9B/669, 4S/346.

28 Archives départementales du Morbihan, Lz 1598.

29 H.C.A.32/552.

30 H.C.A.32/806

31 Benaerts, *Régime consulaire*, p 5.

32 Ibid, pp 54-5.
33 H.C.A.32/607.
34 A.d.Rennes, 15 Rl/5, Archives départementales du Morbihan,Lz 939.
35 H.C.A.32/743, 807.
36 H.C.A.32/806.
37 A.d.Rennes, 15 Rl/5; Benaerts, *Régime consulaire*, pp 48-9.
38 A.d.Rennes, 4S/2.
39 H.C.A.32/1797.
40 H.C.A.32/557, Archives départementales du Morbihan, Lz 939.
41 H.C.A.32/629.
42 H.C.A.32/512.
43 Benaerts, *Régime consulaire*, p 49.
44 A.d.Rennes, 15 Rj/18.
45 Benaerts, *Régime consulaire,* p 49.
46 A.d.Rennes, 15 Rj/18, 15 Rl/5, H.C.A.32/697.
47 Benaerts, *Régime consulaire,* p 49.
48 A.d.Rennes, 15 Rl/5.
49 H.C.A.32/534.
50 H.C.A.32/630.
51 H.C.A.32/630.
52 H.C.A.32/746, 534, 697, A.d.Rennes 15 Rl/5, 15 Rj/18, Segerhof Archives 420 0/1.
53 H.C.A.34/63, Archives départementales du Morbihan, Lz 939, Archives navales, Brest, 2Q/63.
54 Benaerts, *Régime consulaire,* pp 49-55.
55 H.C.A.32/868.
56 H.C.A.32/683, A.d.Rennes, 15 Rl/5, Benaerts, *Régime consulaire,* pp 57-9.
57 Ibid, pp 49-51, A.d.Rennes 15 Rl/5.
58 Benaerts, *Régime consulaire,* p 51.
59 Ibid.
60 Ibid, p 53.
61 H.C.A.32/847, A.d.Rennes, 15 Rl/5.
62 Ibid, 15 Rj/19, H.C.A.32/521.
63 A.d.Rennes 15 Rl/5, 15 Rj/18.
64 Ibid, H.C.A.32/914.
65 H.C.A.32/745, A.d.Rennes, 15 rl/5, 15 Rj/18.
66 Ibid, H.C.A.32/579.
67 Benaerts, *Régime consulaire,* p 51.
68 H.C.A.32/717.
69 Benaerts, *Régime consulaire,* p 53.
70 Ibid, A.d.Rennes 15 Rl/5, 15 Rj/20.
71 Benaerts, *Régime consulaire,* p 51, Archives départementales du Morbihan, Lz 939.
72 A.d.Rennes, 15 Rl/5.

73 Ibid.
74 H.C.A.32/579.
75 H.C.A.32/746, A.d.Rennes 15 Rl/5, 15 Rj/18.
76 H.C.A.32/535, A.d.Rennes 15 Rl/5. Some indication of the relative importance of these is givenin the records of the forced loan, to which the firm of Marion Duguen et Cie. paid 192 *livres* and Jacob Duguen paid 401 *livres*; A.d.Rennes L1392.
77 Archives départmentales de la Loire Inférieur, Marine, 20 JJ/2330.
78 H.C.A.32/645.
79 A.d.Rennes, L 1392.
80 H.C.A.32/538.
81 See for example the details of the release of French prisoners from the prison ship *Camperdown* at Chatham, Adm 103/45, passim.
82 Benaerts, *Régime consulaire*, pp 52-3, A.d.Rennes 15 Rl/5, 15 Rj/19; there is no record of the capture of this vessel in either the H.C.A. 32 or 34 series.
83 Benaerts, *Régime consulaire,* p 55, H.C.A.32/521.
84 A.d.Rennes, 15 Rl/5, 15 Rj/21, Archives navales, Brest 2Q64, Benaerts, *Régime consulaire,* pp 56-7.
85 Ibid,p 53, A.d.Rennes, 2Um/16, Tribunal de Commerce. The latter includes the deails of the sale of the *Eleonor* prize and shows that Benaert's figure of 67,933 *livres* for the sale of ship and cargo is wrong; the ship was sold for 3,500 *livres*, the cargo of butter for 67,730 *livres* and legal charges of 1,003 *livres*, making a nett total of 70,227 *livres.*
86 H.C.A.32/538.
87 A.d.Rennes, 15 Rl/5, Benaerts, *Régime consulaire*, p 55, H.C.A.32/814.
88 A.d.Rennes C 437, Intendance de Bretagne.
89 A.d.Rennes 4S/349.
90 Benaerts, *Régime consulaire,* p 55.
91 A.d.Rennes 15 Rl/5, 15 Rj/20.
92 H.C.A.32/902, Archives de la Marine, Brest 2Q/63.
93 H.C.A.32/1092, Robidou, *Les derniers corsaires malouins*, p 172.
94 Archives nationales, Marine, FF2/13, 2/38, Archives navales, Brest 2Q/77, 79, 81, Pc 6, A.d.Rennes 15Rj/21,24.
95 H.C.A.32/1174, Robidou, *Derniers corsaires malouins,* p 172, A.d.Rennes 15 Rj/20.
96 Robidou, *Derniers corsaires malouins,* pp 172-4, Archives navales, Brest 2Q66-8.
97 H.C.A.32/983, Robidou, *Derniers corsaires malouins,* pp 1733-4, Archives nationales, marine, FF2/11, Archivesnavales, Brest, 2Q/68, A.d.Rennes 15 Rj/21.
98 Ibid, 15 Rj/22, Robidou, *Derniers corsaires malouins,* p 173.
99 Ibid, pp 176-8, 181.
100 H.C.A.32/1268.

101 H.C.A.32/1109, A.d.Rennes 15 Rj/22.
102 Archives nationales, Marine FF2/13.
103 H.C.A.32/977.
104 H.C.A.32/1093.
105 A.d.Rennes 15 Rj/24, Archives navales, Brest 2Q/77, Archives navales, Charbourg 12P Corsaires et prises de l'An XI à 1814, Archives nationales, marine FF2/38.
106 Ibid FF2/13.
107 Robidou, *Derniers corsaires malouins*, p 172, Archives navales, Rochefort 13 P8/213.
108 H.C.A.32/964, Archives nationales, marine FF2/11, 13, Archives navales, Brest 2Q/66.
109 R. Surcouf, *Robert Surcouf* (new ed. Paris 1925), for details of his exploits in the Indian Ocean, see Sir Evan Cotton, *East Indiamen; the East India Company's maritime service* (1949), pp 156-8.
110 Robidou, *Derniers corsaires malouins*, p 172.
111 A.d.Rennes 15 Rj/21.
112 Archives navales, Brest 2Q/67.
113 Ibid 2Q/68, Archives départementales des Côtes du Nord 1M, 6U, Archives nationales, Marine FF2/137.
114 A.d.Rennes 15 Rj/21, Archives navales, Brest 2Q/69.
115 Robidou, *Derniers corsaires malouins,* p 175, Archives navales, Brest 2Q/71, H.C.A.32/1103.
116 Maistre, 'Corsaires de la Manche', no pagination.
117 H.C.A.32/1165, A.d.Rennes 15 Rj/22.
118 Ibid.
119 Ibid, H.C.A.32/1005.
120 H.C.A.32/961.
121 H.C.A.32/1292, Archives nationales, Marine FF2/38, Archives navales, Brest 2Q/80.
122 Ibid Pc6/109, Robidou, *Derniers corsaires malouins,* pp 179-80, A.d.Rennes 15 Rj/25. He may also have been the managing owner for the 113 ton *Ville de Paris*, Maistre, 'Corsaires de la Manche'.
123 A.d.Rennes 15 Rj/20,21, Robidou, *Derniers corsaries malouins,* pp 172-3, Archives navales, Brest 2Q/66-7, Archives nationales, Marine FF2/11.
124 H.C.A.32/1046.
125 A.d.Rennes 15 Rj/21-2, Archives navales, Brest 2Q/68-9.
126 Ibid,2Q/72,Archives nationales, Marine FF2/13, A.d.Rennes 15 Rj/22, H.C.A.32/1189.
127 Archives navales, Cherbourg 12P, Corsaires et prises de l'An XI à 1814.
128 H.C.A.32/1193.
129 Robidou, *Derniers corsaires malouins,* p 173. Ile de France was often used as a base for commerce raiding, A. Toussaint, *Histoire des corsaires* (Paris 1978), pp 81-92 for a description of privateering in the Far East.

130 A.d.Rennes 15 Rj/22.
131 Robidou, *Derniers corsaires malouins,* p 181.
132 Ibid.
133 Ibid, p 173.
134 H.C.A.32/1269.
135 H.C.A.32/983.
136 Robidou, *Derniers corsaires malouins,* p 173.
137 H.C.A.32/967.
138 Archives navales, Brest 2Q/68,70.
139 Ibids 2Q/69,71-3, A.d.Rennes 15 Rj/22; it is probably the same *Speculateur* that was fitted out by Amiel and Thomazeau late in 1809.
140 H.C.A.32/1046, A.d.Rennes 15 Rj/22.
141 Robidou, *Derniers corsaires malouins,*p 173, H.C.A.32/1041, Archives navales, Brest 2Q/69, Archives nationales, Marine FF2/11, A.d.Rennes 15 Rj/22; the prizes included the *Mercurial, United Brothers, Alfred* and a Portuguese prize.
142 H.C.A.32/1041.
143 A.d.Rennes 15 Rj/22, H.C.A.32/1046.
144 H.C.A.32/967, A.d.Rennes 15 Rj/22, Archives navales, Brest 2Q/68-9,72, Robidou, *Derniers corsaires malouins*, pp 173-5.
145 A.d.Rennes 15 Rj/22, H.C.A.32/1240.
146 H.C.A.32/962, A.d.Rennes 15 Rj/22.
147 H.C.A.32/1090, Archives navales, Brest 2Q/74. Some indication is given of his standing in commercial society by the payment by François Olive Jallobert of 701 *livres* 5 *sous* 8 *deniers* in the forced loan and anothr tenth in the extraordinary contribution to the war in Messidor Year II, A.d.Rennes L1392.
148 A.d.Rennes 15 Rj/22, Robidou, *Derniers corsaires malouins,* p 175.
149 Its full title was Tribunal de Commerce de Terre et de Mer; H. Malo, *Les derniers corsaires; Dunkerque (1715-1815)* (Paris 1925), p 187.
150 It was roughly comparable to the Seamen's Sixpences levied in England.
151 The following is based on Maistre, 'Corsaires de la Manche'.
152 See for example the Extraits des Régistres du Greffe for the *Brave sans Culotte, César,* and *Hirondelle* in the Archives Navales, Toulon 2Q/125.
153 See below pp 272-3.
154 Pfister, 'Dunkerque'.
155 Ibid, p 341.
156 Ibid, p 334.
157 H.C.A.32/876, 731.
158 Pfister, 'Dunkerque', pp 332,334.
159 Archives départementales du Pas de Calais, 'Notices généalogiques', p146.
160 H.C.A.32/825.
161 Pfister, ' Dunkerque', p 333.
162 Archives départementales du Pas de Calais, 'Notices généalogiques', p 35.

163 H.C.A.32/538.
164 Malo, *Derniers corsaires*, P 267, Archives nationales, Marine FF2/12, Archives du Ministère des Affaires Etrangères, Correspondance consulaire et commerciale, Bergen, 2, no pagination.
165 Malo, *Derniers corsaires*, p 266.
166 Ibid, p 277, Archives nationales, Marine FF2/12.
167 Ibid, p 38
168 Ibid, p 12.
169 H.C.A.32/808.
170 H.C.A.32/1014, Archives nationales, Marine FF2/12.
171 Ibid, H.C.A.32/1089, Pfister, 'Dunkerque', p 374.
172 Ibid, p 251, H.C.A.32/541, 621.
173 H.C.A.32/609, 812.
174 Pfister, 'Dunkerque', pp 374-5.
175 Ibid, p 334, Archives nationales, Marine FF2/12.
176 Archives départementales du Pas-de-Calais, 'Noitces généalogiques', p 160; for details of Stival see P. Daudrey, *Familles de la marine dunkerquoise,* (Dunkirk 1979), p 556.
177 Pfister, 'Dunkerque', p 343.
178 H.C.A.32/1075, Archives nationales, Marine FF2/12.
179 Ibid.
180 H.C.A.32/630, 511.
181 H.C.A.32/613.
182 H.C.A.32/558.
183 H.C.A.32/536, 782, Archives navales, Brest 2P6/34, Archives départementales des Côtes du Nord, 144 l/34.
184 H.C.A.32/675.
185 H.C.A.32640, 897.
186 *Brave, Chasseur, Contre Amiral Magon, Général Dorsenne, Single en Baptiste, H.C.A.32/967, 983, 979, 1290, 1192* for details of de Vries, Daudry, *Familles de la Marine,* p 316.
187 Archives nationales, Marine Ff2/12, Malo, *Derniers corsaires,* p 264.
188 P. Butel, *Les négotiants bordelais; l'Europe et les Iles au XVIIIe Siècle* (Paris 1974), p 182.
189 Ibid, pp 194-5.
190 P. Butel, 'L'armement en course à Bordeaux sous la Révolutiopn et l'Empire', *Revue historique de Bordeaux et du département de la Gironde* (1966), new, xv, p 24.
191 Ibid, p 28.
192 Ibid, p 25.
193 Ibid, p 312.
194 H.C.A.32/586, 849.
195 Butel, *Négotiants bordelais*, pp 41, 199.
196 Archives mavales, Brest 2P6/31.

197 Archives nationales, Marine Ff2/11.
198 Ibid.
199 Butel, 'L'armement en course', p 20.
200 Archives départmentales des Basses Pyrénées, 95L/37, Archives navales, Rochefort 13P8/148, 58, 13P9/1, 13, H.C.A.32/673.
210 H.C.A.34/65.
211 Butel, 'L'armement en course', p 34.
212 H.C.A.32/611.
213 H.C.A.32/556.
214 H.C.A.32/581.
215 H.C.A.32/660.
216 For a study of his career see P.Bécamps, *La Révolution à Bordeaux; J.-B.-M. Lacombe, Président de la Commission Militaire* (Bordeaux 1953).
217 H.C.A.32/516, Archives navales, Rochefort, 13P8/148, 212, Butel, 'L'armement en course', p 47.
218 H.C.A.32/892.
219 H.C.A.32/638.
220 H.C.A.32/1213.
221 Butel, 'L'armement en course', pp 49, 58.
222 H.C.A.32/1164, Archives nationales, Marine FF2/11, Archives navales, Rochefort 13P9/201.
223 Ibid, 13P8/213, Archives nationales, Marine FF2/38.
224 Butel, 'L'armement en course', p 55.
225 H.C.A.32/834, 650.
226 H.C.A.32/609.
227 H.C.A.32/611.
228 H.C.A.32/797.
229 H.C.A.32/675.
230 H.C.A.32/896.
231 For an account of the capture of the *Kent* see Sir Evan Cotton, *East Indiamen; the East India Company's maritime service* (1949), pp 156-7.
232 See above, p 101.
233 Archives nationales, Marine FF2/11.
234 Cotton, *East Indiamen*. p 165.
235 Archives navales, Rochefort 13P8/64.
236 Marcus, *Naval History of England, vol 2,* pp 379-80.
237 Archives nationales, Marine FF2/11.
238 Archives départementales de la Loire-Atlantique, Marine 20JJ/1965.
239 H.C.A.32/1157
240 Butel, *Négotiants bordelais',* p 328.
241 H.C.A.32/522.
242 Butel, *Négotiants bordelais,* p 334.
243 H.C.A.32/535.
244 Archives navales, Rochefort 13P8/60, 148, 13P9/1, 13, H.C.A.32/564.

245 Butel, *Négotiants bordelais,* p 304.
246 H.C.A.32/635.
247 Archives nationales, Marine FF2/11.
248 Ibid, H.C.A.32/1046.
249 J. Meyer, *L'armement nantais dans la dernière moitié du XVIIIe Siècle* (Paris 1969), p 77.
250 Ibid, p 78.
251 P. Jeulin, *L'évolution du trafic du port de Nantes; organisation et trafic depuis les origines* (Paris 1929), table No 6, pp 282-3, J. Everaerts, 'Les fluctuations du trafic négrier nantais (1763-1792)' *Cahiers de Tunisie,* (1963), xxxiii, p 56, J.G. Clark, *La Rochelle and the Atlantic economy during the eighteenth century* (Baltimore 1981), p 32.
252 Jeulin, *Evolution de Nantes,* table No 8, pp 284-5.
253 R. Stein, 'The French sugar industry in the eighteenth century: a quantitative study', *Business History,* (1980), xxii, p 13.
254 R. Dion, 'Orléans et l'ancienne navigation de la Loire', *Annales de Géographie,* (1938), pp 134-42.
255 Stein, 'French sugar business', p 8.
256 Everaerts, 'Trafic négrier', p 54.
257 Ibid, pp 52-3.
258 Jeulin, *Evolution de Nantes,* table No 9, pp 288-9.
259 Segerhof Archives 420 D2, p 170.
260 H.C.A.32/650, 835, 574, 593, 799; Segerhof Archives, Grand Livre 420/03, D2, p 167, Archives départementales de la Loire-Atlantique, Marine 20JJ/2329, *Georgette, Sans Culotte, Didon, Espoir, Espérance, Perkin, Intrépide, Père Duchesne, Républicain, Eugénie.*
261 H.C.A.32/807, Archives départementales de la Loire-Atlantique, Marine 20JJ/2329.
262 Everaerts, 'Trafic négrier', pp 54-5.
263 H.C.A.32/593, Segerhof Archives 420/02,03.
264 Archives départementales de la Loire-Atlantique, Marine 20JJ/2329; H.C.A.32/611.
265 Archives départementales du Morbihan, Lz939.
266 Archives départementales de la Loire-Atlantique, Marine 20JJ/2330.
267 Segerhof Archives 420 D2, p 167.
268 Archives départementales de la Loire-Atlantique, Marine 20JJ/2329, 20JJ/2330.
269 Ibid, 20JJ/2329, Archives départementales du Morbihan Lz 939, H.C.A.32/769.
270 Archives départementales de la Loire-Atlantique 20JJ/1969.
271 Butel, 'L'armement en course', p 47.
272 Archives départementales de la Loire-Atlantique, Marine 20JJ/1965, H.C.A.32/810.
273 L. Bergeron, *Banquiers, négotiants et manufacturiers parisiens du Directoire*

à l'Empire (2 vols, Paris 1975), i, 139.

274 Archives nationales, Marine FF2/11, Archives départementales de la Loire-Atlantique, Marine 20JJ/1965.

275 Bourcard bought half a share for 500 *livres*, Segerhof Archives 420/01.

276 Ibid, Archives nationales, Marine Ff2/12.

277 Ibid, FF2/11, Archives départementales d'Ille-et-Vilaine 15 Rj/22, H.C.A.32/1110, Archives départementales de la Loire-Atlantique, Marine 20JJ/1965, Archives navales, Brest 2Q/75, Segerhof Archives 420/01.

278 Archives départementales du Morbihan Lz 1598, Segerhof Archives 420/03, H.C.A.32/835, 807.

279 H.C.A.32/620.

280 Segerhof Archives 420/02, Bourcard invested 500 *livres* but does not appear to have made a profit.

281 Archives départementales de la Loire-Atlantique 20JJ/1965.

282 Archives nationales, Marine FF2/11.

283 Archives départementales de la Loire-Atlantique 20JJ/1965.

284 Ibid.

285 Ibid, H.C.A.32/746.

286 Archives départementales de la Loire-Atlantique 20JJ/1965, Archives nationales, Marine FF2/11, Archives navales, Brest 2Q/74, H.C.A.32/1130.

287 For details of Bayonne privateering in the mid-eighteenth century, Crowhurst 'Bayonne privateering, 1744-1763', pp 453-68.

288 Clark, *La Rochelle,* Chapts 1 and 2.

289 Ibid, p 29.

290 Ibid, p 33.

291 Ibid, p 73.

292 The ship was later captured, H.C.A.32/846, Archives navales, Rochefort 13P8/59, 148.

293 L. Charbonnel, *Commerce et course sous la Révolution et le Consulat à la Rochelle* (Paris 1977), p 74.

294 Ibid, pp 75-82.

295 H.C.A.32/774.

296 Charbonne, *Commerce et course,* pp 82-8.

297 Ibid, pp 90-2, Archives départementales de la Charente Maritime, Inscription Maritime 395, Archives nationales, Marine FF2/11, Archives navales, Brest 2Q/64.

298 H.C.A.32/542.

299 Archives nationales, Marine FF2/11.

300 Ibid, Archives navales, Rochefort 13P8/198, 13P9/1.

301 Ibid, 13P8/65, 13P9/1.

302 Ibid, 15P6/26, Archives nationales, Marine FF2/11.

303 The link with Bordeaux had been through the elder Chegaray, Bergeron, *Banquiers,* i, 142.

304 Archives nationales, Marine FF2/11.

305 Archives départementales des Basses-Pyrénées 95L/36, Archives navales, Rochefort 13P8/197.
306 H.C.A.32/513, Archives navales, Rochefort 13P9/1.
307 Ibid, 13P8/59, 13P9/1, 15P4/56.
308 Ibids, 13P8/59, 13P9/1, 15P4/56.
309 Ibid, 13P8/59, 60, 148, 13P9/1.
310 H.C.A.32/515.
311 Archives navales, Rochefort 13P8/60, 13P9/1.
312 Ibid, 15P6/1.
313 Ibid, 13P9/13, 198, Archives nationales, Marine FF2/11.
314 Ibid, Archives navales, Rochefort 13P8/69, 13P9/1.
315 Ibid, 13P8/213, Archives nationales, Marine FF2/38.
316 Ibid, FF2/11, Archives navales, Rochefort 13P9/2, H.C.A.32/1130.
317 Archives nationales, Marine FF2/11, Archives navales, Rochefort 13P8/72, 213, 13P9/2.
318 Ibid, 13P8/70-1, Archives nationales, Marine FF2/11.
319 Archives navales, Rochefort 13P8/71, 213, 13P9/2.
320 Archives départementales des Basses-Pyrénées, Amirauté de Bayonne, Série B Supplément, 15, 56.
321 H.C.A.32/497, Rochefort 13P8/197, 13P9/1.
322 Archives départementales des Basses-Pyrénées, Minutes notariales, Duhalde, Paul.
323 Archives navales, Rochefort 13P8/57, 59, 60, 146, 13P9/1, 15P6/13, Archives du Ministère des Affaires Etrangères, Correspondance Cunsulaire et Commerciale, St Ander, 179301810, no pagination.
324 H.C.A.32/1075, Archives navales, Rochefort 13P8/68, 13P9/1.
325 Ibid, 13P4/57, 15P6/12, Archives nationales, Marine FF2/11.
326 Ibid, H.C.A.32/1097, Archives navales, Rochefort 13P9/2.
327 Ibid, 13P8/148, 13P9/1, 16P4/57.
328 H.C.A.32/732, 828, Archives navales, Rochefort 13P8/60, 15P4/56, 15P6/1.
329 The ship was captured in 38°30'N 18°30'W in October 1797, H.C.A.32/673, Archives départementales des Basses-Pyrénées 95L/37, Archives navales, Rochefort 13P8/58, 148, 13P9/1, 13.
330 Ibid, 13P8/73, 13P9/2, 15P4/57.
331 C. Carrière, *Négotiants marseillais au XVIII siècle; contribution à l'étude des économies maritimes* (Institut Historique de Provence, no date), pp 316-7.
332 For the development of Marseilles commerce with the West Indies see ibid, pp 331-6.
333 Stein, 'French sugar business', p 9, Carrière, *Marseille*, p 331.
334 Ibid, pp 336-46.
335 C. Carrière and M. Courdurie, 'L'espace commerciale marseillais au XVIIe et XVIIIe siècles', in *Aires et structures du commerce français au XVIIIe siècle* (Paris 1973), P.Léon (ed), p 85. For Marseilles commerce,

Négotiants marseillais aux XVIIIe siècle; contribution à l'étude des économies maritimes (2 vols, Marseilles, no date), i, 34-116.

336 W.Scott, *Terror and repression in revolutionary Marseilles* (1973), pp 24-5.
337 Ibid, p 44.
338 J. S. Bromley, 'Projets et contrats d'armement en course marseillais 1705-1712', *Revue d'histoire économique et sociale* (1972), pp 76, 89, J. S. Bromley, 'The importance of Dunkirk (1688-1713) reconsidered' (paper presented at the XVI International Colloquium on Maritime History, 1976), p 246.
339 C. Taillefer, 'La guerre de course à Marseilles de 1793 à 1802', *Provincia,* (1963), p 114.
340 Ibid.
341 C. Carrière, 'Les entrées dans le port de Marseilles pendant la Révolution', *Provence historique* (1957), vii, p 200-25, Carrière, 'Négotiants marseillais', i, 113.
342 C. de Tournadre, 'Les entrées de navires dans le portt de Marseille sous le Consulat', (D.E.S., University of Aix-en-Provence, 1957), p 19.
343 Archives navales, Toulon 13P3/4.
344 Ibid, 13P3/6.
345 Scott, *Revolutionary Marseilles,* p 16.
346 Archives départementales desBouches-du-Rhône 531 U/1.
347 Archives navales, Toulon 2Q/125.
348 Ibid.
349 Archives départementales des Bouches-du-Rhône 13B/1598.
350 Archives navales, Toulon 2Q/125.
351 Archives départementales des Bouches-du-Rhône 13B/1598.
352 Archives navales, Toulon 2Q/132.
353 De Tournadre, 'Entrées de navires à Marseille', p 105.
354 Archives navales, Toulon 2Q/125.
355 Archives navales, Rochefort 13P8/158.
356 Archives départementales des Bouches-du-Rhône 13B/1598.
357 Bergeron, *Banquiers*, i, 100.
358 De Tournadre, 'Entrées de navires', p 106.
359 Archives navales, Toulon 2Q/125.
360 Ibid.
361 Ibid, 19P3/26.
362 Ibid, 19P3/22.
363 Ibid, 20P3/100.
364 Ibid, 19P3/22.
365 Ibid, 19P3/22, 2Q/81, 20P3/100.

5 Profit and loss

It is reasonable to ask two questions about privateering: was it profitable, and if so who benefited? These apparently straight forward questions are difficult to answer, partly because of lack of evidence and partly because of difficulties in interpreting the surviving evidence. The second question begs a third: what is meant by 'benefit'? As will be seen later, it is possible to argue that many people benefited from French commerce raiding, sometimes in a purely financial way and sometimes because it provided an occupation at a time of serious unemployment. Few economic historians have tried to establish whether commerce raiding was profitable, and the most forthright statement was made by Léon Vignols in an article published in 1927.[1] He stated categorically that the *guerre de course* was never profitable in any French port at any time. This reflected a view based on research on Saint Malo and with that port. Half a century later one cannot hold such a view with any certainty although, as will be seen in this chapter, it was extremely difficult to make a profit unless at least one richly laden ship was captured. On the subject of benefit the position is even less clear, though it cannot be denied that privateering provided employment to a great many people at times of economic difficulty.

Profit in term of income is only one side of the coin. The other was the ability to minimise outlay as a means of maximising profit. There were some areas in which no economies could be made: wage rates were well established and could not be reduced; there does not seem to have been any opportunity for cutting the costs of fitting out ships and the proceeds of any captures were divided according to a legal formula. But the managing owner, on whom fell the responsibility for organising the voyage, had a range of options which could affect the nature of the voyage even if he could not predict its outcome.

The managing owner could also do much to reduce the risk of a disputed capture being taken to court, for this was expensive and in an extreme case - as in Dickens' novel *Bleak House* - legal fees could consume all the available finance.

The way in which commerce raiding was organised, the opportunities for profit and occasions of loss can be shown by a number of examples of different voyages. The first is that of the *Hirondelle* of Marseille, which was fitted out in June 1812 by Michel Martin, a wholesale merchant.[2] The first man to be appointed captain, Antoine Monnier, fell ill and was replaced by his second-in-command. Paul Marcellin in July. The cruise began sucessfully: a small Spanish vessel from Port Hahon, the *Saint Antoine de Padoue* was taken jointly with another privateer, the *Dorade*, and sent to the small Catalan port of Cadaquès in June. The prize was declared just and was sold there; the decision was approved provisionally on the 10th and 12th of July before being sent to the Conseil Impèrial des Prises in Paris for final ratification. On the 26th, again in company with the *Dorade*, the *Hirondelle* seized another Spanish vessel the *Carolina* which was taken to the French port of Port-Vendre and the proceeds paid to the Treasurer of the Invalides de la Marine at Marseille. At this point no accounts had been prepared. On 2nd July the *Hirondelle* captured another Spanish vessel, the *Vierge del Torré*, but this was sunk after a few objects had been taken out. It seems that the vessel was small and not worth the trouble and expense of taking to port for legal condemnation. On the 6th two Spanish pinnances were seized, the *Saint Joseph* and *Saint Joseph alias Pepa*. They too were taken to the port of Cadaquès, provisionally declared just prize by the Sous Commissaire de las Marine and sold on 10th August. The decision was later approved by the naval administration at Toulon. More captures followed: on 9th July another Spanish ship -subsequently retaken by two Spanish privateers from Port Mahon - another Spanish prize on the 10th., which was sold on 5th August with the approval of the Conseil Impérial des Prises at Paris, and on the 12th, a Spanish vessel laden with planks bound for Minorca. The proceeds of this sale went to the Commissaire de la Marine at Palamos. Four more Spanish vessels were captured on the 14th., all bound from Port Mahon to Spain with wheat, and the sale was approved on 12th November. When yet another Spanish prize was captured the *Hirondelle* was carrying more Spanish prisoners than French members of her crew and the prisoners were transferred to the prize and released. In his account of this voyage the managing owner began by ignoring three of the Spanish prizes, because their case had not been heard by the Conseil Impériale des Prises. It was not until 28th June 1813 that the Préfet Maritime of the Sixth Arrondissement at Toulon began proceedings to establish the shares of these prizes due to the crew of the *Hirondelle* and to the Caisse des Invalides de la Marine. The Sous Commissaire de la Marine also participated in the proceedings; his responsibility was to ensure that the regulations concerning the hiring of the crew and the fitting out of the vessel had been correctly carried out. The ship's managing owner, Martin, was summoned to appear before the Tribunal de Céans on 5th July and ordered to deposit all the documents that would be required to draw up the final accounts. The captain and members of the crew were also ordered to be present to answer any questions. The result was the passing of final judgment on 9th July which took the following form:

	Fr.	C.
To the sale of the two Spanish pinnaces *Saint Joseph alias Pepa* and *Saint Joseph*	10,141	50
To the sale of the four remaining Spanish vessels, 31,877 *piecettes*	31,877	
Rebate on changing *piecettes* and *duros* into francs	1,090	
Sundry items saved from the *Vierge del Torré*	628	30
	43,736	80
Less		
Captain Marcellin's expenses by land from Cadaquès to Marseille	685	
Further expenses by Captain Marcellin	1,635	50
Millon's account for safeguarding prizes at Cadaquès	701	
Captain's commission of 2% in lieu of the prize captains' sea chest, on 43,7376 fr. 80 c.	864	72
Managing owner's commission, 1%	432	36
Negotiating commission, ½%	216	18
Sundry expenses and letters	250	
Sundry express letters	60	
Two powers of attorney	12	
Translation of documents	78	
Gift to the prize captain	288	
Sundry charges relating to the Conseil des Prises	1,000	
TOTAL	6,222fr.76c.	
Leaving a balance of	37,514fr. 4c.	

One third to crew 12,504fr.68c.
Two thirds to shareholders 25,009fr.36c.

	Profit and loss	
From the shareholders account the following to be deducted:		
Captain Monnier's expenses while the ship was being repaired	89	20
Captain Marcellin's expenses while cruising	2,733	25
Captain Monnier's expenses while ill	360	75
The account of Daubeuque et Cie. while the corsair was repaired	666	82
Managing owner's expenses in supervising sale of prizes	848	
Further expenses while the ship was repaired	649	
Expenses of Martin of Marseille while the corsair was in quarantine	633	85
Expenses of paying off the ship	233	69
Sundry legal fees	68	44
Further expenses of Captain Monnier	18	90
Managing owner's commission on above	167	66
TOTAL	6,499fr.56c.	
BALANCE	22,038fr.80c.	
Less advance payments to crew from sale of prizes	470	
Money paid to the wife of Captain Marcellin on account	300	
Payment to Captain Monnier	300	
Pilot's fee	12	
Payment to Soulary, a sailor	50	
TOTAL	1,132	
BALANCE	20,907fr.80c.	
Less the value of articles taken from a Spanish prize	628	
BALANCE	20,279fr.80c.	
To which add sums held by the captains on account	960	
Final sum due to shareholders	21,239fr.80c.	

This was not the final account of the venture, for it omitted the sum due to the Invalides de la Marine, but it had taken almost a year to reach this point. The other issue to be decided was the amount to be deducted from the sum due to the crew to compensate for advance payments already made to them. The final amount could not be calculated until the outstanding accounts on other Spanish prizes had been agreed and approved by the Conseil des Prises in Paris. Another difficulty was that this version of the expenses was challenged by a group which included the petty officers and crew and by Captain Monnier. The papers were re-examined by the Préfet Maritime and then referrred to M. Lazare Gaudin for adjudication. The dispute centred on eight points:

1. Were the accounts of sales of prizes at Cadaqùs establised by the preliminary hearings?
2. Should the expenses of selling the prizes at Cadquès be divided equally among the prizes, since the *Saint Antoine* had not been sold?
3. Should the expenses of 1,635 fr. concerning the sale of wheat, which formed the cargoes of four Spanish prizes, be reduced to 327 fr. since they should have been borne by the purchasers of the grain?
4. Should all the expenses relating to items sold be borne by the purchasers of those items?
5. Should the commission paid to the managing owner and captain by the order of 2 Prairial Year XI be allowed?
6. Should the proceeds of the sale of the corsair be included in the account of the shareholders?
7. Should the amount allocated to the shareholders include the cost of buying and fitting out the vessel, which is included in the sum deducted from the crew's third?
8. Should the sale of each ship be approved separately or only be included in the final account?

Some of these questions reveal the ignorance of the crew as many of the points they raised were covered by the order of Year XI which laid down the procedure to be followed in these cases. The Tribunal accordingly decided that preliminary judgments should always precede final accounts, that expenses of selling prize goods should be paid by the purchasers and that the general expenses should be shared equally among the prizes that were sold. The Tribunal also stated that the shareholders should be given the proceeds of the sale of the corsair and that the sum paid to the Invalides de la Marine should amount to 5c. per franc. On the final points it was stated that the cost of buying and fitting out the corsair was an expense carried by the shareholders, who were to be compensated for the payment of wages by deducting this from the one third due to the crew. The court did not state the corollary to this, that the members of the crew received their wages for their voyage and a proportion of the profits when all relevant expenditure had been met. The Tribunal also stated that preliminary accounts should be drawn up as preliminaries to the final presentation of accounts. As a result of these decisions and observations the amount allocated to shareholders rose to 28,664 fr. 46 c., though they had to bear 30,837 fr. 11 c. expenses.[3] Thus at the end the shareholders made a nett loss on the voyage, but the matter did not end there. The Tribunal had not included the *Vierge des Carmes* and the supplementary accounts presented at the end of December 1814 set the modest sum of 524 fr. 65c. against the earlier loss.

The example of the *Hirondelle* is interesting for a number of reasons, not least because it shows that a voyage in which a number of prizes were taken nevertheless resulted in a loss to the investors. This was not because the captain had made a mistake over his choice of cruising ground. He was clearly ordered to sail off the Catalan coast to intercept shipping trying to reach the Spanish mainland from Port Mahon. It is also clear from the experiences of the captain that prizes could be captured in that area, where shipping was forced to sail undefended. The loss can be attributed to two points: the captain's failure to capture more ships to compensate for the cost of fitting out and repairing the *Hirondelle*, the decision to send the Spanish prizes to a Catalan port instead one in France, which increased the legal fees and contributed to the expenses of the voyage. Put simply, the managing owner should have spent less than 24,000fr. on buying and fitting out the ship - a sum which included 5,900fr. for wages in advance - or the captain should have kept the subsequent expenses of refitting down. At the heart of the problem is the total of 33,247fr. nett for prizes against 24,100fr. for buying and fitting the ship out and another 6,737fr. for repairs during a voyage which lasted for only twenty days. The additional expenses of travelling between Marseille and the Catalan coast and extra legal fees only made matters worse.

It is easy to criticise the captains and managing owner for what appear to be errors of judgment and in some cases of inefficiency in allocating expenditure correctly. It is much harder to suggest ways in which the voyage might have been a financial success other than by capturing more Spanish ships. This is particularly important since by no means all the nett proceeds of captures went to the shareholders. The profits were divided one third to the crew, less money already advanced, and two thirds to the shareholders. Any money paid to the crew above the wages already advanced was divided according to a scale: the captain received twelve shares, his deputy ten, the first lieutenant eight, ensigns four, coastal pilots and petty officers three, volunteers one and a half and cabin boys one.[4]

This was a just reward, for it made each voyage a shared venture and provided the crew both with agreed wages and a share in any profits. Although the tonnage of the *Hirondelle* is not known, the accounts do show the costs of fitting her out - 24,100 fr., which include advance wages to the crew of 5,900 fr. This points to the *Hirondelle* as a ship of moderate size, perhaps around 30 or 40 tons.[5] If that is indeed so, the *Hirondelle* was too large for the task she was given: to catch small Spanish coasters. Captain Monnier undoubtedly did his best; he captured a great many vessels in a comparatively short time. To succeed however he had to keep his presence secret from his potential victims; once news reached Port Mahon of his cruise no more Spanish coasters would put to sea and Spanish coast trade would be paralysed until he had left the area. Monnier's problem was that before taking all his ships he had so many Spanish prisoners on board the *Hirondelle* that there was a danger that they might attempt to seize his ship. Instead of taking them to a port and releasing or imprisoning them he continued his cruise and put the prisoners on the prize after taking out the most valuable parts of the cargo. Obviously the *Hirondelle* was only a relatively small ship and the release of the prisoners marked the end of the cruise, since the prisoners announced to Spanish shipping that there was a French privateer in the area and were able to give precise details of the size, distinguishing features and size of crew. The *Hirondelle* could no longer cruise along the Spanish coast in the guise of an unarmed vessel, even though she probably flew a Spanish flag until cleared for action, to complete the disguise. Seen in this light, the captain had taken as many prizes as he could have hoped for, and he was unlucky only in that he had lost two which were retaken by Spanish ships from Port Mahon. Even if these two vessels had also reached a Catalan or French port they could only have contributed a modest amount to the proceeds of the voyage. In view of the sales of the other ships, it is not unreasonable to assume that they could have been sold for around 2,000 fr. which would not have covered the loss. Even at its most optimistic, it seems that the shareholders were lucky to have made only a small loss instead of a much larger one.

The case of the *Hirondelle* demonstrates some of the difficulties of commerce raiding in the Mediterranean. A more astute plan would have been to use a much smaller craft and reduce costs, or a larger one against potentially bigger and more profitable prey. There were a number of strategies open to a managing owner. He could instruct his captain to intercept the larger neutral ships from northern Europe and America which continued to trade spasmodically with Mediterranean ports. If successful, this policy would have paid handsome dividends. This was a risky plan, for there were comparatively few potential prizes of this type. If this plan was not adopted the captain could be ordered to attack the coasting trade, using a small vessel and covering a large area, to avoid the problems faced by the *Hirondelle*. Both of these plans could be effective.

One successful small vessel was the *Expéditif* fitted out at Barcelona with a letter of marque supplied by the French consul. This vessel cost Polan, a Nice wholesale merchant, only 13,813 fr. to fit out in 1811, but she took prizes which realised a gross total of 34,526 fr. After comparatively modest expenses of 3,071 fr. had been deducted for the voyage, the cruise gave a profit of 31,455 fr.[6] There were further expenses of disposing of the prizes but each shareholder received 7,156 fr. from 1,000 fr. share, which was an excellent return for a small vessel. The *Etoile de Bonaparte*, a larger ship fitted out by Dominique Olmetta of Saint Florent cost 29,456 fr. for its third cruise in 1807 and realised a total of 396,824 fr. from the sale of prizes. The costs incurred in approving the capture and sale were likewise modest, 6,557 fr., against the *Expéditif's* 3,071 fr. The outcome of the voyage was a balance to the shareholders of 230,721 fr. Another successful venture was that of the *Victoire* fitted out by another wholesale merchant, Louis Rollin, at Naples in the summer of 1812. This ship took prizes which realised 233,265 fr., less expenses of 14,366 fr.[7] This was divided between the crew and the shareholders in the usual way and the final profit to the shareholders was 123,985 fr., a considerable sum. It was the prospects of returns on this scale that drove men to take risks and look for the opportunities of taking 'rich prizes'.

The key to these ventures was the close cooperation between the captain and managing owner, and the *Jean Bart* of Marseille shows how efficient management by both could help to make a voyage profitable.[8] The *Jean Bart* concentrated her attack mainly on English and neutral ships. She was a comparatively large vessel of around 100 tons with a crew of 121 and an armament of 3 cannon, one of which was a 16 pounder, and 4 swivel guns.[9] The *Jean Bart* began her first cruise in May 1809; it was to last for six months and in the first three a number of prizes were taken. To reduce the costs of administration the prizes were taken to French ports: Sète, La Ciotat and Ajjacio as well as Marseille and Toulon. This prevented delays in a foreign port which would involve the payment of additional fees for translation and legal charges and it also ensured that the cargo would fetch the best prices.

After the first cruise the policy was changed. The managing owner and captain realised that it was a mistake to cruise for six months for this was very expensive - not least for the cost of provisions and wages. In spite of this the first voyage had produced an enormous profit. Prizes to a total value of 617,719 fr. had been sold and the shareholders received 243,361 fr. This profit sustained the other voyages, for none was as successful as the first. Some of the prizes had been Spanish, but these were all small coasters, two of which had been bought by the navy for 2,433 fr. and 36 fr. and most of these ships had been taken during a short trading season. The captain and managing owner realised after the first voyage that it was far better to attack the English and large neutral ships and accordingly to limit the voyages to the period when they would be in the Mediterranean and only sail off the ports which they were known to use. Accordingly the second cruise was much shorter than the first. The *Jean Bart* sailed early in 1810 and soon took an English polacca bound from Malta to Bristol which was sold in Tunis, presumably because it was risky to try and sail it back to Marseille and because the cargo would fetch a good price in Tunis, where French merchants had many commercial contracts.[10] The following month another English ship was taken and this time sent to Bizerta: the *Jean Bart* then returned to port. This marks the turning point of the venture. The third cruise began in mid-October 1810 and at first showed every prospect of success: a Maltese ship was sold at Toulon for 80,760 fr. and another three ships, English, American and Swedish, were captured within a week. In all they raised 78,727 fr., less expenses of 8,255 fr. which gave the shareholders 46,981 fr. But set against this had to be set the huge sum of 145,206 fr., most of which had been incurred in fitting out the ship. What seems to have happened is that very little had been spent on the ship for two years and it became necessary to make extensive repairs. Wear and tear in the winter months at sea had also contributed to this price, although it was during the winter that the prizes were taken. The fourth cruise began in April and it follows the familiar pattern. Prizes were sold to a total value of 82,901 fr., expenses were 18,527 fr. - high because of the cost of wear and tear on the ship - prizes were being sold in foreign ports, and the shareholders finally received 51,071 fr. This was apparently the final cruise. The shareholders made a final profit of 366,408 fr. on four voyages in about two years, but this was largely because of the very successful first cruise; the profits for subsequent voyages never approached this. As to the *Jean Bart*, it is not known what became of her after the summer of 1811. She may have been too old to use again - the extensive repairs may have been a stopgap measure or a symptom of serious weaknesses which were beginning to appear, or the owner may have decided that the prospects of trade were better; there had always been more opportunity to continue trading in the Mediterranean than in northern waters. The Marseille privateer *Dubordieu*, fitted out by Isaac Tama, wholesale merchant at Marseille in December 1809 tells a similar story.[11] The *Dubordieu* took an English brig, the *Leeds*, bound from Brazil with a cargo of brasil wood, sugar, coffee, hides and tobacco bound for Malta. Shortly afterwards, in January 1810 he captured another English ship the *Loyalty* of 450 tons, armed with 14 cannon and carrying a crew of 22. The *Leeds* was taken to an Algerian port and the ship and cargo realised a total of 251,825 fr. after expenses had been paid. The cost of fitting out the *Dubordieu* had been 69,367 fr., including 12,750 fr. for advance wages and the total administrative costs and commisions amounted to 79,426 fr., leaving the sum of 106,481 fr. to the shareholders. No details of the subsequent sale of the other large prize have survived, but it is clear that the voyage was extremely profitable. The captain and crew of the *Dubordieu* were particularly lucky; there were few ships as rich as this sailing independently and she was only sailing alone because, sailing from Brazil, she could not join a convoy.

It would be wrong to give the impression that all voyages were successful. Many were not and the voyage of the *Paysan La Tour*, fitted out by Xavier Benet, a wholesale merchant at Marseille in 1811, was a disaster. The ship made a loss of 31,362 fr. partly because only one ship was taken - the sale of which raised 5,682 fr. expenses paid - but principally because the cost of maintaining her at sea amounted to 38,147 fr.[12] Of the other voyages which made a loss, the *Marie Louise* of Marseille had a deficit of 41,250 fr. on her voyage in 1810, the *Agathe* of La Seyne lost, 16,120 fr. in 1810 and the *Ecureuil* of the same port had a deficit of 17,446 fr. in 1811.[13]

So far all the privateers that have been discussed returned safely to port and their value was added to the sum to be divided among the shareholders. In one case where the details have survived the ship was captured by the English.It might be assumed that this would automatically mean a loss. In the case of the *César* fitted out by Prosper Petit in 1810 at Marseille the ship would have had to capture more prizes to compensate for this loss. Two prizes were taken during the cruise, the first a small Spanish vessel which, together with cargo raised 12,411 fr. and an English ship the *Kitty* or *Catherine*, which was sold for 22,980 fr.[14] Expenses reduced this to 30,306 fr. The heart of the matter was the cost of fitting the ship out for her voyage: 59,484 fr. which included 8,730 fr. for the crew. Even this rather lavish sum did not prevent the captain spending another 1,913 fr. while at Algiers with his prizes and sundry small sums which together made a total of 63,933 fr. The shareholders faced a total loss of 43,729 fr.

All the above cases are relatively straightforward and were resolved to the satisfaction of all parties within a year or two of the cruise ending, as regulated by the legal code of Year XI. But there were cases where the final decision was delayed and the example of the *Brave sans Culotte* reveals other, more complicated issues that could delay and confuse the outcome. This was a ship fitted out by Antoine Boucanier and Aimé Charles Fabré et Cie. wholesale merchants at Marseille.[15] The vessel was a chebec, a fast, lateen rigged galley that was ideally suited to the task of commerce raiding for she could be rowed like a galley in calm weather when other ships were immobilised. The agreement to send her to sea was signed in March 1793 and had certain features which were different from those already described, principally because the voyage of the *Brave sans Culotte* took place before the introduction of the privateering regulations of the Year XI. One important feature was that the proceeds of the cruise should be divided equally between the shareholders and crew instead of two thirds and one third as was the common practice. The captain also received a commission of 5 per cent and the managing owners 4 per cent on the gross value of the prizes, whether sold in Marseille or elsewhere. Except for the unusual division of the profits, these terms were essentially the common practice throughout France, though in 1793 had not been codified. The 5 per cent commission for Captain Debergue was in lieu of the former privilege of the right to plunder the sea chest of the captain of the captured vessel. The agreement for the *Brave sans Culotte* also included an allowance for the prize captain of 48 fr., plus an additional 24 fr. for the safe arrival of the prize in port. The man who had first sighted the prize also received 30 fr. One of the two managing owners was also appointed quarter master and given an allowance of 2 per cent of the gross value of all prizes. In other words, the agreement reflected traditional custom.

To begin with all went well. A Spanish ship, the *Saint Christ de la Croix*, was captured laden with corn, declared fair prize and sold in June. A second prize, the Swedish *Sophie*, was also declared just prize and sold in September. The third capture however, that of the Venetian *Belle Venise*, which was sent to Messina and her cargo consigned to Joseph Condoleo, was declared invalid and cargo and the ship were ordered to be returned to the captain, who was given leave to institute a claim for damages against the owner of the corsair. There the matter rested until 22 Messidor Year VII (10 July 1799) when a judgement was made ordering the owners of the *Brave sans Culotte* to pay 10,644 fr. to Condoleo. No action was taken and on 20 Prairial Year XII (9 June 1804) the Préfet Maritime demanded all the papers of the case so that a final account could be drawn up. By this time Aimé Charles Fabré had died and the case was delayed until 26 May 1814. When the Tribunal de Commerce finally met to consider the case they were not faced by any lack of evidence but there was one unusual problem: all the accounts of the voyage were in *livres*, *sous* and *deniers* and the transactions had been in *assignats*. It was decided that the current values should be calculated according to a table of depreciation of *assignats* established by law on 5 Messidor Year V (23 June 1797) in the département; this had valued the notes at 36 per cent of their face value.

It should be emphasised that at this point, twenty years after the voyage had been made, no final decision had been reached over the share of the proceeds from the voyage to be paid either to the shareholders or the crew, though some form of payment on account must have been given after the voyage. It was finally agreed by the tribunal that the values of the two prizes and their cargoes had been 91,825 *livres* in *assignats*, reduced to 33,057 *livres* and finally to 32,633 fr. by calculating 1¼ *livres* to the *franc*. After taking all expenses into account the sum of 17,648 fr. was left to be divided equally between shareholders and crew, many of whom by that time were probably dead. Even this did not end the complicated arrangement, for the money paid in advance wages had to be deducted from the crew's half share and this had to be recalculated into *livres* at the rate of 52 *livres* 10 *sous* in *assignats* per cent and then recalculated into *francs* at the rate of 1¼ *livres* per *franc*. This variation in the exchange rate, between *livres assignats* and *livres* reflects the difference in time between the payment of the advance wages and of the other expenses. Finally, the tribunal decided that it was not necessary to deduct the 5 *centimes* per *franc* formerly paid to Invalides de la Marine or the 10 *centimes* per *franc* due under the order of 14 Brumaire Year VIII (5 November 1799). It is doubtful whether the case of the *Brave sans Culotte* was any more than administrative delay; there was no suggestion that the managing owner had tried to defraud the crew of their share and the legal judgement in 1814 was to finally establish the sum due to the Invalides de la Marine.

The case of the tiny 6 ton felucca *Aventure* of Marseille was different. This developed into a legal wrangle of the utmost complexity and was never fully settled. The final judgement, made after eighteen years, was no more than a compromise. At that stage nothing else was possible and the cost of reaching it had been enormous.[16] At the heart of the matter lay a mistaken judgement by a French consul. The *Aventure* was fitted out in Year IV (1805-6) and took a number of prizes to the port of Genoa, at that time part of the Republic of Liguria, under French control. The French consul was asked to carry out the legal formalities of declaring the vessels fair prize and disposing of them, but he made what proved to be a fatal mistake. After judging the vessels to be fair prize he handed the cargoes over to a group of Genoese merchants to be sold without first ordering an inventory to be made or caution money to be paid. Inevitably there was a wrangle later about the quantity and the quality of the cargo and the price paid. What made the dispute particularly difficult to solve was that the merchants were not a single group or company who could be sued collectively and in 1798 the managing owner, Chiappe, agreed to act as the legal representatives of the shareholders to try and recover the money, a decision which was confirmed in 1801. Chiappe was evidently a man of great determination; he continued to bring actions against the sixty four Genoese merchants and their heirs for the next thirteen years in French and Italian courts including Lyons, Aix-on-Provence (on at least ten occasions), Genoa, the Cour de Cassation at Paris (the final appeal court) and finally before the Tribunal de Commerce at Marseille - a total of around one hundred judgements. Chiappe spent more than 250,000 fr. and the shareholders another 11,800 fr. The final loss was approximately 19,000 fr. on a total income of 265,074 fr. Even this result was a compromise: the Republic of Liguria had by then disappeared and with it legal jurisdiction in the case.

Chiappe was a man of integrity and determination and his actions emphasise the special responsibility of the managing owner in financial matters relating to the ship. It would be easy to assume that the success of a voyage depended on no more than an ability, or luck, in capturing rich prizes; but the examples given above show that much more was at stake. One of the managing owner's responsibilities was to keep costs to a minimum, and the payment of wages is one factor that has been touched on. At the outbreak of war in 1793 wages had become reasonably stable although there was some variety from port to port and ship to ship. By comparison with the cost of buying and fitting out the ship the wages were a comparatively small sum - usually around half the cost of the ship - but they were probably higher than in merchant ships. The main attraction, apart from employment, was that the crew had the prospect of gaining an additional amount if the voyage was successful, as some of the voyages described above undoubtedly were. The evidence of the *rôle d'armement* of the 87 ton *Génie* of Boulogne in 1813 shows how much the officers and men were paid and how the rates varied slightly from voyage to voyage according to the experience of the men.

For the first cruise in September 1813, sixty days at sea excluding days spend in port for repair, the captain was paid 400 fr., his deputy 350 fr., and the five lieutenants 300 fr. each.[17] Next in importance were the boatswain and boatswain's mate and two ensigns who received 250 fr. each. The surgeon merited 240 fr., the writer 200 fr. and a group of petty officers: prize captain, master gunner, purser, master carpenter, master sail maker and his mate, 180 fr. The remainder of the crew, except for two landmen aged fourteen and sixteen received between 120 fr. and 160 fr. The two youths were paid 80 fr. each. This scale indicates the importance placed on each: the boatswain played an essential part in controlling the crew, the surgeon was needed to try and maintain the fighting efficiency of the ship. So too, in different ways did the other petty officers. Below them the difference in experience was matched by a slight variation in the levels of pay. These wages were not high. They were apparently fixed by custom, and differences were the result of variation in the size of the ship, the experience of the man and the port, the largest and best found ships at the major ports setting the standard for the others. In the case of the *Genie* the wages for the first voyage cost 8,840 fr. but a number of men were captured on a prize which was trying to return to port and the additional cost of hiring replacements raised the expense of the second voyage to 10,755 fr. At the end of the second cruise the *Genie* returned to Fécamp and replenished the stocks of provisions. The crew were paid a further 10,725 fr. and the ship returned to sea. While the ship was in port she remained a financial burden to her shareholders. Provisions were supplied to the crew at an agreed rate which ranged from 6 fr. a day for the captain to 2 fr. per day for the volunteer and sailor, 1 fr. 50 c. for a landman and 1 fr. 25 c. for a cabin boy.[18]

This question of the cost of wages was important in assessing profitability because it was one of the cost components over which the managing owner and captain had to exercise discretion. To some extent this specialised labour was very cheap - a new mast by comparison cost over 900 fr., which was more than twice the captain's wages for a voyage - and there was every encouragement to fill up the ship with men in the hope that many would be needed to form prize crews. But these men also had to be fed, and provisions for eighty men were a considerable expense. The cost of fitting out a ship for a privateering voyage could also be high, particularly for cannon, shot and powder, which explains why in earlier wars governments had been prepared to lend them to corsairs. At the same time, because prizes captured jointly by two or more ships were divided between their captors according to the number and calibre of their guns there was a strong financial inducement for managing owners to invest in cannon. The consequence of this was that the *Genie*, which was only 87 tons, cost 58,027 fr. to fit out for her first voyage, which included the crew's wages, and 55,967 fr. for her second. Bearing in mind that only two thirds of the value of prizes would pass to the shareholders after expenses had been met, it can readily be seen how difficult it was for a captain to hope to make a profitable voyage unless he was fortunate enough to take at least one rich prize. The residual value of the corsair contributed to the sharesholders' final profit, but this was normally a very small amount.

From the point of view of the shareholders, the duty of the managing owner was to spend as little as possible on preparing the ship for the voyage. From the managing owner's point of view the reverse was true. Whereas the shareholder only made a profit on his investment if prizes were taken and the ship returned safely to port, the managing owner received a commission on all the work he carried out. He had certain expenses to meet: the wages and bills for fitting out the corsair, but he was also the banker who received the share money and any supplement that became necessary if prices rose beyond his expected budget. The example of Benoît Bourcard, a Nantes merchant, illustrates this: Bourcard was paid commission -and thereby made a personal profit - even though the venture was a loss. Bourcard was a merchant of Swiss origin who had become established at Nantes as a commission agent before the outbreak of the Revolutionary War. For a time after 1793 he bought shares in a number of ventures and in 1798 fitted out the *Adélaide*, a 45 ton schooner-rigged ship.[19] In a generally unlucky venture his decision to attack trade proved to be his first mistake; Bourcard had seen commerce raiding rise to its peak the previous year and, more important, had seen its problems. 1798 proved an inauspicious year for commerce raiding, at least for Bourcard and his shareholders. The venture began in a conventional way; on 22 Pluviôse Year VI - 2 February 1798 - Bourcard published his prospectus and solicited support from among his friends and business associates. He claimed that the proposed voyage would cost 55,000 *livres*, which would be raised from the sale of 1,000 *livres* shares. When he published his prospectus Bourcard did not have a ship, and he waited until the money was fully subscribed before he bought the *Adélaide* and arranged for her to be fitted out at Paimboeuf under the supervision of his captain, Binard.[20] The officers and crew were paid slightly less than those of the *Genie*: the second captain was paid 300 *l.* (350 fr. on the Boulogne vessel), the first lieutentant 240 *l.* (300 fr.) and other ranks were scaled down in a similar way to the volunteers who received 120 *l.* (130-140 fr.). The total wage bill for the 49 men was 9,602 *livres*, which includes a number of men who had to be hired in Spain later after some had deserted.

The cost of hiring the crew was reasonable but the other costs were alarmingly high. One of Bourcard's problems was that most of the ship building and repairing was carried out at Paimboeuf, not at Nantes, where he could easily supervise it. Between Minden and Paimboeuf on the Loire estuary and Nantes the river was shallow and navigation hindered by sandbanks. Well before the outbreak of the Revolution the larger ships were beginning and ending their voyages at Minden and Paimboeuf and Nantes merchants were in some danger of losing control of the arrangements for shipping, though they could not leave Nantes where they sold their cargoes. It was because of this separation that cost rose; instead of 55,000 *livres*, the cost of fitting out rose to 73,000 *livres*, an amazing sum for a small vessel of 45 tons. The usual ratio of cost of wages to cost of fitting out should have been round 1:2 which would have given a final bill for fitting out of around 27,000 *l.* An examination of the accounts reveals that the ship cost 16,000 *livres* which was slightly higher than it should have been and that the major items of expenditure were the work of the carpenter, Dubigeon fils at 1,537 *l.*, ropemaker Temple jeune et Cuisinier fils 2763 *l.*, Angers sailcloth supplied by Donetteau 1,467 *l.*, sailmaker Brillant 995 *l.* and pig iron ballast from Demangeat 2,222 *l.* Two pounder cannon from Coffé cost 5,848 *l.* and cannon balls and shot another 1,330 *l.* The armourers Jugeur and

Charbonnier charged 796 *l.* and gunpowder, fine and coarse was 810 *l.* In all, the artillery cost 9,242 *l.* Provisions were another 6,431 *l.* and advance wages and sundry items came to another 12,692 *l.* On this Bourcard charged 5 per cent commission: 3,466 *l.* The cost had far exceeded the amount promised in the prospectus, which fortunately for Bourcard was not legally binding, and it is worth noting that Bourcard had promised prospective shareholders six 12 pounder cannon and swivels but the *Adélaide* carried only two cannon. Bourcard had also seriously underestimated the cost of fitting out the ship; against an estimate of 8,000 *l.* the actual cost proved to be almost 27,000 *l.* Bourcard either did not appreciate what a managing owner had to pay for in buying and fitting out a privateer or was badly cheated by his contractors. The former is the more likely; he had experience of commercial shipping but this was his first privateer. The result of the venture seriously reduced the chances of another.

The *Adélaide* sailed early in May and cruised off the coast of Spain and Portugal. At the end of the month she took three prizes, but all were recaptured before they could reach port. Then the *Adélaide* put in to Santander and remained there for a fortnight but on leaving was chased by a British warship and had to take refuge in San Vicenze, a small port a short distance away. Here the crew, frustrated by lack of progress or merely drunk, threw a church statue into the sea and the captain had to pay 100 *livres* as compensation to the church. On 28 June the ship put to sea again and took three more ships, an American and two Dutch. The French consul at Corunna condemned all three as fair prize but two were later returned to their owners on appeal. At the end of June the *Adélaide* returned to Santander because the captain was seriously ill. This effectively ended the voyage. Nothing happened for over a month while every effort was made to cure the captain and although the ship made a short cruise in November no ship was captured and the *Adélaide* returned to Santander. From there the captain returned by land to Nantes via Saint Jean-de-Luz, Bayonne and Bordeaux. Meanwhile costs continued to rise; the visits to Santander and San Vicenze, medical treatment and transport for the captain, provisions and sundry payments cost almost 4,000 *livres*. Bourcard did not appoint another captain and left his ship at Santander until it was eventually sold in 1800 for 29,886 *livres*, less 2 per cent commission of 597 *livres* to Vial, Cie. et fils the agents at Santander. Bourcard abandoned the venture when it became clear that it would be a financial loss. On the credit side the Dutch prize *Onwerwagt*, one of three to reach Vigo was declared fair prize. She had been bound from Setuval to Liebau in Courland with a cargo of salt. She was a small coaster; she was sold for 16,000 *reals* - 4,000 *livres* - and her cargo for another 4,925 *reals* (1,073 *livres*). Against this sum were expenses of almost 3,000 *reals* and each shareholder of a 1,000 *livre* share received 1 *livre* 10 *sous* 5 $^{14}/_{73}$ *deniers*. Another prize the American ship *Hornet* was commanded by a determined captain who fought to establish the ship's neutrality at every stage. After his ship had been declared fair prize at Corunna by the French concul the case was transferred to the civil court of the Loire Inférieure in December 1798.

This court found in favour of the owners and ordered the ship and cargo to be returned to the captain with compensation for wrongful seizure. Bourcard took the case to the Tribunal de Cassation, where a compromise was reached. The *Hornet* and cargo were returned to the owners, who paid all legal expenses and 113 *livres* to each shareholder.[21] It is not known what happened to the other prize, except that the income was small. The outcome of this short cruise was that the ship which had cost 73,000 *livres* to buy and fit out and which had incurred charges of approximately 4,000 *livres* subsequently realised 27,175 *livres*.[22] It is hard to avoid the conclusion that Bourcard, though an able and experienced commission merchant, was a disastrous managing owner of a privateer. He made a small personal profit but never fitted out any more corsairs. Bourcard was not unique; even experienced managing owners could run up heavy debts and make a loss. One dramatic example of a heavy loss by an experienced managing owner was that of the 69 ton *Rancunier*, fitted out by Fontaine and Lunel in 1808. In an eight month cruise from October 1808 repairs cost 93,628 *francs*. Total costs for the voyage were more than 170,000 fr. and income was only 9,197 fr.[23]

If single voyages such as those of the *Adélaide* and *Rancunier* might be disastrous, could not a merchant make a profit by judiciously investing in ventures organised by more experienced men? Bourcard evidently believed so; he bought his first shares in 1793, when he spent 8,625 *livres* on shares and part shares in nine ships.[24] Financially this was not successful; his income from commerce raiding was only 1,622 *livres*, though he did receive a payment of 1,979 *livres* in Frimaire Year IV, when the final accounts of the *Intrépide* of Nantes were ratified. This was followed by a gap when commerce raiding halted and only recovered slowly from 1796. In 1797 Bourcard purchased shares in two Brest ships, the 340 ton *Heureuse Nouvelle* and 250 ton *Difficile*, the small *Entreprise* of Le Croisic, the 120 ton *Hasard* of La Rochelle, three ships at Lorient: the *Aigle* and *Minerve* (tonnage unknown) and the 450 ton *Coureur* as well as fourteen at Nantes: the *Adonis*, *Jeune Adéle, Nantais, Figaro* and *Indien* (tonnage unknown), the 600 ton *Mars*, 140 ton *Aimable Nanette* the *Hydre* and *Chéri*, both 600 tons, the 154 ton *Marianne*, the *Julie* and *Félicité*, both 120 tons and the 80 ton *Intrépide*. He also invested in four Saint Malo ships: the 280 ton *Belliqueuse*, the 25 ton *Incroyable*, the 15 ton *Passe par tout* and the 32 ton *Buonaparte*. This was a considerable investment in full and half shares and Bourcard spread his purchases among as many different sizes and ports as he could. His shares also reveal how extensive the network of commercial contacts was, for each of the shares was bought from a friend or business colleague who was either managing owner or agent for selling shares. In these investments Bourcard followed the same policy as the insurance broker, for he spread his purchases among ships which were likely to cruise in different areas as well as different times of the year. It is hard to think of anything else that he could have done, though it is worth noting that he did not consider buying and fitting out his own ship, until commercial enthusiasm had run much of its course.

In 1798 he invested additional money, though on a more cautious basis, perhaps because he realised that commerce raiding was proving less lucrative than he had expected and partly because he was already thinking of managing his his own ship to earn commission. He bought a share in the large *Barbier de Séville* (tonnage unknown but with a crew of 208) at Bayonne, two ships at La Rochelle (tonnage unknown), the *Lynx* and *Vautour*, nine at Nantes: the 200 ton *Henri*, *Clarice* (tonnage unknown), the 600 ton *Brave*, 200 ton *Minerve*, 100 ton *Papillon*, 150 ton *Constance*, 120 ton *Levrier* and 400 ton *Indéfatigable*. He had chosen a corsair at Bayonne because there was a surge of interest there - forty five ships were fitted out compared with nineteen the previous year, and the other new investments seem to have been attempts to follow earlier purchases which had appeared promising. As interest in commerce raiding fell, so too did Bourcard's investments: in 1799 one ship at Brest, the 90 ton *Aventurier* and only one more at Nantes, the 120 ton *Heureux Hasard*. He bought his last share in 1800 in the *Nouveau Vigilant* of Nantes (tonnage unknown). During the course of the war of 1793-1801 Bourcard invested 118,616 *livres* in commerce raiding.[25]

In Germinal Year VII (April 1799) all accounts show that Bourcard was making a profit of 4,391 *livres* on investments which at that point stood at 101,515 *livres* and at the end of the Revolutionary War his profit stood at 8,652 *livres*, slightly more than seven per cent on his investment over a period of six years. His real profit was of course greater, for there was a delay in the approval of the final accounts and payments continued to be made for several years. Bourcard's experience in the Napoleonic War was less successful. He continued to invest, though at a slower rate - 54,452 fr. for the whole war, which was approximately half his investment in the Revolutionary War. His profits were down as well; at the end of May 1806 his accounts show a loss of 3,768 *francs*, which fell to a loss of 29,170 *francs* by the end of the war. He does not appear to have received any income after July 1814 and his purchases ended a year earlier. Bourcard's experiences may have been typical of many if not all investors in privateering; his policy was undoubtedly correct in buying shares in a wide range of ships at many ports and to begin with was successful. The policy failed during the Napoleonic War because of the general reduction of commerce raiding, which reflects the general malaise among merchants as the ports declined and the British navy tightened its defence of trade and the blockade of the coast. Whether merchants in the Mediterranean were any more successful is another matter; as noted already, commerce raiding followed a different pattern and the Mediterranean area may been less damaged by Napoleon's policies.

If a careful investor like Bourcard could make a profit during the Revolutionary War, would it have been better for managing owners to try and spread their risks among many ships at different ports or encourage their captains to range more widely? This is a difficult question to answer, for so much depended on the quality of the men appointed to command the ships and on their experience. The disadvantage in this respect, which was reflected in the difficulties facing French marine insurance, was that ports, and the men who sailed from them, tended to specialised. Another problem was that there was often delay in receiving payment even when the voyage had been successful and it was difficult to obtain payment. The appointment of a member of the crew to represent crew's interests helped, but the only recourse at times to appeal to the Tribunal de Commerce when payment was unduly delayed or irregularities had occurred. As to the managing owners who apparently made their fortunes from privateering, Robert Surcouf is perhaps the best known. Yet it is not clear whether this is because he also invested heavily in his own corsairs, which would have given him additional profits from successful voyages on top of his com-misssion as managing owner. At the same time it is not easy to separate his career as managing owner of a number of Saint Malo privateers from that of captain of a privateer in the Indian Ocean. That undoubtedly brought him wealth. Without doubt he was one of the most successful captains during the Revolutionary and Napoleonic wars, although his activities in the Indian Ocean stand outside the scope of this study. it is interesting to note that all of the six ships he fitted out at Saint Malo between 1804 and 1812 were small to medium size. This must have been from choice, because his reputation from commerce raiding in the previous was would have led men to flock to serve under him. The following table shows the detail of his ships:

Name	Tonnage	Built	Cruised
Confiance	70	1803	27/ 6/1804 - 19/ 4/1806
Marsouin	55	1805	Year XIV (1805-6) 13/ 2/1806
			23/ 2/1806 - 17/ 3/1807
			5/10/1807 - 30/10/1807
			15/11/1807 - 24/ 1/1808 Captured
Dorade	30	1810	1/ 5/1810 - 10/ 5/1810 Captured
Biscayenne	12	1810	26/ 3/1810 - 22/ 9/1810
Auguste	150	1810	31/ 8/1810 - 17/ 9/1810 Captured

Edouard	50	1811	19/ 3/1811 - 30/ 3/1812	
			27/ 8/1812 - 7/ 2/1813 Captured	

Source: Archives départementales d'Ille-et-Villaine, 15Rj 21,22,25 and H.C.A. 34/65, 32/961, 1005, 1103, 1292.

Surcouf's experience in the Indian Ocean had showed him that size was no advantage in commerce raiding - he had achieved his most spectacular success in a pilot boat which he had captured at the mouth of the Ganges at the Sand-heads in 1796 and it was there that he had taken the Indiaman *Triton* almost without a fight.[26] In 1800 he had made another notable prize when he took the Indiaman *Arniston* with the *Confiance* sloop off Bencoolen.[27] These set the pattern for Surcouf's activities in European waters, for the first ship that he sent to sea was also called the *Confiance*, though this was a smaller ship than the one he had used in the Indian Ocean. She was virtually new when it sailed in 1804 and this seems to have been the pattern for all his ventures. The *Confiance* was probably built for commerce raiding; the others certainly were and Surcouf probably supervised their construction. His luck held for almost a four years - his first loss was not until January 1808 - though there is no way of knowing whether all his ventures were profitable. After 1808 his luck was more mixed, though with the exception of the *Auguste* and *Dorade* his ships were at sea long enough to make a number of prizes. These ships cruised in the areas normally frequented by ships from Saint Malo and took prizes off the Lizard and far to the west of Cape Clear. Surcouf's career as a managing owner probably reflects the trend already noted for Bourcard: early success followed by decline in the second half of the Napoleonic War. Surouf's ships were victims of the tight British blockade.

Other managing owners followed a policy that was more similar to Bourcard's. The family company Basterréche Fréres, connected to a Paris bank, fitted out twenty ships during the Revolutionary and Napoleonic wars and spread their risks between a wide variety of ships, from the 10 ton *Aventure* to the *Amiral Martin* of 210 tons. All but two of the voyages were made from Bayonne and only six of the raiders were captured - a demonstration of the relative security of commerce raiding from Bayonne and Saint Jean-de-Lux. The full list of ships is given below:

Name	Tonnage	Crew	Year of cruise	Fitted out
Sans Souci	100	114	1793	Bayonne
Aventure	10	18	Year IV [1795-6]	Saint Jean-de-Luz

		7	Year VI [1797-8]	Bayonne
Hirondelle	41	25	Year IV [1795-6] Captured	Bayonne
Adour	150	147	1797 Captured	Bayonne
Impatient	150	83	Year VI [1797-8] Year VII [1798-9]	" "
Impromptu	70	18	Year VI [1797-8]	Saint Jean-de-Luz
Husard	250	142	Year VII [1798-9] Captured	Bayonne
Amiral Martin	165	100	1807 1808 1809-Captured	" " "
Eve	165	110	1807	"
Dauphin	?	65	1809	"
Navarrois	?	140	1809-Captured	"
Pérignon	?	67	1809-Captured	"
Prince de Neuffchâtel	170	98	1809	"
Amiral Martin	165	100	1810 1811-Captured	" "
Général d'Armagnac	28	22	1810 1811 1812	" " "

Beau Noir	?	14	1813	".

Source: Archives Nationales, Martine FF[5] 11,38, Archives départementales des basses Pyrenées 95 L 36,Archives de la Marine, Rochefort, 13 P[4] 56, 13 P[6] 13, 13 P[8] 57, 59, 60, 68-72, 97, 148, 212-4, 13 P[9] 1,2,13 198; H.C.A. 34/60, 62, 65, 32/513, 958, 1130.

At first sight it would appear that these ventures of Basterréche Fréres were more likely to have been likely to have been profitable; only six of the ships were captured and the brothers continued to send ships to sea up to 1813. One possible explanation is that Bayonne was able to attack British shipping at its weakest point off the Iberian Peninsula, provided the raiders cruised well off shore on the line taken by ships coming from North America and the Newfoundland fisheries. There were also neutral and Spanish ships as the revolt in Spain developed. Bourcard's efforts in the *Adélaide* had been in vain, but this was a much smaller ship than the ones fitted out by Bastérreche Fréres, which could sail further out to sea. It is also likely that the efforts by Bastérreche Fréres also represent a final attempt to arrest the decline of Bayonne at a time when Bordeaux was in serious difficulties, with economic life virtually at a standstill. Whatever the reason, Bastérreche Fréres had considerable financial resources to back them as the managing owners, were able to benefit both from commissions on the work they carried out and and as shareholders.

The above examples have been shown the prospects for commerce raiding at different ports, and although shortage of material has focussed attention on the latter part of the Napoleonic War, the Bourcard papers have revealed much of what was happening at other ports for the period in general. The examples do not give a general view, and the information given in the following table may go some way towards fulfilling that need. It should be noted however that the details are in many cases for single voyages and take no account of whether the ship was captured at the end of the venture or whether her value could be added to the shareholders' profit. If it is accepted that profits were higher in the Revolutionary War than the Napoleonic - as Bourcard has shown for the Breton and Atlantic ports - then one may assume that the profits for the first war, for which detailed information is sparse, were higher.

Voyages which made a profit

Name	Port	Year of Cruise	Profit
Railleur	Marseille	Year V [1796-7]	348,051 livres
Hirondelle	Corsica	1800	4,852 francs

			Profit and loss
Prudent	Granville	1803	105,188 francs
Eglé	Dieppe	1805	153,877 francs
Espoir	Saint Valery-sur-Somme	1805	14,800 fr. per share
Heureuse	Elba	1008	4,831 francs
Intrépide	Barcelona	1809	133,824 francs
Général Moncey	Bordeaux	1809	163,126 francs
Dubordieu	Marseille	1808-10	36,532 francs
Général Emeriau	Marseille	1809	19,573 francs
Ligurie	Marseille	1809	58,612 francs
Favori	San Lucar du Barrameda	1810-12	58,632 francs
Intrépide	Marseille	1810	125,956 francs
Intrépide	Valencia	1812	26,737 francs
Etoile de Bonaparte	Taranto	1807	360,809 francs
Maréchal Moncey	St Jean-de -Luz	1808	163,319 francs

French war on trade

Harpe	Marseille	1811-13	112,074 francs
Expéditif	Barcelona	1811	31,453 francs
Themis	Leghorn	1811	63,508 francs
Médelin	San Maria, Spain	1810-11	155,491 francs
Mélanie	San Lucar	1811	1,341 francs
Marie Louise	Dieppe	1811	544 fr. per share
Marie Louise	Naples	1811	323,830 francs
Petit Médelin	San Lucar	1811	48,304 francs
Roi de Rome	San Lucar	1811	11,557 francs
Incomparable	San Maria Spain	1811	9,939 francs
Trois Amis	San Lucar	1811-12	84,856 francs
Ucles	San Maria Spain	1812	25,937 francs
Guadalquivir	San Maria Spain	1811-12	93,051 francs
Espérance	San Maria	1811-12	9,371 francs

			Profit and loss
Espadon	Binic	1811	16,187 francs
Dominicain	San Lucar	1812	2,518 francs
Vautour	Calais	1812	3,552 fr. per share
Victoire	Naples	1812	123,985 francs
Ville de Caen	Saint Malo	1812	37,560 francs
Seraphine	Portoferrajo	1814	15,844 francs

Source: Archives de la Marine, Toulon, 2 Q 80, 125, 126, 127, 132; 1 P^7 31 19 P^3 22; Archives Nationales, Marine, FF^2 11-13, 38; Archives de la Marine, Brest 2 Q 66; Archives de la Marine, Rochefort, 15 P^6 19, 15 P^4 57; Archives départementales du Pas de Calais, 9 U 4, Archives départmentales des Bouches du Rhône, 13 B 1597.

Voyages which made a loss

Afélaide	Nantes	1798	48,825 livres
Félicité	Ajaccio	1801	15,506 frncs
Etoile	Dieppe	1805-06	17,568 francs
Ecureuil	Toulon	1811 (3rd cruise)	17,446 francs

Foudre	Marseille	1811	41,007 francs
Vengeance	St Jean-de-Luz	1809	7,387 francs
Agathe	Toulon	1810	16,120 francs
Lively	Saint Brieuc	1810	21,209 francs
Jean Bart	Toulon	1809-10	145,206 francs
Paysan La Tour	Marseille	1811	31,362 francs
Marie Louise	Marseille	1811	41,250 francs
Martinet	Marseille	1811	29,605 francs
Dorade	Marseille	1812	26,992 francs
Sans Souci	Valencia	1812 (1st cruise)	37,588 francs
Dorothée	Marseille	1812	38,204 francs

Source: Archives de la Marine, Toulon, 2 Q 26, 80, 125, 132: 19 P^3 26; Archives Nationales, Marine, FF^2 11-13, 38 Archives départementales des Côtes du Nord, 6 U.

In addition there are many examples of corsairs taking prizes with a value that was likely to exceed the fitting out costs plus any additional expenses and thereby make a profit as well as examples of ships that seem to have had unsuccessful voyages. The information given above is concerned mostly with the Mediterranean, but this merely reflects the available evidence. There is one further aspect of profitability that deserves attention: the expenses of voyages.

Expenses as a percentage of prize value

Name	Port	Value of prize(s)	Expenses as % of value	Final A/c
Athalante *1796	Marseille	83,595rls	24	1808
Auguste *1807	St Jean-de-Luz	76,536frs	0.08	1808
Adventurier *1796	Marseille	265,074frs	96	1805
Bonaparte *1797	Leghorn	262,414frs	43	1805
Brave Sans Culotte *1793	Marseille	49,842frs	64	1815
Confiance *1805	Saint Malo	17,682frs	62	1805
Curieux *1811	Boulogne	421,490frs	15	1812
Décidé *1812	Balancelles	94,842frs	0.07	1813
Droits de l'Homme *1797	Nice	489,919frs	71	1811
Heurex Marins *1797	Marseille	30,065frs	12	1806
Reciprocité *?	Dieppe	11,360frs	24	1807

* = Dates of cruise.

Source: Archives de la Marine, Toulon, 2 Q 81, 125, 19 P[3] 22; Archives de la Marine, Rochefort 13 P[4] 57; Archives Nationales, Marine FF[2] 12; Archives départementales du Pas Calais 9 U 12; Archives départmentales d'Ille-et-Vilaine 15 Rj 21; Archives départmentales des Côtes du Nord 6U.

The figures show that it was possible to keep most of the proceeds of a voyage, but only if the prize was brought back to a French port, preferably the one where the managing owner lived and from where the corsair had sailed. It should be noted however that this became increasing difficult for ships at the northern ports after 1806 because of the British naval blockade, and the Mediterranean examples probably reflects what really happened. One thing that the figures do not show is the profit to be made from ransoms as compared with the sales of prizes and their cargoes, though it is usually accepted that profits from ransoms were lower. At the same time, though the majority of profitable voyages seem to have been made in the Mediterranean, where the opportunities were greater, it was also possible to make a loss as well. There was only one certain way of making a profit: capture at least one richly laiden ship, bring it back safely to the corsair's home port, take it quickly before the Tribunal de Commerce and draw up the accounts correctly and in accordance with accepted principles. This guaranteed that no counter charges could be brought which would incur legal costs. At the same time the investor, as Bourcard has indicated, was well advised to spread his purchases as widely as possible among different ships and separate ports and rely on experienced colleagues.

As a final note, although the discussion has been concerned with profits and expenses which could easily be measured, there remains an area of profitability which was also important and yet more difficult to quantify. This is the profit to be made by a wide variety of individuals. During the course of the two wars commerce raiding contributed to the profits and in many cases the survival of ship yards, sail makers, a wide range of artisans, the seaman and through all these to the survival of all those within the community at the sea ports who supplied the daily needs of the inhabitants. The economic life of the sea ports depended so much on the success of maritime ventures, and although it is well known that Bordeaux declined when its colonial trade fell, it is not appreciated that at least in some years privateering contributed to the well being of ports. In 1797, the best year in this repect, the boom in commerce raiding provided employment for many who otherwise would have been destitute and the decline of privateering thereafter, coupled with the collapse of neutral trade, contributed to the decline of the ports. In the Napoleonic War the same is true; neutral commerce provided employment and profits in the early years but when this was halted and privateering failed to grow many people drifted away.[28] The effect was a long term one and was part of the drift from the Atlantic coast to the north east of France. Profitability in commerce raiding effected more than the success or failure of merchants.

NOTES

1 L. Vignols, 'La course maritime; ses conséquences économiques, sociales et intérnationales, *Revue d'Histoire Economique et Sociale,* (1927), xv, p 207.
2 The following is based on the account in the *liquidation générale*, Archives navals, Toulon 2Q/125, Extrait des régistres du Greffe du Tribunal de Commerce de Marseille.
3 Ibid, 28 December 1814.
4 Archives départementales du Pas-de-Calais 6U, Tribulal de Commerce, Etat des sommes restant à payer à l'équipage du corsaire le Génie et de celles qui ne pourront être remboursées par les marins n'ayant part qu'à la prise le Swallow.
5 Two other examples are the *Expéditif,* fitted out at Barcelona in 1811 for 13,813 fr. and the *Etoile de Bonaparte,* fitted out at Taranto for a third cruise for 27,456 fr. Archives navales, Toulon 2Q/125.
6 Ibid.
7 Ibid. Nothing is known of the identity of Rollin.
8 Archives navales, Toulon 2Q/125, 132.
9 Archives nationales, Marine FF2/387.
10 The polacca was a Mediterranean craft which carried a mixture of square and lateen sails on its three masts; for an illustration of this unusual rig P. Earl, *Corsairs of Malta and Barbary* (1970), p 65.
11 Archives navales, Toulon 2Q/125.
12 Ibid, 2Q/132, 125.
13 Ibid, 2Q/126, 125, 132.
14 Ibid, 2Q/125.
15 Ibid.
16 Ibid, the details are also included in R.P. Crowhurst, 'Profitability in French privateering, 1793-1815', *Business History,* (1982), xxiv, p 56.
17 Archives départementales du Pas-de-Calais 6U, Tribunal de Commerce, Boulogne.
18 Archives départementales du Pas-de-Calais 9U/9, *Entreprenant.*
19 Segerhof Archives, 420 0/5, 6, 420 Grand Livre, 1790-9, f. 249.
20 The vessel was paid for on 30 Prairial (18 June); Segerhof Archives 420 0/6, D/2, f 249; Archives départementales de la Loire-Atlantique, Marine 20JJ/2330.
21 Segerhof Archives 420 V/1.
22 Ibid, 420 D/2, ff 43, 75, 249, 267.
23 Archives départementales du Pas-de-Calais 9U/10, Archives nationales, Marine FF2/12.
24 Segerhof Archives 420 D/2, f 167.
25 Ibid, D/2, ff 167, 247, D/4, f 40.
26 Cotton, *East Indiamen*, pp 157-8.

27 Ibid, p 156.

28 See for example F.G. Pariset (ed), *Histoire de Bordeaux; Bordeaux au XVIIIe siècle* (Bordeaux 1968), p 327.

6 French prisoners of war in Britain, 1793-1815

The revolutionary and Napoleonic wars mark a turning point in the treatment of prisoners of war in Britain. In general the prisoners were treated no better and no worse than others held in Britain during the earlier eighteenth century wars but a number of fundamental changes were made in the organisation of the prison service. During the earlier wars the responsibility for feeding and clothing the prisoners had been considered the responsibility of the country from which they had come. Towards the end of the Revolutionary War the Consulate abandoned the care of its French prisoners to the British government and declared that it would only maintain the (smaller) number of British prisoners of war held in France. The exchange of prisoners of war according to an agreed scale of rank, which had helped to shorten the period of imprisonment for many men, gradually came to a temporary halt during the Revolutionary War and was used less during the Napoleonic. A third difference concerns the housing of prisoners, for the practice of keeping them in prison hulks and civil gaols developed into the practice of building special wooden prisons at Norman Cross and elsewhere and a new permanent prison on Dartmoor. These new prisons were designed according to the new attitude to prison design and reflected the influence of John Howard. Whether it was easier or more difficult to escape from these new prisons it is impossible to say, for men continued to escape, even from the newest.

From the moment that a man was made prisoner it was extremely difficult for him to escape. The first act when a ship was taken was for the captor to put a prize crew on board to sail her and put the French crew into a place of security, often the hold. The French vessel was then taken to a British port, usually a naval base, as most of the captors were naval vessels. In the first year of the war, for example, the *Malbaise* of Cherbourg and *Expervier* of St Malo, both captured by the *Swan* cutter, were taken into Plymouth.[1] At the same time the Calais vessel *Petite Victoire* and Dunkirk *Ambitieux* and *Sans Pareil* were taken to Portsmouth.[2] In both cases the lieutenants commanding the small naval vessels which made the captures were anxious to have their prizes in a port where they could supervise the proceedings against them. In the same way the *Greyhound* cutter escorted the *Custine* of Cherbourg into Weymouth after taking her off Alderney, no doubt because this was conveniently close.[3] Others were taken to different ports: the Dunkirk *Hirondelle*, taken by the *Boston* in March 1793, was escorted into the Thames, the Boulogne *Enfant de la Patrie* was seen into Shoreham after her capture off Beachy Head and the *Patriote* of Calais which fell to the *Childers* sloop off the Flemish coast, was taken into Dover.[4] Deal, conveniently close to the naval station of the Downs, was also used: the *Childers* escorted its prize the *Patriote* of Dunkirk there in April 1793 after taking her off the Flemish coast and the Dieppe privateers *Sans Peur* and *Jean Bart* were taken there too.[5] It was only when the captor was a privateer that the prize was taken into a port outside Britain: the *Lucan* privateer escorted her prize the *Ami des Planteurs* into Guernsey.[6]

The first responsibility of the captain of the British ship was to establish the nationality and port of origin of the captured vessel and the port from which she had sailed. On arrival at an English port the seamen were transferred to a prison or prison ship and the officers were sent under guard to London to be examined at Doctors Commons. The captain and one or two officers were asked a series of standard questions which were designed to discover who they were, where they had been born and where they had been living prior to the voyage. The Admiralty also wanted to know where the ship had been constructed, how old it was, where the officers and joined it, and where the vessels had been when it was captured. In each case they gave the information from the ship's log, and where the position was given in Longitude as well as Latitude, it was frequently in degrees West of Paris, not London. Whether these questions ever elicited the whole truth about the ship and its crew is debatable, for in many cases the captain and officers had no knowledge of the ship before they were appointed to command it. This information was often given on the record of the Inscription Maritime, but there was little opportunity of checking it.[7] In the course of this examination the court also examined the bundle of papers found on board at the time of capture, unless they had been thrown overboard. This included the letter of marque, the crew list (which showed the advance payment to each person) and sundry papers regarding the appointment of prize crews. At the beginning of the Revolutionary War it was relatively easy to check these papers, for there was little need to falsify the records. Later however, as it became more difficult for French merchants to transport their goods many used neutrals and false papers and during the Napoleonic War many ship owners were encouraged to assume a neutral identity until the end of war. Under these conditions it became increasingly important, and increasingly difficult, to establish the true identity of the ship and her crew, as well as the goods she was carrying. In the case of privateers, it was important to establish the nationality of the men on board her, since occasionally British sailors had joined the crew.

This was a difficult problem to solve. Most French privateers were manned by a polyglot crew drawn from throughout the French coastal ports as well as northern Europe, the Mediterranean and even North America. When the men were from French ports - in Metropolitan France or a colony - they were acting legally, and men from other states were treated in the same way, provided their country was not at war with Britain. Their place of origin was entered in the prison records but their nationality was hidden in the general lists which categorised prisoners as 'French' or 'Dutch' depending on the ship on which they had been captured. Where problems arose was when a man was found to be British. Seamen captured by the French were given the option of being imprisoned or serving in a French ship - the British followed a similar policy - and sometimes a British sailor joined a French privateer. In December 1797 William Brannon was found on board a French ship and was charged with treason.[8] The witnesses against him in the Admiralty Sessions were André le Vergue of the *Audacieux* privateer and an African, William Thomas, who had been captured on board the same ship. This provides an unusual case because both the accused and the African appear to have been British. To judge from the latter's name, William Thomas, the African was to all intents a British subject. He may originally have been a slave, but after the famous ruling by Lord Mansfield in 1772 it became more difficult to enforce slavery in Britain. In English law Thomas occupied an anomalous position, since he was not accused of treason. Brennon was less successful; his charge carried the death penalty, though it is not clear whether he was convicted.

Another difficult case was that of fifteen men who were captured as crew members on board a Dutch East India ship either late in 1795 or early the following year and who claimed they were Prussian. Their nationality was considered irrelevant; more important was their position on board an enemy ship. In February 1976 it was decided that the men should be released because when they had left India they had not known about the outbreak of war between Holland and Britain.[10] Another problem facing the Admiralty was to decide the status of men who claimed they were merely passengers on enemy ships. Jacob Nielson, who was taken on board the Dutch privateer *Einheid* and taken to Edinburgh, claimed that he was a merchant and merely a passenger on the ship.[11] His explanation was that he had been born at Apenrade in Denmark and had moved to Christainsand - the modern Oslo - ten years earlier. There he had traded in a small way as a merchant and had then decided to go to Bergen. Leaving his wife to manage the business he had sailed on the Dutch privateer as a passenger and had been captured. Whatever the outcome the story is plausible, because war had interrupted normal communications and the quickest way from Oslo to Bergen in winter was by sea. It is not known whether he was released or imprisoned. The Board was less likely to release a Swedish sailor, Carl Frederick Ribe, born at Karlskrona, who was captured on the privateer *Vautour*.[12] His account was a familiar one. He had sailed from Hamburg to Morlaix on an American ship, which was then sold. He went to Brest to seek work but was then taken ill and used his savings on medical treatment. He then signed on with the crew of a privateer because that was the only work he could get. Problems such as these were usually dealt with soon after the privateer was brought into an English port, since the neutral sailor's case was weakened if he did not present it to the Admiralty quickly.

After these preliminary cases, which arose out of the legal enquiry into the nature of the voyage, the men were committed to a prison or prison hulk. In the first year of the Revolutionary War the prisoners from privateers, merchant vessels and warships were all confined in prison on land. Some were sent to Forton, later the Fortune Hospital at Gosport, others to Plymouth, Falmouth, Bristol, Pembroke, Kinsale and Liverpool.[13] Forton was situated approximately one mile from Gosport and two miles from Portsmouth. The prison consisted of two main buildings, one of which measured 230 ft. x 25 ft. and the other, a double prison, 115 ft. x 45 ft. with an airing ground between. In the American War of Independence officers and sailors had been placed in one building and higher ranking officers in the other.[14] There was also a hospital, built in 1777 and capable of holding one eighth of the total number of prisoners, a separate house for the surgeon and the whole prison was surrounded by a high wooden fence.There were also three guard houses placed at strategic points on the perimeter. Kinsale, to which prisoners who had been captured off South West Ireland were consigned, was a receiving prison from which men were later sent to Liverpool. The other prisons were civil goals which were requisitioned by the Admiralty and in which prisoners were lodged in much the same manner as criminals and felons during peace time. Conditions were not necessarily bad by contemporary standards: to an American in the War of American Independance imprisonment had been infinitely better than life on a warship.[15] The same was undoubtedly true of the Revolutionary and Napoleonic wars. These prisons were solid, stone built and were provided with some form of heating in winter. The best housed prisoners were probably those in Liverpool, where the prison had been completed in 1786 and had been designed according to plans approved by the penal reformer John Howard.[16]

Prisoners at Liverpool were fortunate to be housed in a new prison,though conditions elsewhere were not likely to be very harsh - overcrowding was the worst problem-but that only came later. The Revolutionary War took place at a time when considerable effort was being made by many local authorities to improve conditions in English prisons and the prisoners of war benefitted from these reforms. During the two Anglo-French wars of the mid-eighteenth century French prisoners of war had been lodged with common prisoners, including felons and debtors, in an old tower in Water Street close to the dock. Five men had died there between 1744 and 1748. During the American War of Independance it had been too small to hold the American and Spanish prisoners and 1,432 were kept in an old powder magazine on Brownlow Hill, about a mile from the river. This building was demolished at the end of the war in 1783 to make room for new housing as the town expanded. The town council decided, in view of Howard's harsh comments on the old town gaol in 1780: 'a foul, dirty place', to build a new prison using plans provided by Howard and the work was carried out in 1786. The new prison blocks contained six buildings radiating from a central courtyard, in which stood some of the administrative buildings. The whole was surrounded by a 20 ft. high wall and other buildings were built against the north wall and enclosed the entrance. The area measured 127 yds. x 124 yds. This was by no means the only prison that had benefitted Howard's pioneering work and prisoners of war in some of the smaller receiving prisons were better housed in consequence.

By the end of 1793 these prisons were becoming full and the Sick and Hurt Board was foced to look for more buildings. In 1794 the prison at Yarmouth was used for the handful of men who were landed at east coast ports - 13 in the course of the year - and men who came ashore at Portsmouth were put into Portchester Castle.[17] As the number of prisoners increased during the year three old warships were turned into prison hulks, by having their interior fittings removed, bars put over the port holes and the topmasts removed.[18] The ships were the third rate *Hero* and fourth rate *Bristol* at Chatham and fifth rate *Prudente* at Plymouth. The first was a former French warship which had been captured in 1793 and had been condemned to be broken up.[19] The *Bristol* was considered to be too old for continued naval service - she had been built in 1775 - and the *Prudente* was also French and had been captured in 1779. The Admiralty was probably reluctant to use these old ships, for prisons ships had had a chequered history. The first time that prison hulks had been used in England was in 1776, when an act was passed which permitted the use of prisoners condemned to transportation to be employed on local river works and to be housed in hulks.[20] Many convicts were employed on work in the Thames, but the disadvantage of using these old ships was that they were extremely unhealthy - 150 of the 600 convicts had died in the firth 20 months and under a further act in 1779 the only criminals to be kept on the hulks were the most notorious and daring.[21]

Prison ships had also been used during the American War of Independance to house prisoners in North America. Here too they had been used to provide security when the available accomodation - the Provost Building, three sugar warehouses and some churches - were full.[22] The first ship to be used in this way was the transport *Witby*, which was moored in Wallabout Bay on Long Island. Others were subsequently pressed into service in the Hudson and East Rivers and during the course of the war a total of forty two ships were used, the majority in Wallabout Bay, where escapers had to cross open water and mud flats to reach the safety of the shore.[23] These provided the model of the use of prison ships in the Revolutionary and Napoleonic wars.

After the first two years of the war the number of prisoners entering Britain slowed and in 1795 only one new prison was used, at Dover.[24] The first men entered in December and included one who had escaped from Deal after landing in England and subsequently had been recaptured. In 1796 the naval action off Lorient in June, in which Lord Bridport captured the *Alexandre*, *Tigre* and *Formidable* brought many more Frenchmen into England besides a handful of privateer crews. These new prisoners were lodged at Deal, Dartmouth, Stapleton, Weymouth, Harwich, Edinburgh, Greenock and Guernsey, and three more ships were turned into prisons hulks: the *Captivity* and *Vigilant* at Portsmouth and *Eagle* at Chatham.[25] The *Eagle* was an old third rate built in 1774; the other two do not appear to have been in regular Admiralty use and were probably old ships renamed or prizes.[26] Deal prison took 399 in the course of the year, Dartmouth held two who were subsequently sent to the Mill Prison near Plymouth and Weymouth and Harwich also provided short term security: 18 men were held at Weymouth before being sent to Portchester Castle and another 18 at Harwich were later sent to Yarmouth.[27] Stapleton Prison, built in 1782, took its first prisoners in 1796 when Bristol Prison became crowded. North of the Border men were lodged in Edinburgh Castle and Greenock, which remained in use until the end of the Napoleonic War and appear to have to have been used for men who caused trouble or tried to escape from other prisons.[28] The other prison used for the first time in 1796 was on Guernsey and this reflects the efforts of Channel Island privateers during this year, though they usually captured small merchant ships rather than privateers.

Some prisoners were exchanged in 1796 but this did little to ease the problem of finding suitable accomodation, especially when further naval victories in 1797 provided a fresh stream of prisoners and naval patrols sent in more privateers. To cope with this influx the Admiralty planned a large new prison on a 40 acre site at Norman Cross, on the Great North Road not far from Stamford. This was an open site on top of a hill and was considered very healthy, though the clay soil made the exercise ground a quagmire after heavy rain. The buildings were of wood and were prefabricated in London. During March the first buildings were brought to the site and erected, and it is claimed that 500 carpenters were employed, working seven days a week.[29] The prison consisted of 16 large wooden buildings of which 12 were for prisoners and 4 for a hospital and buildings for the prison staff, with walls of rough sawn, ¾ in. thick deal boards that had not been primed or painted.[30] There were no windows and the walls were only a single plank thick. Problems arose because the prisoners bored holes in the walls to let in some light and air. When the buildings were inspected in September 1797 it was clear that they would not be warm enough in the winter. The boards which formed the walls had been split by the weather and by the nails and the Medical Board's agent, Sir Rupert George, recommended that the walls be given an extra thickness of $\frac{3}{4}$ in. planed and tongued boards to help keep out the wind and rain. To provide an adequate water supply 21 wells were sunk within the camp and the prison was surrounded by a high wooden stockade which in turn was enclosed by a deep ditch. Besides these the site itself was chosen to deter escape. To the North and East lay the fens and the only escape routes were either South towards London and the South Coast along the Great North Road or, avoiding the fens, to the ports on the North East coast or East Anglia. There was little point for an escaped prisoner to strike westwards. It was also an ideal place to site a large prisoner of war camp because it lay conveniently within an important agricultural area and this could provide food for the prisoners. When Norman Cross was open it became possible to close the prisons at Forton, Falmouth, Dartmouth and Harwich and transfer their prisoners to Norman Cross. The men were carried by ship to King's Lynn and thence to Yaxley by barge at a charge of 1s 1d per man before completing the journey on foot.[31] This was by no means harsh for the prisoners for the daily stages were short and food was provided at points along the route.

The growing numbers of prisoners of war also forced the Transport Office, which had been appointed in October 1795 to take responsibility for healthy prisoners, to house men in other prisons.[32] Hull and North Shields were used as receiving prisons and many more were put into four old warships: *Fame, Portland, Royal Oak* and *Prothée*, which were moored at Portsmouth.[33] These joined the other prison ships moored in line astern and separated from the shore by mud flats which made it extremely difficult to escape. The *Fame* was a very old third rate, built in 1759 and renamed the *Guildford* in 1799. The *Portland* was a fourth rate of 1770, the *Royal Oak* a third rate of 1769 and the *Prothée* a third rate retaken in 1780.[34]

The use of these old ships set the pattern for the rest of the war, for in 1798, when the Battle of the Nile and the capture of more privateers increased the number of French prisoners. Three more ships were used at Chatham: the *Camperdown*, *Vryheid* and *Sandwich* and three more, the *Crown*, *San Damaso* and *Sultan* at Portsmouth.[35] The *Camperdown*, formerly the *Jupiter*, and *Vryheid* were two Dutch ships - the latter the flagship - captured by Admiral Duncan in the Battle of Camperdown in 1797.[36] The *Sandwich* was a second rate, rebuilt in 1759, the *Crown* a third rate built in 1782 and the *Sultan* was a third rate from 1775. Nothing is known of the *San Damaso*, though it is likely to be a former Spanish ship taken as prize but never considered suitable for service in the British navy. The use of these ships in 1798 enabled the Transport Office to take prisoners from the *Prudente* at Plymouth, which was now put to other use and the last prisoners at Kinsale were transferred to Liverpool. No more prisons or prison ships were brought into service during the Revolutionary War. The *Captivity*, *Eagle* and *Bristol* were taken out of service as prison ships in 1800 and prisoners were removed from Dover and Yarmouth. The remaining men were returned to France after the signing of the Peace of Amiens.

When war broke out again prisoners were again sent to Yarmouth and three new prisons were opened at Chatham, Portsmouth and Greenlaw and the *Bienfaisant* and *Europa* were used at Plymouth.[37] Greenlaw had not been used as a prison camp before and the men were housed initially in an old mansion. This was situated at Glenorse, approximately one and a half miles from Penicuik on the Edinburgh road. At first no more than 200 prisoners were sent there.[38] As the need to house more men increased other buildings were added, most of which were of wood. When completed the camp consisted of eight blocks, each holding 660 men and measuring 100 ft. x 30 ft. and arranged in a semicircle.[39] At the centre of the semicircle lay the cook house and workshops and the whole was enclosed by a palisade or high wall. In another adjoining enclosure were the water reservoir, agent's office, canteen and a hospital, barracks for the officers and men guarding the prison and stone built houses for the principal officers. The first guards were Scottish regulars from Edinburgh, but as the demand for troops to fight on the continent grew they were withdrawn and replaced by a company of militia: a captain, 4 subalterns, 8 sergeants, 4 drummers and 155 men. Until 1811 this was the only Scottish prison south of Edinburgh.

The other prisons were situated in the large naval dockyards at Chatham and Portsmouth where they could be guarded easily and the remaining prisoners were put on the *Beinfaisant* - a former prize - and *Europa*. No further prisons were needed in 1804 but in 1805, after the battle of Trafalgar four more ships were brought into service: the *Kron Prinds* at Chatham, the *San Isadoro* and *Hector* at Plymouth and the *Gvildford* at Portsmouth.[40] All were former prizes except the third rate *Hector*, which dated from 1774.[41] From this point the naval blockade and superiority at sea continued to produce a stream of prisoners and new prisons were brought into use and others were planned. In 1806 three old third rates were pressed into service at Portsmouth: the *Suffolk*, built in 1765, the *Vengeance* of 1774 and *Veteran* of 1787.[42] As the number of prisoners continued to grow, two more ships, the former prizes *Waldemar* and *El Firme* were turned into prison hulks at Portsmouth and Plymouth and a prison was opened at Bath, which housed 298 men who had been captured off Santo Diego and Havana. It was only used for two years.[43] The *Waldemar* was taken out of service at the end of the year and the prisoners were turned over to other ships. In 1808 the old fourth rates *Panther* and *Brave* were used together with the *Sainte Antoine* at Portsmouth.[44] The *Panther* was one of the oldest ships afloat. She had been built in 1758 and was only used as a bulk until 1811; two years later she was broken up.[45] Prisoners continued to reach Britain in 1809. The fifth rate *Glory* - the former *Gloire* taken in 1806 - was turned into a hulk at Chatham and for a short time the *St Nicholas* also a former prize, was employed at Plymouth. The new Dartmoor Prison received its first inmates in May.[46] Most of the 1,936 men who were sent there had been captured at the Battle of Trafalgar and had formerly been held at the Mill Prison.

Dartmoor was the largest and the most modern of all the prisons used in these wars. The first proposal to build a prison was made in 1805, when Thomas Tyrwhitt had proposed building a settlement on Dartmoor to be called Princeton in honour of the Prince Regent. In July Tyrwhitt, who was Lord Warden of the Stanneries, suggested that the settlement should house the prisoners of war currently in six hulks at Hamoaze in Plymouth, which were costing £18,000 a year to maintain, and prisoners from the Mill Prison. The site was agreed the same month and the foundation stone laid in March 1806. The initial proposal had been for a prison covering 23 acres and costing £86,000 but this was reduced to 15 acres and £70,000. When completed, the prisoners were housed in five large, two storied rectangular buildings, each with a capacity of 1,500 men. Most were in double tiers of hammocks hung on cast iron pillars and a third tier was hung in the roof space, which was also used as a promenade in fine weather. There was also a hospital and a separate building for petty officers and the whole was enclosed by an inner wall, which had a walkway for the guards. Between this and the outer wall were situated the governor's house and other buildings.

In 1810 the old third rates *Canada* and *Irrestible* - the former *Swiftsure* - dating from 1765 and 1787 were turned into prison hulks at Chatham and they were followed in the final stage of the war by a series of stop gap measures.[47] In 1811 the *Guildford* and *Panther* were taken out of service at Portsmouth and Plymouth and men were transferred to the *Ganges* a third rate built in 1782, at Plymouth.[48] The following year prisoners were moved from the *Canada* and *Brave* at Chatham and Plymouth and the prison at Greenlaw was closed. In their place the third rate *Brunswick* of 1790 and *Kron Princessa* were used at Chatham. Prisons were opened at Perth and, temporarily, at Esk Mills.[49] Both the latter were substantial and were intended to hold 1,140 and 5,000 respectively. The prison at Perth consisted of five three story buildings, each holding 1,140 men. In addition there was another building to the South for 1,100 petty officers and there was also a building to the North for another 150 men. The whole area was enclosed by a 10 ft. wide moat and iron palisade and beyond that was a wall 12ft. 6in. high. The guards were drawn from the local militia. The first prisoners were sent from Plymouth via Dundee; later others were landed at Kirkaldy on the Forth. The prison at Esk Mills was at Valleyfield. 9 miles South of Edinburgh on the Peebles road. The prison is reported to have cost £73,000. Both prisons were relatively close to Edinburgh Castle, which was used as the administrative head quarters of the prison service in Scotland.[50] In the last two years of the war most prisoners were returned to France. In 1813 the *Kron Prinds*, *Brunswick* and *Irrestible* were taken out of service at Chatham, the *Suffolk* was closed at Portsmouth, and Perth was closed. Four ships were temporarily brought into service at Plymouth: the second rate *St George* and *Temeraire* built in 1785 and 1798, the former fifth rate prize *Oiseau* - previously the *Cléopatra* - and the third rate *Vanguard* which dated from

1787.[51] At Portsmouth the third rate *Sampson* built in 1781 and the *Sophia Frederica* were used.[52] In 1814 many of the prisons were closed and men were returned to France in the belief that the war had ended, though the Battles of Jamappes, Amiens and Waterloo provided more prisoners, most of whom were sent to Dartmoor but were returned to France within six months.[53]

These men incarcerated in the prisons and prison ships were, in the main, sailors, soldiers and petty officers. Few naval or military officers were held in the prisons; they were sent to a town on parole. To begin with, privateer officers were not considered to possess the social status of naval and military officers and were imprisoned with their men. But in 1795 the Transport Office was created and given responsibility for the healthy prisoners. As soon as this news reached the prisoners a flood of requests was received by the commissioners asking for parole. Two men, Grosjean and Lefevre, who had signed on as volunteers on a privateer and had been captured applied for parole and were granted it in February on the grounds of good conduct.[54] On 15 February Masson and Leblanc, the first and second lieutenants of the privateer *Franklin* which had been captured by the frigate *Latona* in May 1793, were also granted parole.[55] But on the 18th the Transport Office suspended all further parole for the time being. This did not last long, for Jean Cesnard, captain of the *Dame Angélique* merchant ship and his son were granted parole in June two days after being landed at Deal.[56] From August it was decreed that the officers of privateers should be imprisoned with their men but before long it was necessary to recognise that some of the privateer captains also held the rank of *lieutenant de vaisseau* and had been naval officers.[57] In the cartel agreement of October 1796 it was agreed that the captains of privateers carrying a minimum of fourteen carriage guns should be able to claim parole.[58] This made it easier to decide whether a man was entitled to parole, but occasionally difficulties arose. Dibeldotz was a privateer officer who was put on board a prize master to see it to a French port.[59] Before he could reach port the ship was recaptured and he petitioned the Admiralty for parole. In reply he was reminded of the cartel agreement and told that he had to produce evidence that the privateer on which he had sailed had carried at least fourteen carriage guns. It was extremely difficult to satisfy this demand, for the only evidence was the crew list for the Inscription Maritime or a sworn statement by another man from the same ship. Neither seems to have been forthcoming and Dibeldotz remained in prison.

The result of these restrictions on parole was that the numbers who were allowed it remained relatively small during the revolutionary War, and as late as 1801 there were 367 privateer officers on the prison ships *San Isadoro* and *Commerce de Marseille* in Plymouth because they were not entitled to parole.[60] For those who did obtain parole the arrangements were relatively straightforward. All took an oath that they would abide by the parole regulations. This limited their movements to the immediate vicinity of the town in which they were living, ordered them to walk only on roads and to stay at home at night. The men were given a copy of the parole certificate and had to pay their own expenses to go there. After arriving at their destination they were paid 1s 6d per day - an increase of 6d per day on the American War of Independence - 9d per day for servants, which was an increase of 3d. An agent was appointed for each town who received 5 per cent of the prisoners' allowances.[61] When a prisoner was moved, as when French prisoners were sent from Kinsale to Bristol, they were ordered to give up their original parole certificate and sign new ones before going to Chippenham. While in transit they were kept under strict guard since their parole was temporarily in abeyance.[62]

The first men were granted parole in 1793; 60 officers were sent to Bishop's Waltham, a small village South East of Winchester, which was chosen because it was close to Portsmouth and could be supervised easily.[63] As more men were granted parole from 1794 they were sent to one of two areas: the South West of England or the district North of Portsmouth. In 1794 18 men were sent to Bodmin and 8 to Tavistock.[64] The next two years men were sent to Bishop's Waltham, Alresford, Petersfield and Hambledon and in the South West to Callington and Ashburton. In 1797 Tiverton was added to the list.[65] The advantage of these small towns and villages was that they not only lay close to naval bases from which prisoners could be bought but they could also be supervised easily from Portsmouth and Plymouth. Bishop's Waltham, Alresford and Petersfield all lay on main roads and Hambleton was only a few miles from Bishop's Waltham. The other towns, with the exception of Bodmin, were on main roads to the north of Plymouth and even Bodmin could be reached relatively easily via Liskeard or by sea via the River Fowey and Lostwithiel. One exception was in 1796 when some French officers were landed at Liverpool and were sent to Ormskirk; Dutch officers were paroled at Wigan.[66] Others were sent from Bristol to Chippenham but plans to send officers from Pembroke to Norberth or Carmarthen in 1796 were apparently abandoned because of difficulties in employing a suitable agent.[67]

During the Napoleonic War the policy changed. Although some officers were again sent to Tavistock and Bishop's Waltham in 1803 the majority were sent further away. In October 1803 the Admiralty considered sending prisoners to North Staffordshire or North West Derbyshire and asked the Transport Office to suggest suitable sites. In their reply the Transport Office suggested Chesterfield, Ashbourne and Leek and indicated that the magistrates there had no objections to the proposal.[68] From a number of possible sites Ashbourne and Leek were chosen, together with Ashby-de-la-Zouch in Leicestershire and Peebles in southern Scotland.[69] Thame was added to the list in 1804 and Wincanton, Reading, Launceston, and Montgomery the following year.[70] As still more men were paroled in the remaining years of the war officers were sent to towns which were relatively close to the centres that had already been established. Men were sent to Brecon in 1806, to Moreton Hampstead in 1807, Wantage in 1808 and Oswestry, Okehampton and North Tawton in 1809.[71] The next year Andover and Kelso were used and in 1811 no fewer than five new centres were opened: Welshpool, Bishop's Castle, Chatham, Chesterfield and Lauder.[72] Finally in 1812 Greenlaw and Llanfyllin were added.[73] Thus by the end of the war officers were grouped in five towns in the Welsh Marches, five more in a band covering Staffordshire, North Derbyshire and Leicestershire, three towns in southern Scotland and also in Devon and eastern Cornwall and the Home Counties. The only isolated towns were Northampton and Brecon, but the first lay on one of the principal routes from London to the North and only Brecon was difficult to reach, either by the valley route from Swansea which passed over the Black Mountains or from Newport via Abergavenny.

Feeding and clothing the very large numbers of men in the prison camps and hulks posed formidable difficulties. The usual practice was for the state which had captured prisoners to feed and clothe them and be reimbursed for the costs - though not for the charge of paying prison staff and maintaining the prisons. This convention was observed until 1798 and the French agent for prisoners of war in Britain made efforts to provide sufficient money. But in 1798 the Directory claimed that it had received information that French prisoners of war in Britain were badly treated and Vochez was sent to Britain to examine the allegations.[74] He later returned to France and said that the allegations were greatly exaggerated. However, the result was that the daily rations were reduced by a quarter, because the Directory could not afford to pay the considerable sum required and the following year ceased payment altogether. In an attempt to justify this action it said that henceforth it would support the British prisoners held in france and it was the British government's responsibility to support the French in Britain.[75] For a time the British government ignored this statement, believing that the Directory would revert to the former convention. It was only when prisoners were almost starving and it was clear that no more money would come from France that the British government finally accepted responsibility for the French.

The prison diet is a matter of some controversy. In theory it was similar to that given to British seamen and adequate, though British naval history contains many examples of poor quality provisions being given to sailors. One student of naval history considers that '...the quality was often so bad that most of it was uneatable - Weevilly biscuits, sour beer and salt beef or pork so hard that it could not be masticated.'[76] The nominal allowance to sailors was 1 lb of biscuit and 1 gallon of beer per day, 2 lbs of beef twice a week (Tuesdays and Saturdays), 1 lb of pork twice a week (Sundays and Thursdays), ½ pint of peas four times a week, 1 pint of oatmeal three times a week, 2 oz of butter three times a week and 4 oz of cheese three times a week.[77] By comparison the prisoners of war nominally received a daily ration of 1½ lbs of bread (biscuit) and a quart of beer, ¾ lb of beef (except on Saturdays when 4 oz of butter and 6 oz of cheese were substituted), ½ pint of peas or 1 lb of cabbage and 1/3 oz of salt. The Admiralty tried to ensure that these provisions were of a proper standard. The contracting obligations stated in 1797 that the beer should be equal to the issue in H.M. ships and that eight bushels of the strongest amber malt and six or seven pounds of good hops at £1.18s per ton should be used to make seven barrels of beer.[78] In the same way, bread was to be as good as that issued to the Navy, the beef was to be wholesome and clear, the cheese to be good Gloucester or Wiltshire or an equivalent, the peas were to be white and good boilers and the cabbages were to be stripped of their outer leaves. As a check on quality, a sample of the bread was to be sent to the Transport Office by prison ship commanders and prison agents. The latter were ordered to ensure that poor quality provisions were rejected and the Admiralty tried to ensure that it received value for money by ordering agents to to put contracts out to tender and even prescribed the form that the public advertisement should take and the number of times that it had to be displayed.[79] Problems remained however. Although the provisions supplied to the prisons were not salted and stored for long periods like those supplied to the navy, food for the prisons was often below the required standard, and at times there was collusion between the contractors and prison officials. One agent, Allard, was ordered in 1797 not to accept bull beef because it was considered inferior.[80] Another check on quality was the supervision of deliveries to the prison. The contractor presented the food and this was examined by the agent or his representative and at least one representative elected by the prisoners. Dr Johnston, the agent at Bristol, reported to the Transport Office that each evening one of his clerks received the beef for the following day. In the morning the agent inspected and weighed it and a receipt was given. To avoid collusion between the contractor and agent, contractors were forbidden to give gratuities to the agent's clerks and no agent was allowed to supply provisions. Prisoners' representatives were ordered to report any irregularity.[81] To try and enforce these orders, Dr Johnston reported that he visited the prison twice a week and posted notices forbidding clerks to take illegal payments. Regulations concerning the bread supply were equally strict; it was to be made from white flour and properly baked. In an effort to maintain the standard of bread - one of the few that could be standardised - the Admiralty ordered that a model loaf should be baked, using wheat flour sifted through an 11s cloth.[82] Occasionally supplies reached the prisons that had not been fully cooked but more serious was the discovery in 1801 that at Bottley Mills, which made the flour for the Portsmouth bread, the contractors had been found using a mixture of good and lean grain as well as cockle and other weed seeds.[83]

It is extremely difficult to know how well or badly the diet matched that laid down in the Admiralty regulations. Dishonesty was a common problem among naval contractors and may have been in the case of the men who supplied the prisons, though the Transport Office instituted a system of visits by commissioners to try and enforce the regulations. The most serious problem, apart from the decision by the Directory not to pay for French prisoners' in Britain, was the rise in the price of food in 1800. The contractors were allowed 5d per man per day and were forced to find cheaper alternatrives. In March the Commissioners received news that the price of flour had risen considerably in the north.

The average prices in England and Wales for wheat, barley and oats per Imperial quarter rose from 69s, 36s 2d and 27s 6d in 1799 to 113s 10d, 59s 10d and 39s 4d in 1800 and 119s 6d, 68s 6d and 37s in 1801.[84] There were however considerable regional variations and the records for wheat purchase at Exeter, Eton College and Winchester College show prices reaching a peak in 1799-1800 as well as differences within each year.[85]

In an effort to ease the problem, the Admiralty repatriated 8,000 French and Dutch prisoners under the Convention of Alkmaar, which eased the problem to some extent.[86] At the end of the month the Commissioners, replying to a proposal that the prisoners should be fed on soup like the poor, said that they could not obtain sufficient pieces of cheap meat in the neighbourhood of the prisons.[87] The current allowance of $\frac{1}{2}$ lb of beef produced about a quart of soup, leaving the meat to be eaten as well, and cost about 2d. Soup made of legs, shins and other coarse pieces of meat would cost the same. In any case, because soup kitchens had been set up in London to feed the poor, the cost of even this meat had risen from 2d to $3\frac{1}{2}$d. With regard to the bread, the current supplies were being made with a coarse quality of flour. The current ration of 1 lb of bread, $\frac{1}{2}$ lb of beef and $\frac{1}{4}$ pint of peas and water was all that the prisoners received and could not be reduced. The soup supplied to the poor in London was intended to supplement the meagre amount of food that they could buy for themselves. The result, as the Portsmouth agents and the evidence of contemporary prices showed, was that the men could not be fed on the allowance provided. The bread ration was reduced from $1\frac{1}{2}$ lbs to 1 lb and the men also received $\frac{1}{2}$ lb of fresh beef, $\frac{1}{4}$ pint of peas and $^{1}/_{3}$ oz of salt. This now cost 8d per man per day instead of $4^{13}/_{32}$d allowed under the contract.[88] In an effort to save money the bread was made with foreign wheat - part of the large imports which entered England and Wales. Much of the wheat used by contractors was meagre or damaged and the bread was not always properly baked.[89]

This problem was not confined to London. At Liverpool when the food shortage became severe, the plight of the prisoners came to the notice of Dr. Currie. He considered that the government should take more vigorous action to preserve the health of the men and conducted a campaign on their behalf. Sir Joseph Banks, on behalf of the government, claimed that the diet was adequate for people who were not taking any exercise. Currie persisted in his demands and tried to raise money for the prisoners; he pointed out in Jan. 1801 that the prisoners who could afford to had bought a total of 260,470 lbs of flour, 61,144 lbs of bread and 11,291 measures of potatoes (1,016,190 lbs @ 90 lbs to one measure).[90] Banks pointed out that the poor were suffering the same hardship and the French should not be treated any better. The efforts of Currie helped to make the Transport Office and Admiralty more efficient in their organisation of supplies of food, and during the Napoleonic War, when the British government again had to feed and clothe the French prisoners there seems to have been greater care taken in administration.[91] The first step was taken in March 1800 when the Transport Office decided to send a naval lieutenant, Fisher, to Liverpool Prison to supervise the delivery of provisions and Lieutenant Ormsby to Stapleton Prison. In both cases this was because the agents did not live at the prison. This gave rise to the occasional practice of replacing agents by naval lieutenants, who were not only subject to naval discipline but who were believed to be experienced in judging the suitability of provisions for naval use. Under this administration the Transport Office also experimented more widely with variations of diet during the Napoleonic War. When the food prices again rose the Transport Office substituted turnips for cabbages and Scottish barley, onions, herrings and cod for meat. In 1812, a year of high prices, the weekly rations consisted of: Sunday 1½ lbs of bread, Monday ½ lb of beef, Tuesday ½ lb of cabbage or turnip, Wednesday 1½ lbs of bread, 1 lb of herrings, 1 lb of potatoes, Thursday 1 oz of Scottish barley, Friday 1½ lbs of bread, 1 lb of cod, 1 lb of potatoes, Saturday 1/3 oz of salt, ¼ lb of onions.[92] These provisions were not given to the men but to the cooks who prepared the meals and efforts were made to try and prevent them stealing part of the food. The coppers in which the food was cooked were kept locked when not in use and any food left over was divided as fairly as possible among the prisoners. The bones which formed part of the meat ration were given to prisoners who carved various objects which were later sold to the traders who visited the prison.

One important question remains: is the claim by Louis Garneray that the prisoners were frail and emaciated true, and if so was this the result of inadequate diet or deliberate semi-starvation by the contractors who supplied the food? Garneray had personal experience of the hulks; he spent nine years in captivity, most of them in the *Prothée* in Portchester River. It is possible that when he wrote his account of the imprisonment time had dulled his memory, but his account of being given herrings that were so salt that they were sold back to the contractor in exchange for butter or cheese rings true.[93] It is also evident that the method of cooking the food was relatively crude and destroyed much of the nutriment. The real problem appears to lie in the nature of the diet provided. The British naval seaman had a similar diet to that given to prisoners of war. But there was an important difference: whereas the sailor was given 1 gallon of beer a day, the prisoner only received 1 quart, and even this seems to have been stopped after 1799. Sir James Watt has recently shown that the naval diet in theory produced 42,500 Kcalories per week when the sailor received the full ration and it was all in good condition.[94] It has also been shown that, on average, men leading an active life require around 3,000 Kcalories per day, or 21,000 Kcalories per week.[95] This is however only a rough guide, because the metabolic rate varies considerably and within a group of apparently similar people the energy needs can vary at a standard deviation of ± 15 per cent of the mean. In practice this means that within a group of moderately active men who require on average 2,900 Kcalories per day the actual need will vary from 2,000 Kcalories to 3,800 Kcalories. As a result, the theoretical diet of the prisoner of war up to 1798: 1½ lbs of bread and 1 quart of beer per day, ¾ lb of beef (except on Saturdays, when 4 oz of butter and 6 oz of cheese were substituted) amounted to a total energy yield of 29,625 Kcalories per week, or 4,232 Kcalories per day. When the ration was reduced to 1 lb of bread a day and the supply of beer was stopped the energy intake fell to 16,875 Kcalories per week or 2,410 Kcalories per day. Prisoners needed 2,500 Kcalories per day on average. These were the maximum yields possible; when the quality of any of these items declined the energy intake fell as well. Beer and biscuit were thus crucial to the survival of prisoners of war; the first was apparently not given after 1798 and the quality of the second frequently fell below the standard considered acceptable by the Transport Office. It is small wonder that some prisoners, especially those with a high metabolic rate, became emaciated. The diet also caused other problems, for it lacked Vitamin C. The diet did include a quantity of cabbage, but the vitamin content was destroyed by boiling and there was no fresh fruit provided. For those enclosed in the hulks there was also a problem over lack of Vitamin D which was normally acquired from sunlight, for they were not allowed very long in the open air in summer because of the large number on each ship - up to 600 on an old second rate - and in winter when weather was bad men were often unable to come on deck for long periods. Supplies of butter and cheese provided Vitamin A and even the small amount of meat (weights of beef for the daily ration included bone) included Vitamin B. Of the mineral elements necessary for health the prisoners received calcium in the butter, cheese and bread, iron in the meat and iodine in the fish which was added to the diet as a substitute for meat in the Napoleonic War. Thus in theory the diet was generally adequate for the needs of the prisoners of war and could reasonably be considered generous by the standards of the age, when many people were undernourished. However, it does show that Garneray's description of life in the hulks was accurate. Many were underfed and the prisoners were able to survive largely because they were able, in most cases, to buy additional food.

Money was thus essential. Some men turned to gambling, and in extreme cases this led to severe hardship, when men gambled their clothing, food ration and all their possessions, leaving themselves naked. This problem seems to have been worst at Dartmoor Prison, where there was a large number of prisoners. Some, known in the prison as *Les Miserables*, spent much of their waking hours in this but it was the 'Romans' who disposed of all their possessions, and subsisted on scraps of food and tobacco. They always formed a social problem; at Dartmoor they were confined to the roof space of one of the buildings; at Norman Cross they were limited to the North West quadrangle to keep them away from visitors.[96] In the winter these men suffered considerable hardship, but when the prison authorities provided them with additional clothing they sold it. One of the worst cases was at Portsmouth, where gamblers sold new shirts for 6d, new handkerchiefs for 2d or 3d and a pair of shoes for about the same price. A complete suit, which had cost the government about 30s was sold for 2s 6d. As a result a prisoner had only a paliasse to cover himself and the agent reported that he thought about 500 men would die from cold and starvation as a result during the coming winter. Efforts to solve the problem by making it an offence to buy or sell clothing failed, as did the rule that prisoners who were given extra clothing would not be given any more for eighteen months.[97] The distinctive yellow clothing was finally issued in the hope that it could not be sold outside the prison and the Transport Office also offered a reward of 10 gns for information leading to the conviction of any person who bought or sold prison clothing.[98] The prevalence of gambling helps to explain why Dr. Currie noticed men at Liverpool Prison who were without clothes in 1800.[99]

Those who did not gamble tried to earn money by making a variety of items which they sold at the daily prison market, when traders brought a variety of items of food for sale to the prisoners. Many of the prisoners turned to carving, using bone from the carcases. Another popular occupation was straw plaiting, making baskets, bonnets and small ornaments, except in some areas, such as Bedfordshire and Northamptonshire, where bonnet making was an important industry and the prisoners were forbidden to compete.[100] Other men were shoe makers and the educated offered classes in mathematics and science. Louis Garneray discovered a talent for sketching and painting. All were probably underpaid for their work. There were also men who turned to forgery, especially of banknotes. This posed the authorities some difficulty for until 1810 forgery was not considered a 'crime against the laws of nations', though it was a capital offence in Britain. Those caught before 1810 were confined to the hulks as punishment, as were murderers, who were subject to the authority of the Admiralty and not to the jurisdiction of the municipal tribunals. However, even 1810 prisoners caught committing these crimes were liable to be executed. Other, legitimate, occupations were to act as gardener, barber, carpenter or washerman, who were paid 3d per day, medical orderly, who received 6d per day, sweeper, who was paid 4½d, as were cooks; the last two were employed at the ratio of 1:100 and 1:400 respectively. At Norman Cross men were also employed making rope from junk pieces and buckets from old casks, for which they were paid 3d per day.[101] The extra food earned in this way, or bought with money sent from home, helped to keep the majority in a reasonable state of health. For those who fell ill every effort was made to provide adequate medical services. Each prison had its own hospital at which a surgeon and dispensers were expected to be present every day. The principal surgeon at Bristol was dismissed because he was unable to attend every day because of his extensive practice.[102] Sick prisoners also received a special ration. Those on a 'low diet' received tea and sugar, or 1½ pints of milk pottage, rice milk or panada - a mixture of flour and water - together with 8 oz of bread, 2 oz of butter or 1 pint of milk or broth at the surgeon's discretion.[103] The half diet consisted of: breakfast, tea and sugar and 1½ pints of milk pottage; dinner, 8 oz of mutton, 1 pint of broth, 8oz of light bread pudding, 8 oz of greens, 16 oz of bread, 3 pints of small beer. The full diet was the same for breakfast as the half diet; dinner consisted of 16 oz of beef or mutton, 1 pint of broth, 16 oz of greens, 16 oz of bread and 2 quarts of small beer. Supper for those on half diet was the broth left over from dinner or milk pottage, $\frac{3}{4}$ oz of oatmeal or Scottish barley. $\frac{1}{2}$ pint of milk was allowed for $1\frac{1}{2}$ pints of pottage and $\frac{1}{2}$ oz of oatmeal to 1 pint of broth with a sufficient quantity of onions, leaks or pot herbs. Convalescent prisoners were given 1 pint of warm gruel made from 1 oz of Scottish barley, $\frac{1}{2}$ oz of rice, $\frac{1}{8}$ oz of sugar and 5 grains of pimento each morning at 7 a.m. in addition to normal prison rations. This was an expensive diet and in 1801 the Commissioners had contracted to pay 5d per day for each patient. The contractor who provided the food paid for the hire of the washermen, nurses, cooks, bakers and barbers and was paid 1s 3d per man per day. Earlier in the war prisoners who had 'the itch' had been sent to the prison hospital, but this merely transferred the lice to other patients and it was remedied by burning bedding and clothing instead from 1801. In any case, healthy prisoners were kept out of hospital, partly because accommodation was limited and partly because men tried to escape by tunnelling from the hospitals, which were often close to the prison walls.[104] Efforts were also made to keep prisoners on the hulks healthy by cutting scuttles in the deck and fitting wind pumps to circulate air, but these were seldom very successful.

This close confinement in ill-ventilated hulks and with inadequate diet did not however lead to unusually high rates of mortality. This is hardly surprising, for the majority of the men were in the prime of their life and separated from illness. Out of prison population at Dartmoor of approximately 6,000 at the end of 1809, 150 men died in the cource of the year.[105] The next year, from a slightly larger prison population 424 died and thereafter, although the total numbers at the prison rose to around 7,000 the number of deaths remained low: 85 in 1811, 143 in 1812 and 239 in 1813. The picture at Norman Cross and Chatham is similar.[106] In each case the picture is slightly distorted because a man who was considered to be very ill was often sent back to France. One of the most common diseases was smallpox, but Dartmoor was the only prison to have a serious epidemic: in February - June 1815 70 of the 150 American prisoners who died were killed by it.[107] The normal rate was only one or two a year; a more serious disease was phthisis, or pulmonary tuberculosis. But although smallpox killed comparatively few men directly, it was a major contributor to many of the other deaths. The 'bloody flux' was possibly a form of fulminating smallpox and it is possible that diarrhoea was also a form of the disease.[108] Moreover, because it was an extremely common disease both in England and in France many of the prisoners had caught it in some form as children and recovered, though in a form which left no distinguishing pock marks on the face.[109] The consequence of this early infection was that men lost their early resistance to other diseases, especially bronchitis and broncho-pneumonia and smallpox could also release latent tuberculosis bacillus. This accounts for at least some of the deaths which were attributed to phthisis and for the other, less frequent direct causes of death. That comparatively few men died in prison of smallpox can be attributed to the extensive vaccination and inoculation that had been practiced in England and which helped to contribute to the dramatic reduction of the disease in the last third of the eighteenth century. The outbreaks of smallpox which did occur are more likely to have been the result of imprisoning men who were already carriers of the disease or infected by it - it was more common in France - and who were rapidly removed into the prison hospital.

Another common form of death was 'atrophy' - a wasting of the body. This can be explained by the inadequacy of the diet, especially for those with a high rate of metabolism. One of the surprising causes of death is that of the nine men who died in 1804 at Chatham of scurvy, a disease that was easy to remedy and familiar to naval officers in the prison.[110] It is possible that the men were seriously ill when captured, though the physical symptoms of pallid skin and bleeding gums were familiar. Of the other causes of death, 27 died of typhus at Chatham in 1809 and 26 of pneumonia at Dartmoor in 1814. Others died of dysentry, diarrhoea, enteritis, anasarca, venerial disease, apoplexy, scarlet fever and lockjaw. John Francis, an American prisoner at Portsmouth aged 38 died in his hammock in 1815 'by the visitation of God' and Louis le Mangin, former lieutenant of the privateer *Courier de la Manche*, died at Dartmoor in 1812 of posion.[111] Long term imprisonment also took its toll of others: Nicolas Lucas, former cook of the *Revanche* privateer, died in 1811 aged 67 of 'old age and confusion'.[112] Others went mad: 4 at Chatham in 1808, besides 3 who died of a 'hectic fever', and a 51 year old seaman, Louis Machemin, who hanged himself at Chatham in 1813.[113] Bertrans Armandin, a 32 year old seaman, died of rabies at Chatham in April 1808. Of those who survived, the former slaves and mulattoes captured in the West Indies suffered most. They reached England in the late summer of 1796 and were lodged in Forton Prison at Portsmouth. Some lost part of their clothing to other (white) prisoners and during the following winter suffered very severely from the cold. The prison officers tried to alleviate this by providing extra coal but a number became badly frostbitten and later had to have toes, fingers and even in some cases feet amputated.[114]

All prisoners, whether healthy or sick, anxiously waited for the day when they could return to their native country. All were offered their freedom in return for service in the British forces but few accepted. Of the others the most fortunate were those noted already who could prove that they had not knowingly taken arms against Britain and who returned home. Those who became seriously ill were sometimes repatriated, since they would not be able to fight again, and a number of non-combatants and boys were returned, though with the passing of time and a hardening of attitudes the number declined. Of the rest, parole was given to officers and certain others who had been non-combatants: pilots, prize masters, surgeons and their mates, masters of merchant ships and linguists.[115] At the beginning of the war it was accepted that men should be returned with a comparatively short time, though the first men were not released until 1796. However it soon became clear that there were many more

Frenchmen being exchanged than British and by February 1796 the balance was in favour of France by more the 5,000.[116] Exchange of prisoners stopped until 1800. In theory every prisoner had an opportunity of being sent home, because the lists were drawn up in the order in which men had been captured. In practice the crews of privateers were afraid that naval seamen and soldiers were being placed above them on the list. In 1799 the Commissioners for the Transport Office reminded Captain Rowe, the superintendent of prison ships at Portsmouth, that the crews of small privateers had an equal opportunity of being exchanged.[117] The final decision lay with the French agent. Occasionally men did not want to return. Chiron, a prisoner on parole at Bishop's Waltham, deferred his return to France when offered it in 1796 because he was afraid of being denounced for his royalist views by Republican prisoners.[118] Others, who were not French though they had been captured on board French ships, chose to go elsewhere. Matthew Ollibrault, who had been captured on the *Mercure*, refused to go to France and was allowed to go to Hamburg instead.[119]

Many prisoners also tried to escape; some were successful. A number escaped by tunnelling under the outer wall; others bribed guards, who sometimes took the money and then betrayed them. A number escaped by dressing as a visitor or officer, and some even escaped dressed in women's clothes. The chances of reaching France were at least moderately good. The entry books contain a number of references to men who had 'run' i.e. escaped and were not recaptured. The detailed entry books for the Napoleonic War give a number of examples of the successful escapers. In 1810 Pierre Boue, third captain of the *Atalante* privateer, escaped from Chesterfield. He was 34 years old, 5 ft 8½ inches tall with an oval face and dark complexion and spoke English very well.[120] Pierre Petit, alias François Petit, a sailor from *Vengeur* privateer, escaped from Portchester Castle in 1811, probably with a party of workmen.[121] Louis François Vanhille, the commissary of the *Pandour* warship, aged 32, 5ft 3 inches tall escaped from Dartmoor Prison in August 1812; he not only spoke very good English but also had the appearance of an Englishman - he had presumably been able to buy English clothes from one of the traders at the prison.[122] John Black, master of the *Neptune* merchant ship, escaped from Peebles in April 1811 and it was believed that he went to Aberdeen or one of the northern ports to try and get on board a Norwegian boat.[123] Others showed a remarkable persistance: Antonio Altazin, caulker of the *Etoile* privateer escaped three times, though he was 54. The man who stood the best chance of reaching France was probably Louis Pequidaire (or Puandaire), captain of the *Espoir*, privateer, aged 36.[124] He was not only smartly dressed when he escaped - he wore a superfine blue coat - but spoke pretty good English and had a considerable quantity of gold and silver. This was important, for he could afford to stay in respectable inns and to buy a passage to France with smugglers, though they sometimes took the money and murdered the men. There was also a reward for all recaptured prisoners.

Those who were recaptured faced a period of imprisonment in the Black Hole. This was the small cell within each prison in which men were incarcerated for any offence against prison discipline. Sometimes it was below ground level and there were occasions when it was crowded with too many prisoners. Under these conditions it became a severe punishment, for there was little air: the men were fed only once a day and there was no form of sanitation. Prisoners who had been recaptured were put here as a matter of course, and the men who shared their accommodation were put on half scale provisions until the cost of the recapture had been recovered.[125] But no prisoner could be handcuffed unless he was considered particularly unruly or dangerous and the agent at Bristol was ordered to do no more than put extra guards round the black hole there when men causing a commotion.[126] This relatively generous treatment, by the standards of the age, suggests that the Commissioners recognised that the prisoners felt a deep sense of frustration and despair and severe punishment would only deepen this.

The Revolutionary and Napoleonic wars placed considerable burdens on the administration of prisoners of war. There were more men in prison for a longer time than in previous wars, because the system of exchanges broke down, as did arrangements for feeding and clothing them. This placed particular strain on the men, for whom lengthy imprisonment was not only a severe personal trial but weakened their health. Life was worst on the hulks because of the lack of adequate ventilation, but much depended ultimately on the agent responsible for the prison. A brutal and unfeeling man could make life intolerable, a more tolerant man could do much to keep the men active and enable them to buy extra food and make the existence more tolerable. For some it was an opportunity to learn a skill, or receive a basic education in mathematics or science, but for the majority it was a period of severe deprivation. The officers on parole suffered far less; they had relative freedom, sufficient money and some of them even married local girls. But at best even this life was only tolerable and the worst aspect for all men was to be separated from their family and friends for years at a time.

NOTES

1 H.C.A.32/734, 513.
2 H.C.A.32/800, 847.
3 H.C.A.32/541.
4 H.C.A.32/664, 593, 799.
5 H.C.A.32/799, 832, 686.
6 H.C.A.32/497.
7 The information shown in the privateers' papers in inaccurate; there was no advantage in falsifying the records.
8 Adm 98/213.

9 Adm 98/109, Medical Board to Admiralty, 5 Aug 1799; there is a similar case in Adm 98/107, Medical Board to Admiralty, 1 July 1797. Details of the Somerset case, in which Chief Justice Mansfield judged, on 22 June 1772, that a former Virginia slave was to be freed are to be found in C. Duncan Rice, *The rise and fall of Black Slavery* (1975), pp 214-5 and R. Anstey, *The Atlantic slave trade and British abolition 1760-1810* (1975), pp 244-5.
10 Adm 99/92, Minutes of the Transport Office, ff 68, 92, 6 and 16 Feb 1796.
11 Adm 98/107, Transport Office to Admiralty 29 Dec 1797.
12 Ibid, 26 Dec 1797.
13 Adm 103/41, 411, 128, 213, 221, 275, 133, 103.
14 J.K. Alexander, 'Forton Prison during the American Revolution: a case study of British prisoner of war policy and the American prisoner response to that policy', *Essex Institute Historical Collections* (1967), ciii, pp 369-70. A plan of the prison is in T62/94.
15 O. Anderson, 'The treatment of prisoners of war in Britain during the American War of Independence', *Bulletin of the Institute of Historical Research* (1955), xxviii, p 76.
16 For a description of the treatment of French prisoners at Liverpool see A. de Curzon, *Dr. James Currie and the French prisoners of war in Liverpool 1800-1801* (Liverpool 1926), passim; Adm 105/44, Sir Rupert George to the Transport Office. 20 Sept 1797; for a plan of the prison see R. Evans, *The fabrication of virtue; English prison architecture 1750-1840* (1982), p 129.
17 The entry books are Adm 103/103, 318.
18 The entry books are Adm/186, 109, 381.
19 Manning and Walker, *British warship names*, pp 230, 356, 116.
20 Evans, *Fabrication of virtue*, p 119; the act was 16 Geo III, c 56. Details of the work on the Thames is given in W. Branch Johnson, *The English prison hulks* (rev. ed. 1970), pp 4-6.
21 19 Geo III, c 74.
22 L.G. Bowman, *Captive Americans; prisoners during the American Revolution* (Athens, Ohio 1976), pp 12-3. Other Americans were held at the Mill Prison, J.K. Alexander, 'American privatersmen in the Mill Prison during 1777-1782: an evaluation' *Essex Institute Historical Collections* (1966), cii, pp 318-40.
23 Bowman, '*Captive Americans*, pp 41-3.
24 Adm 103/103.
25 The plan of Stapleton Prison is in T62/94.
26 Manning and Walker, *British warship names,* p 199.
27 Adm 103/103. One agent, Dr. Johnston, argued that it was cheaper to keep healthy prisoners in prison ships than in Portchester Castle, Adm 99/92, f 36v, minutes of the Transport Office, 20 Jan 1796.
28 Abel claims that most of the prisoners in Edinburgh Castle were privateer

crews; F. Abel, *Prisoners of war in Britain, 1756-1815* (1914), p 271.
29 Ibid, pp 133, 136.
30 Adm 105/44, Sir Rupert George to the Transport Office, 20 Sept 1797. Maarten Schaap, a Dutch sailor from Satwyck, was imprisoned in Morman Cross Prison in 1798 and considered it very healthy, though the diet was inadequate. I am grateful to Professor Bruijn for this information.
31 Abel, *Prisoners of war,* pp 137-8.
32 Anderson, 'Treatment of prisoners of war in Britain', p 60; the minutes of the new Transoort Office are listed, confusingly, in the PRO Index as Minutes of the Sick and Hurt Board and the new Board's minutes begin in January 1796 with a minute to send a circular to all prison and parole agents to acquaint them at the the care if all prisoners in health had been transferred to the new board; Adm 99/92, f 1.
33 Adm 103/129, 341, 383, 377.
34 Manning and Walker, *British warship names,* pp 192, 347, 383, 356.
35 Adm 103/45, 185, 406, 82, 388, 426.
36 Marcus, *Naval history of England, vol II,* pp 96-7.
37 Manning and Walker, *British warship names,* pp 127, 393.
38 Abel, *Prisoners of war in Britain,* p 196.
39 Manning and Walker, *British warship names,* p 186.
40 Adm 103/217, 395, 179, 163.
41 Manning and Walker, *British warship names,* p 227.
42 Adm 103/421, 442, 432.
43 Adm 103/453, 119, 25.
44 Adm 103/262, 36, 384.
45 Manning and Walker, *British warship names,* p 333.
46 Ibid, p 211, Adm 103/149, 400, 92, for a history of Dartmoor Prison see A.J. Rhodes, *Dartmoor Prison; a record of one hundred and twenty six years of prisoner of war and convict life, 1806-1932* (1933), pp 21-4.
47 Adm 103/46, 189, Manning and Walker, *British warship names,* pp 128, 245, 428.
48 Ibid, p 205, Adm 103/136.
49 Adm 103/44, 215, 263, 124, Abel, *Prisoners of war in Britain*, pp 196-7.
50 Ibid, pp 155, 197. Jacques Coteux, master gunner of the *Aigle*, escaped from Valley Field Prison on 6 April 1811 and was retaken at Dover on 3 May 1811, Adm 103/491, Escaped Prisoners of War.
51 Adm 103/393, 430, 261, 437; Manning and Walker, *British warship names,* pp 388, 436, 323, 465.
52 Ibid, p 392, Adm 103/404, 408.
53 Prisoners taken at Jemappes entered Dartmoor in June 1815 and returned to France between August and December; 24 taken at Amiens entered in July and returned in December, 1,879 captured at Waterloo entered in July and returned in December, Adm 103/98.
54 Adm 98/213, Transport Board to Allard, 13, 16 Feb 1796.

55 Adm 99/92, Transport Board Minutes, 10, 15 Feb 1796, H.C.A.32/620.
56 Ibid. This followed the precedent set during the War of American Independence when captains, lieutenants, ensigns, masters, *gardes marines*, clerks, surgeons and their mates, chaplains and 'volunteers of family' from ships of war, and captains, second captains, prize masters, lieutenants, pilots, clerks, surgeons, chaplains and passengers of rank from merchant ships and privateers were granted parole. Officers above the rank of second captain were entitled to have their servants with them, Anderson, 'Treatment of prisoners of war in Britain', p 74.
57 It appears that when the French abandoned hope of challenging Britain's naval power, a number of the younger naval officers were released to serve on privateers. In view of the shortage of naval officers many of those appointed during the Revolutionary War were probably former captains of merchant ships.
58 Reported in Adm 98/107, Transport Office to Admiralty, 17 May 1797.
59 Adm 98/109, Transport Board to Admiralty, 4 May 1799.
60 The *Commerce de Marseille* does not appear in the PRO Index and was a merchant ship whose prisoners were entered on the books of one of the other prison ships. Adm 103/395-9, Adm 105/44, Dacres, Serle and Harness to Transport Office, Plymouth, 7 May 1801.
61 Adm 98/213, Transport Office to Mansel, 8 Nov 1796.
62 Ibid, Transport Office to Allard, 10 Nov 1796.
63 Adm 103/551.
64 Adm 103/601.
65 Adm 103/607.
66 Adm 99/92, Transport Office Minutes, 16 Jan 1796.
67 Adm 98/213, Transport Office to Mansel, 2 Nov 1796.
68 Adm 98/111, Transport Office to Admialrty, 26 Oct 1803.
69 Adm 103/602, 562, 554, 584, 555, 569.
70 Adm 103/605, 598, 582, 590.
71 Adm 103/564, 591, 608, 594, 604.
72 Adm 103/553, 580, 609, 561, 566, 567, 581.
73 Adm 103/570, 588. Adm 10/14, a schedule of the accounts, correspondence &c for the service of prisoners of war in health 1796-1816, in sickness 1806-16 is inaccurate. It excludes a number of parole centres. The total of 67,785 French prisoners may be reasonably accurate as a record of the period as a whole.
74 Abel, *Prisoners of war in Britain*, p 12.
75 Adm 98/109, Transport Office to Admiralty, 15 Aug 1799, report that the French agent, Niou, had no money for provisions or clothing.
76 C. Lloyd, *St Vincent and Camperdown* (1933), p 96.
77 C. Lloyd (ed), *The health of seamen* (1965), p 164.
78 Abel, *Prisoners of war*, p 47.
79 Adm 98/213, Transport Office to Allard, 6 Mar 1796.

80 Ibid, 2 Oct 1797.
81 Abel, *Prisoners of war in Britain*, p 47.
82 Adm 99/92, Transport Office minutes, 3 Feb 1796.
83 Adm 105/44, Serle to Transport Office, 12 Aug 1801; 'cockle' in this context denotes the weeds that were normally found growing in wheat.
84 B.R. Mitchell and P. Deane, *Abstract of British historical statistics* (1971), p 488.
85 Ibid, p 487.
86 Adm 98/109, Transport Office to Admiralty, 23 Jan 1800.
87 Ibid, 28 Jan 1800.
88 Adm 105/44, A. Phillip, Ambrose Serle and John Harness to Transport Office, 27 Apr 1801; see also de Curzon, *Dr James Currie,* p 50.
89 Ibid, p 43.
90 Ibid, p 79. There was a similar complaint from the Mayor of Bristol regarding prisoners of war at Stapleton Prison, Adm 105/44, Ambrose Serle to Transport Office.
91 Adm 98/109, Transport Office to Admiralty, 4 Mar 1800.
92 Abel, *Prisoners of war in Britain,* p 48.
93 L. Garneray, *The French prisoner* (new ed 1957), p 9.
94 Sir James Watt, 'Some consequences of nutritional disorders in 18th-century British circumnavigations', in *Starving sailors: the influence of nutrition upon naval and maritime history* (1984), J. Watt, E.J. Freeman and W.F. Bynum (eds), p 68.
95 J.V.G.A. Durnin, 'Energy requirements in health', ibid, pp 2-4.
96 Adm 105/44, Rupert George to Transport Office, 8 Oct 1805.
97 Ibid.
98 Ibid, Additional Instructions for the agent at Portchester, 25 Apr 1801.
99 de Curzon, *Dr James Currie,* p 34.
100 Abel, *Prisoners of war in Britain,* p 148.
101 Adm 105/44, Rupert George to Transport Office, 8 Oct 1805.
102 Adm 105/44, Report on Stapleton Prison, 2 Jan 1801.
103 Adm 105/44, A. Phillip, Ambrose Serle and J. Harness to Transport Office, 27 Apr 1801.
104 Adm 98/213, Transport Office to R.J. Allard, 25 Sept 1797.
105 Adm 103/623, Death certificates at Dartmoor.
106 Adm 103/628, Death certificates at Norman Cross and Chatham.
107 Adm 103/640. death certificates at Dartmoor Hospital.
108 The following is based on P. Rozzell, *The conquest of smallpox; the impact of inoculation on smallpox mortality in eighteenth century England* (1977), pp ix, 104.
109 The entry books for the Napoleonic War list all distinguishing features of prisoners, presumably to make it easier to provide a description when any of them escaped; few are described as 'marked by smallpox'.
110 Adm 103/622.

111 Adm 103/640, 623.
112 Adm 103/623.
113 Adm 103/68, Entry book, Chatham.
114 Adm 105/44, William Otway to Transport Office, 7 Aug 1797.
115 Adm 103/128, Entry book, Falmouth, 1793, Pierre Evans, linguist on the privateer *Georgette* Adm 98/213 Transport Office to Allard, 25 Mar 1796, Pierre Nobertentote, pilot of the *Jean Bart*, was sent on parole to Chippenham.
116 Adm 99/92 Transport Office Minutes, 9 Feb 1796.
117 Adm 98/109, Admiralty to Transport Office, 18 Jan 1799.
118 Adm 99/92, Transport Office Minutes, 11 Feb 1796.
119 Adm 98/214, Transport Office to Allard, 29 Apr 1799.
120 Adm 105/45, parole and prison escape reports.
121 Ibid, 10 Feb 1811.
122 Ibid, 22 Feb 1812.
123 Ibid, Peebles, 23 Apr 1811.
124 Ibid, from Chatham, 22 Sept 1811.
125 Adm 98/214, Transport Office to Allard, 22 Apr 1799; Adm 103/491, Prisoners of war, escaped; the cost of recapturing J.C. Aubertin, who escaped from Andover in October 1812 and was recaptured the same month was 113.7s.6d. He escaped again from Portsmouth in June 1813 and was discovered in Andover in November.
126 Adm 98/214, Transport Office to Allard, 22 Apr 1799.

Conclusion

This study has shown that during the Revolutionary and Napoleonic wars merchants invested in privateering as a substitute for trade. In addition, the men who served on board the ships, from the captain to the youngest boy and volunteer did so primarily because there was no other work for them to do. Commerce raiding also provided employment for all who worked in the dockyards building and repairing the ships and making the ropes, sails, anchors, cannon and personal weapons that were used on the corsairs. Privateering also helped to sustain the merchants who supplied clothing and provisions for the men; indirectly, commerce raiding helped for a time to sustain the maritime community as a whole.

Privateering was not a desperate response to the collapse of trade. Few of the merchants who invested in it spent more than modest amounts and fewer privateers sailed to attack enemy merchant shipping than had traded in peacetime. Furthermore, there is a pattern to this form of warfare which demonstrates its close relationship to merchants' hopes that this might form an alternative to normal trade and thus enable them to continue their normal occupation during war. The rise of privateering to a peak in 1797-8 - the exact point varies slightly from port to port -reflects the conditions in each area and it is significant that when the internal trade collapsed so too did privateering.

During the Napoleonic War there was comparatively little interest in commerce raiding, partly because it was possible on the Atlantic coast to continue trade with American merchants until 1807, and partly because men had re-alised that commerce raiding paid few dividends. There were some exceptions, notably Robert Surcouf, but they were rare and even Surcouf made his fortune from his success as captain of a corsair in the Indian Ocean towards the end of the Revolutionary War and not as the managing owners of Malouin privateers during the Napoleonic. The decline of ports from 1807, which resulted from the imposition of Napoleon's Continental System, failed to stimulate commerce raiding as an alternative. There was no shortage of ships, and although Napoleon demanded increasing numbers of men for his continental campaigns there remained suitable merchant seamen at the ports. The critical factors were a shortage of finance to pay for the ventures, a lack of business confidence and the certain knowledge that increased British naval patrols had made it more likely that privateers would be captured.

Privateering was by no means a haphazard activity; everything was very carefully planned. The most important features were the skill of individual merchants, officers and men. Success depended partly on luck as in any form of activity but even more important was the managerial skill of the merchant appointed as managing owner, his choice of a suitable vessel, captain, officers and crew besides the selection of a cruising area, which the instructions left to the captain's discretion. Little was left to chance. Men at Dunkirk, a port with a long and distinguished record in privateering, were familiar with the pattern of English trade, the places where masters of merchant ships lay waiting for suitable wind or tides to continue a voyage or enter a small harbour. Dunkirkers know the run of tides off the English coast, the navigational hazards and the pattern of winds. They were also familiar with the deeply indented coastline of Norway and the main trading ports and were equally at home off the coast of north east Europe. They also knew the times when the Baltic fleets sailed and the routes they took.

At the western end of the English Channel the Malouins, rivals of Dunkirk, knew the landfalls that merchant ships used at the end of trans Atlantic voyages, not only off south west Ireland but also in the English Channel. They were familiar with the coastal waters off south west England as well as the Scilly Isles and Channel Islands. The same skills were shared by men from the other ports and harbours along the north coast of France and southern Brittany. Most of the vessels were relatively small but carried a rig that was appropriate to the navigational conditions. The most popular was some form of fore-and-aft rig, often a lug sail which enabled the well-handled vessel to tack rapidly when the wind changed direction, and provided great manoeuvrability when handled by an experienced crew.

Corsairs from the Atlantic ports were crewed by men with different skills and all had experience of deep water navigation. They were all familiar with the Caribbean but ships from Nantes also traded with the west coast of Africa for slaves in peacetime and Bordeaux was engaged in important commerce with the Indian Ocean. Privateers from Bordeaux, Nantes and La Rochelle tended to be larger than those from ports in the English Channel. They tended to be at sea for longer periods of time and used the additional space for larger crew and for provisions. They also cruised in the Atlantic and the Bay of Biscay where the weather could be more severe and the winds more regular. For this reason the vessels were normally square rigged in the prevailing winds which gave them maximum speed to pursue a merchant vessel or escape from a naval warship. There was some variation in the pattern of commerce raiding in this area. Not only were the spring, early summer and autumn cruising grounds different because of the routes taken by convoys outward bound for the Mediterranean and East and West India trade and for their return, but during the summer a number of corsairs sailed to the West Indies. Many of these carried trade goods to sell in the southern Caribbean, outside the area patrolled by British warships and also carried letters of marque *en guerre et merchandise* which enabled them to capture any merchant ships they encountered during the voyage.

The men of Bayonne and its associated port St Jean-de-Luz possessed other qualifications for commerce raiding. A century earlier they had possessed the reputation of freebooters as well as being hardy and experienced whalers. Although their piratical activities in the Caribbean had been brought under control early in the eighteenth century and the whale fishery had declined, the Basques still retained the reputation of being hardy and experienced deep sea sailors. In practice however they played a comparatively minor role in commerce raiding in this period. Since the beginning of the eighteenth century the River Nive, on which Bayonne was situated, had begun to silt up and much of its early trade had moved north to Bordeaux. Bayonne remained a free port and the smaller vessels which continued to use Bayonne carried a variety of goods which came from northern Spain to Bayonne's annual fair and were thence shipped to markets in northern Europe. The experience of the Basque was thus in the trade of the Iberian peninsula and the vessels they fitted out cruised off the north coast of Spain and off Portugal. Their crews knew the coastal waters, tides and winds and the vessels carried sweeps which enabled them to be rowed in calms. Often these vessels, sometimes little bigger than rowing boats, put out from the shore to attack a convoy that lay becalmed and there was little that the escort could do to stop them. Their small size and shallow draught also enabled vessels to remain close inshore beyond the reach of the naval warships. It was also extremely difficult for the captains of British naval vessels to try and blockade the Basque ports, for the low lying, sandy shore of south west France had few harbours and was a dangerous lee shore for British warships. In consequence the Basque privateers could cruise with relative impunity and their only disadvantage was that their small size limited the scope of the cruises and the size of their captures.

In the Mediterranean the pattern of commerce raiding was different. British naval patrols off Toulon that were intended to stop the fleet putting to sea also controlled the movement of shipping into and out of the port of Marseilles. Only very small vessels from Genoa, Sète and the Rhône could escape. In addition, Marseilles suffered heavy financial losses in the civil war that had also engulfed Toulon. There was little money available for commerce raiding and much of the trade which supplied Marseilles with the necessities of life was in the hands of Genoese merchants. The British trade with the Island of Zante, Leghorn and elsewhere in the Mediterranean was always protected by naval escorts but there were many other vessels from the Italian states and Spain that could be attacked, either because France was at war with them or because they were carrying goods destined for British markets. Neutral ships were sometimes also captured for the same reason. The base for the attack on this trade was Corsica, when it was not in British hands, and corsairs also sailed from Erakleion on the north coast of Crete early in the Revolutionary War and from Spanish ports in the Napoleonic, using letters of marque supplied by French consuls in the ports. The main victims were the isolated ships from the Italian states and neutrals, for the British merchant ships were generally too well protected. This commerce raiding was less seasonal than the others already described, for apart from the citrus fruits and wheat that was carried, there were many other raw materials and manufactured items were shipped throughout the year. The privateer crews had a knowledge of the pattern of this trade and of the best look out points from which to watch for approaching ships; winds were variable and produced their own distinctive rig but there were no tides.

It was important that managing owners chose the best type of ship for commerce raiding, for there was an important difference between the vessel built for bulk carriage and one designed for speed. At the beginning of the Revolutionary War managing owners used whatever ships were available. At this stage speed was not important, for captains hoped to intercept merchant vessels returning from the Caribbean and North America whose captains were not aware that war had broken out. It was relatively easy to approach an unsuspecting vessel, as ships often did at sea to exchange information, and then to capture it. In any case, even a relatively slow sailing ship could sail well when handled by an experienced crew who could quickly and easily adjust the trim of the sails. Under-manned merchant ships had little chance of escape. Later in the war managing owners bought ships that had been specially built for speed and manoeuvrability and had finer lines than merchant vessels. Most were designed especially in 1797-8 when demand for ships was high, and built during the war, but occasionally, an older vessel that had been built in the War of American Independence, was pressed into service. Managing owners made a point of stressing the speed of their ships in the broadsheets that launched the ventures.

Sometimes managing owners tried a different approach and used a ship that had been built in England and had a distinctive appearance. Many of the areas on the south and east coast of England had boats of a special design and managing owners occasionally used these as a disguise. Another alternative was to buy an American built ship and send it to cruise in the area through which the American trade passed, in the hope that the appearance of the ship flying the

American flag would lull merchant vessels and their escorts into a false sense of security. These, and the British built ships, always carried a linguist who could speak English and this disguise was adequate for all but the most astute naval officer.

One of the attractions of commerce raiding for merchants was that they expected that the prizes would provide a regular supply of goods that could be sold profitably. Shareholding added a further advantage for it offered the first choice in the sale of goods condemned by the prize court. The difficulty arose when the market for goods was glutted, as happened relatively quickly in 1798. It then became impossible to sell prize goods and the men who had invested in them suffered loss. This proved a heavy blow, for the same men had earlier survived the financial crisis of the *assignats* and heavy taxation and were often unable to withstand further misfortunes. This helps to explain why privateering declined.

It also proved extremely difficult to make large profits. The cost of the venture: buying or building a vessel and fitting it out, paying the crew advance wages and buying the provisions cost a great deal of money, though the cost was higher at the Atlantic ports than elsewhere. The best prospects were in the Mediterranean, where there were more ships sailing unescorted, but a privateer had to take prizes worth at least the cost of fitting out the ship. Furthermore only two thirds of the profits were paid to the shareholders, for the remaining third was assigned to the crew, to cover the cost of wages. It was by no means uncommon for a corsair to capture a number of prizes but to make a loss on the venture, for the cost of fitting out the ship, hiring and feeding the crew and costs of refitting took all the profits.

Another aspect of privateering is the absence of the men who had directed commerce before the Revolution. Commerce raiding at every port seems to have been controlled by men who had been little known before 1789. Their background was managing vessels in the coasting trade and as officers in the merchant marine and they possessed a great deal of local knowledge. In terms of commerce raiding in the waters of the English Channel, North Sea and the Soundings these were important assets and of more immediate benefit that knowledge of more distant areas such as the coast of Newfoundland. However, this reveals the social and economic effect of the Revolution on the leading merchants for there is evidence that at all the major ports the principal merchants were publicly attacked and the new political leaders looked to them to support the Revolution and taxed them heavily. The result was not only that they became short of money to spend on these ventures but, more important, they kept out of the public limelight and left others to organise the ventures. However it is possible that when privateering reached its peak in 1797-8 many of the former leaders of the commercial community bought shares on a large scale and that it was this factor which created the dramatic surge of activity. It is also evident that in terms of investment, Nantes with a greater number of relatively large and expensive ships spent more money than Dunkirk on commerce raiding. Nantes had escaped the worst effects of the Revolution and in 1797-8 this was the port which led the attack on British trade. In the longer run however it was the northern ports - Dunkirk and St Malo - which sustained the attack.

Finally it may be asked whether the British Admiralty were aware of the nature of French privateering and whether the policy of defending British commerce was based on anything other than the pressure from commercial groups. It is clear from a reading of the minutes of the Board of Admiralty that the Board showed little interest in the corsairs but a great deal in the activities of the London merchants. Such information as did reach the Board from spies in France was of little practical value, for it referred to ships being fitted out or built and gave no indication of the size or when they were likely to sail, for how long and where. Information about privateers seen cruising off the coast of southern and eastern England was similarly confused, for watchers on the shore had little real idea whether a ship was a corsair unless it captured a merchant ship and corsairs were identical in appearance to merchant vessels. In the absence of fact, rumour flourished. However, the Admiralty did have a clear idea of where the British ships normally sailed and made every effort to patrol these areas. It is also evident that there was a graded screen of naval vessels which defended trade. At the western end of the English Channel were larger frigates and warships and in the English Channel much use was made of cutters and other small, manoeuvrable naval vessels. These proved effective for they could often outsail the corsairs and were handled with a greater discipline. The use of patrols off the north and south coast of Brittany as an extension of the Brest blockade and patrols off Dunkirk, the Dutch coast and the south and east coast of England also provided a useful measure of defence and these interlocking measures provided an adequate protection for British trade. Further afield the use of naval escorts to protect convoys and patrol the coast before returning with the trade were also effective. France's naval weakness gave her no opportunity to challenge this as had been done a century before.

Lacking naval support, French privateers were at the mercy of the British navy. Popular support was only given to privateering when conditions appeared favourable for selling prize goods and at Bordeaux, the great commercial centre of the 1780's, the commercial class was fatally weakened by the Revolution. Only at Dunkirk and St Malo, the traditional corsair ports, did commerce raiding continue to attract men in both wars, though on a comparatively modest level. The proximity of British merchant shipping in the English Channel was a temptation that could not be resisted.

Appendix
Captives

Seamen captured on Privateers

	1793	1794	1795	1796	1797	1798	1799	1800	1801	Total
Bayonne	90	-	-	-	456	872	301	267	-	1,986
Bordeaux	370	-	-	68	1165	1306	1210	1871	407	6,397
Boulogne	50	-	-	93	94	39	130	72	33	511
Calais	62	-	-	82	113	74	260	114	42	767
Cherbourg	76	-	-	95	264	64	53	63	125	740
Dieppe	73	-	-	-	75	44	-	-	-	192
Dunkirk	520	-	35	336	563	228	457	47	117	2,306
Fécamp	138	-	-	17	11	-	-	-	-	166
Granville	44	-	-	28	165	60	419	56	-	772
Le Havre	191	-	-	194	253	68	-	-	-	706
Honfleur	29	-	-	-	16	82	8	-	-	135
Lorient	171	-	-	-	329	582	31	-	70	1,185
Marseilles	284*	-	-	-	150*	-	-	-	-	434*
Nantes	564	-	-	126	1170	1293	568	400	-	4,121
Paimpol	25	-	-	-	141	33	-	64	-	263
St Malo	264	-	-	237	585	699	262	348	626	3,381
St Valéry	56	-	-	-	-	-	-	-	-	56
Brest	-	-	30*	1000	518	148	164	75	24	1,959*

	1793	1794	1795	1796	1797	1798	1799	1800	1801	Total
Loano	-	-	58	-	-	-	-	-	-	58
La Hogue	-	-	-	28	-	27	11	-	-	66
La Rochelle	-	-	-	66	741	39	64	131	-	1,041
Caen	-	-	-	-	31	-	-	-	-	31
Conquet	-	-	-	-	31	-	-	-	-	31
Lannion	-	-	-	-	29	-	-	34	-	63
Morlaix	-	-	-	78	123	-	-	20	94	312
St Honoré	-	-	-	-	20*	-	-	-	-	20*
St Jean-de-Luz	-	-	-	-	32	24	60	40	-	156
Cadiz	-	-	-	-	-	135	-	-	-	135
Ostend	-	-	-	-	-	75	80	50	84	289
Corunna	-	-	-	-	-	-	-	85	-	85
Ancona	-	-	-	-	-	-	-	-	92	92
Totals	3367	-	123	2448	7094	5894	4097	3737	1714	28,456

*Indicates an estimated total

Source: Adm 32 passim

	1803	1804	1805	1806	1807	1808	1809	1810	1811	1812	1813	Totals
Bayonne	-	168	-	30	35	-	243	103	-	-	165	744
Bordeaux	678	90	295	-	20	195	154	-	-	-	-	1,432
Boulogne	34	41	-	-	52	128	181	303	177	59	-	975
Calais	-	42	-	85	50	225	-	80	40	-	-	522
Cherbourg	84	-	-	29	-	48	20	-	-	57	-	238
Dunkirk	59	115	92	-	250	66	74	237	-	41	42	976
Fécamp	14	-	-	-	90	-	-	43	-	54	-	201
Hamburg	45	-	-	-	-	-	-	-	-	-	-	45
La Rochelle	69	-	-	-	-	314	53	36	-	-	-	472
Lorient	19	-	-	127	183	-	70	219	-	-	53	671
Nantes	104	-	-	-	-	203	107	320	-	-	-	734
Paimpol	27	-	-	-	-	-	-	-	-	-	-	27
St Malo	66	187	60	197	357	125	450	852	206	489	349	3,338
Conquet	-	30	-	-	-	-	-	-	-	-	20	50
Marseilles	-	-	30	-	-	-	30*	130*	132	30*	101	453*
Dieppe	-	-	-	-	40*	-	-	220	50*	-	-	310*
Granville	-	-	-	-	74	-	-	56	-	-	-	130
Ostend	-	-	-	-	20*	125	80	-	-	-	-	225
Amsterdam	-	-	-	-	-	29	-	30*	-	-	-	59*
Aurai	-	-	-	-	-	19	-	-	-	-	-	19
Danzig	-	-	-	-	-	-	41	20*	-	-	-	61*
Rochefort	-	-	-	-	-	-	130	29	-	-	-	159
Totals	1199	673	477	468	1171	1477	1633	2678	605	730	730	11,841

*Estimated

Source: H.C.A.32 passim.

Prisons and prison hulks

Bristol	1793-1803	*Eagle, Bristol* (Ch)	1796-1800
Stapleton	1793-1814	Edinburgh, Greenock	1796-1814
Falmouth	1793-1796	Guernsey	1796-1801
Kinsale	1793-1801	*Vigilant* (Po)	1796-1815
Liverpool	1793-1801	*Fame* (Po)	1797-1801
Plymouth	1793-1815	Norman Cross	1797-1815
Forton	1793-1797	*Portland, Royal Oak* (Po)	1797-1802
Hero, Bristol (Ch)	1794-1801	*Prothee* (Po)	1797-1815
Portchester	1794-1814	*Camperdown* (Ch)	1798-1801
Prudent (Pl)	1794-1798	*Crown* (Po)	1798-1802
Captivity (Po)	1796-1800	*Vryheid* (Ch)	1798-1802
Deal	1796-1801	*Hero, Sandwich* (Ch)	1798-1802
Dover	1795-1800	*San Damaso* (Po)	1798-1815
Yarmouth	1794-1800	*Sandwich* (Ch)	1798-1811
"	1803-1814	*Sultan* (Po)	1798-1802
Pembroke	1793-1796		
Hull	1797	(Po) - Portsmouth,	
North Shields	1797	(Pl) - Plymouth	
Dartmouth	1796-1797	(Ch) - Chatham	
Weymouth	1796	Source: Adm 103 passim	
Harwich	1796-179		

Bienfaisant (Pl)	1803-1814	*San Antonio* (Po)	1808
Chatham	1803-1814	St Nicholas (Pl)	1809
Europa (Pl)	1803-1814	*Canada* (Ch)	1810-1812
Greenlaw	1803-1812	*Brunswick* (Ch)	1812-1813
Portsmouth	1803-1814	Dartmoor	1809-1815
Kron Prinds (Ch)	1805-1813	Esk Mills	1812
San Isadoro (Pl)	1804-1814	*Ganges* (Pl)	1811-1814
Suffolk (Po)	1806-1813	*Irrestible* (Ch)	1810-1813
Vengeance (Po)	1806-1814	*Kron Princessa* (Ch)	1812-1814
Veteran (Po)	1806-1814	*Oiseau* (Pl)	1813-1814
Waldemar (Po)	1807	Perth	1812-1813
Bath	1807-1808	*St George* (Pl)	1813-1814
El Firme (Pl)	1807-1814	*Sampson* (Po)	1813
Guildford (Po)	1805-1811	*Sophia Frederica*(Po)	1813-1814
Hector (Pl)	1805-1814	*Temeraire* (Pl)	1813
Bravo (Pl)	1808-1812	Valley Field	1811-1814
Glory (Ch)	1809-1814	*Vanguard* (Pl)	1813-1814
Panther (Pl)	1808-1811		

(Po) - Portsmouth,
(Pl) - Plymouth
(Ch) - Chatham
Source: Adm 103 passim

Parole Centres

Centre	Years	Centre	Years
Tavistock	1794-1797	Alresford	1795-1797,1809-1812
Ashburton	1795-1797	Peeble	1803-1811
Callington	1795-1798	Ashbourne	1803-1812
Bodmin	1794-1797	Bishop's Waltham	1803-1811
Tiverton	1797-1799, 1803-11	Leek	1803-1811
Ashby-de-la-Zouch	1803-1812	Oswestry	1809-1812
Thame	1804-1812	Okehampton	1809-1812
Wincanton	1805-1811	North Tawton	1809-1810
Reading	1805-1812	Wantage	1808-1810
Launceston	1805-1812	Welshpool	1811-1812
Montgomery	1805-1811	Bishop's Castle	1811-1812
Brecon	1806-1812	Chatham	1811-1814
Moreton Hampstead	1807-1814	Chesterfield	1811-1813
Northampton	1809-1812	Greenlaw	1812
Andover	1810-1811	Lauder	1811-1813
Kelso	1810-1812	Llanfyllin	1812-1813

Source: Adm 103, passim.

French privateers captured

	1793-1801	1803-1814
English coast		
Firth of Forth to the Wash	14	5
The Wash	1	0
East Anglia	19	11
Thames Estuary to Dungeness	16	10
Dungeness to Isle of Wight	22	6
Isle of Wight to Prawle Point	41	13
Prawle Point to Lands End	35	13
Scilly Isles	22	5
Ireland		
South coast	1	0
South west coast	11	0
Norway		
South west coast	7	0
Netherlands		
West Frisian Islands	1	0
Den Helder to Dunkirk	24	2

	1793–1801	1803–1814
France		
Dunkirk to River Somme	13	7
River Somme to Cherbourg	17	4
Cherbourg to Ushant	18	8
Ushant to Pointe de Penmarch	25	6
Point de Penmarch to River Loire	14	0
River Loire to River Gironde	14	1
River Gironde to San Sebastian	4	0
Spain		
San Sebastian to Cape Ortegal	2	0
Cape Ortegal to Cape Finisterre	23	3
Portugal		
Cape Finisterre to Lisbon	21	2

Sources

MANUSCRIPTS

The major problem faced by the student of privateering is that the archives and libraries of the Conseil d'Etat, the Conseil des Prises, the Cour des Comtes and the Cour de Cassation were burnt in 1871 during the Commune. This has made it impossible to learn the total number and value of prizes captured during these wars. The research has therefore concentrated on surviving records in Paris and the départements. Most of the surviving records for Dunkirk were destroyed by fire after the First World War and the bombardments of Marseilles, Loeient and St Lô towards the end of the Second World War have also destroyed valuable records.

PARIS

Archives Nationales
Series FF2bis:
1-15 Decisions of the Conseil des Prises
17-19 Sale of prize ships
20-27 Port and consular decisions
28-31 Decisions for separate ships

French war on trade

33-35 Spanish prizes
Series FF2

11-15, 37-41	List of privateers and their prizes
42-4,51	List of prizes
113	Alphabetical list of prizes
216	Prizes entered at Boulogne
250	Alphabetical list of captured ships

Archives des Affaires Etrangères
Correspondence consulaire et commerciale, Bergen 1793-1815 and St Ander, 1793-1810

Archives départementales de la Gironde

7B/1099-2003	Letters and accounts of Romberg, 1788-95
C/3688	Shares in trading ventures

Archives départementales des Basses-Pyrénées

95L/35	Declarations by captains of ships
95L/36-7	Tribunal de Commerce, Bayonne
IIIE/3490	Notarial records, Paul Duhalde

Amirauté de Bayonne, Série B Supplément, Bayonne privateers

Chambre de Commerce de Bayonne

A2	Free port
E8	Privateering
G16, 20, 41-2, 47, 64, 70, 75-6, 84-5, 90	Trade with the North
H8-10, 28	Overseas trade
H44-54	Ships fitted out by the Chambre de Commerce
B11	Deliberations of the Chambre de Commerce

Archives départementales des Bouches du Rhône

13B/1598	
531U/1	Tribunal de Commerce

Archives départementales du Calvados

2 II/648-671	Amirauté de Honfleur

Archives départementales des Côtes du Nord

144L/34	Revolutionary period, privateers
1M	General administration
6U	Tribunal de Commerce

Archives de la Charente-Maritime

377-90	Inscription Maritime

Archives départementales du Finistère

11L	Departmental administration and accounts
12L	Communal administration and accounts
13L	Financial contributions
153L	Tribunal de Commerce, Brest
154L	Tribunal de Commerce, Morlaix

Archives départementales de l'Hérault

L2149-58, 3782-5, 433503-5, 5258 War at sea
L1148 Imports and exports, Sète, Year V

Archives départementales d'Ille-et-Vilaine

9B/346, 669	Crew lists, 1790, corsairs, fishing boats
15Ri/5	War at sea, privateers
15Rj/18-25	" "
L654	Report on the Patriotic Contribution from the Disctrict of St Malo, 5 July 1792
4S/346-9	Inscription Maritime, Privateers
6U/2	Tribunal de Commerce
2Um/16	" "
C437	Intendance de Bretagne

Archives départementales de la Loire-Atlantique

20JJ/1965, 1969, 2330 Privateering accounts
L528-30, 635, 764-6 Prize papers
17U/188 Tribunal de Commerce

Archives départementales du Morbihan

Lz 936,9	Declarationof the purchase or construction of ships
Lz1566	Captains' reports
Lz 1589-96	Ship registers
Lz 938	Prize papers
Lz 1598-1610	Prize papers
U 2241	Tribunal de Commerce

Archives départementales du Pas-de-Calais

6U/3	Tribunaux de Commerce, Boulogne, Calais
9U/10, 21	Tribunal de Commerce, Boulogne

Genealogical documentation

Archives départementales de la Seine-Maritime

6P/6-7, 21-2 Inscription Maritime

French war on trade

Archives départementales de la Vendée

2Q/2452	Inventory of the cargo of the *Favourite* of London captured by the *Niverne* of Bordeaux

Archives de la 1ère Région maritime, Cherbourg

3P	Intendance de Dunkerque	
4P	Inscription Maritime,	Cherbourg
6P	" "	Le Havre
8P	" "	Fécamp
7P	" "	Rouen
12P	Privateers and prizes,	Year XI-1814

Archives de la 2ème Région maritime, Brest

2Pc6	Inscription maritime,	Brest
2Q	Prize papers	
1T1-5, 8	Administrative papers, privateers	

Archives de la 2ème Région maritime, Rochefort

13P8-9	Inscription maritime,	Bayonne
15P6	Tribunal de Commerce,	"
13P8	Inscription maritime,	St Jean-de-Luz
15P2-5	Tribunal de Commerce,	" "
13P9	Lists of merchant vessels,	Bayonne
1Q	Prize papers	

Archives de la 3ème Région maritime, Toulon

1P	Inscription Maritime,	Toulon
2Q	Prize papers	

LONDON

Public Records Office

Adm	1/3841-5	Letters from British consuls
Adm	1/3849-57	" " foreign "
Adm	1/3974-6	Intelligence
Adm	1/3977-81	Intercepted letters
Adm	1/6032-40	Intelligence, 3rd series
Adm	2/124-66	Orders and Instructions
Adm	2/941-68	Secretary's letters to commanders-in-chief of squadrons
Adm	2/1090-6	Letters to consuls
Adm	2/1097-14	Letters concerning convoys
Adm	7/60	Register of applications for convoys
Adm	7/64-8	Lists of convoys

Adm 7/354-7 List of prizes
Adm 7/555-9 List of ships' stations
Adm 10/14 List and index of prisoners-of war
Adm 98 passim Medical Department, Out Letters
Adm 99/92-265 Medical Board minutes
Adm 103 passim Registers of prisoners-of-war
Adm 105/44-6, 59-66 Medical Department, Miscellaneous
AO3/874-5 Accounts of expenses of French prisoners
T62/94 Plans of Forton, Stapleton and Greenlaw
HCA32 passim Papers deposited with the High Court of Admiralty
HCA34/60-65 Decisions of the High Court of Admiralty

BASEL

Schweizerisches Wirtschaftsarchiv, Basel
Segerhof Archiv
420 D1-5 Principal account books
420 D45-6 Accounts of goods delivered
420 F, passim Out letters

PRINTED SOURCES

Abell, F, *Prisoners of war in Britain, 1756-1815* (1914)

Alexander, J. K., 'Forton prison during the American Revolution: a case study of the British prisoner of war policy and the American response to that policy' *(Essex Institute Historical Collections)*, ciii, (1967), pp 365-89

Alexander, J. K., 'American privateersmen in the Mill Prison during 1777-1782: an evaluation' *(Essex Institute Historical Collections)*, cii, (1966), pp 318-40

Anderson, O., 'The treatment of prisoners of war in Britain during the American War of Independence', *(Bulletin of the Institute of Historical Research)*, xxviii, (1955), pp 63-83

Anstey, R., *The Atlantic slave trade and British abolition 1760-1810* (1975)

Bécamps, P., *La Revolution à Bordeaux: J.-B.-M. Lacombe, Président de la commission militaire* (Bordeaux 1953).

Bécamps, P., 'Les relations avec les neutres au temps de la Révolution; l'agence commerciale à Bordeaux (23 mars 1794 - 29 janvier 1795)' *(Revue historique de Bordeaux)*, (1955), pp 305-16.

Benaerts, L., *Le régime consulaire en Bretagne; le département d'ille-et-Vilaine sous le Consulat et l'Empire (1799-1804)* (Paris 1914

Bergeron, L., 'Approvisionnement et consommation à Paris sous le premier Empire' *(Mémoires de Paris et Ille-et-Vilaine)*, xiv (1963), pp 197-232

French war on trade

Bergeron, L., *Banquiers, négotiants et manufacturiers parieisns du Directoire à l'Empire* (2 vols, Paris 1975)

Bergeron, L., *L'episode napoléonienne; aspects intérieurs 1799-1815* (Paris 1972)

Bergeron, L., 'Problèmes économiques de la France napoléonienne' *(Revue d'Histoire Moderne et Contemporaine)* (1970), pp 469-505.

Bernard, M., *La municipalité de Brest de 1750 à 1790* (Paris 1915).

Bonnel, U., *La France, les Etats-Unis et la Guerre de course (1797-1815)* (Paris 1961)

Bowman, L. G., *Captive Amnericans: American prisoners during the American Revolution* (Athens, Ohio, 1976)

Bromley, J. S., 'The Channel Islands privateers in the War of the Spanish Succession' *(Transactions of the Societé Guernésiase)*, xiv, (1950), pp 444-78

Bromley, J. S., 'The French privateering war 1702-13' in *Historical essays presented to David Ogg* (1963), Bell, H.E. and Ollard, R. L. (eds)

Bromley, J. S., 'The importance of Dunkirk (1688-1713) reconsidered' (Paper presented at the XV International Colloquium on Maritime History, San Francisco, 1976)

Bromley, J. S., 'The Jacobite privateers in the Nine Years War', in *Statesmen, scholars and merchants; essays in eighteenth century history presented to Dame Lucy Sutherland* (1973), Whiteman, A.,Bromley, J. S. and Dickson P. G. M. (eds)

Bromley, J. S., 'Projets et contrats d'armement en course marseillais, 1705-1712' *(Revue d'Histoire Economique et Sociale)* (1972, pp 74-109

Butel, P., 'Charles Fieffé, commissaire et armateur; contribution à l'étude du négoce bordelais sous la Révolution et l'Empire' (Thèse du 3ème cycle, Univ.of Bordeaux, 1967)

Butel, P., 'Crise et mutation de l'activité économique à Bordeaux sous le Consulat et l'Empire' *(Revue d'Histoire Moderne et Contemporaine)*, xvii, (1970), pp 540-58

Butel, P., 'L'armement en course à Bordeaux sous la Révolution et l'Empire' *(Revue historique de Bordeaux)*, xv, new ser. (1966), pp 17-64.

Butel, P., *Les négotiants bordelais; l'Europe et les Iles au XVIIIe siècle* (Paris 1974)

Butel, P., 'Guerre et commerce: l'activite' du port de Bordeaux sous le régime des licenses, 1808-1815' *(Revue d'Histoire Moderne et Contemporaine)*, (1972), pp 128-49.

Cabantous, A., *La mer et les hommes* (Dunkirk 1979)

Caron, P., *Le maximum géneral; texte et notes* (Paris 1930)

Carrière, C., 'Le commerce de draps à Marseille au XVIIIe siècle' *(Conférences de l'Institut de Provence)*, (1962), pp 120-1

Carrière, C., 'Les débuts du commerce marseillais dans la Mer Noire à la fin du XVIIIe siècle' *(Conférences de l'Institut historique de Provence)* (1963), pp 147-8

Carrière, C., 'Les entrées ne navires dans le port de Marseille pendant la Révolution' *(Provence Historique)* (1957), pp 200-25

Carrière, C., 'Les Marseillais, étaient-ils des corsaires?' *(Conférences de l'Institut historique de Provence)* (1966), pp 204-6

Carriére, C., *Négotiants marseillais au XVIIIe siècle; contribution à l'étude des économies maritimes* (2 vols, Marsailles, no date)

Carrière, C., 'Le problème des grains et farines à Marsaille pendant la période du Maximum (4 mai 1793, 24 décembre 1794)' *(Conférences de l'Institut historique de Provence* (1955), pp 161-84

Carrière, C., 'Protestantisme et commerce à Marseille au XVIIIe siècle' *(Conférences de l'Institut historique de Provence)* (1965), pp 150-1

Carrière, C. and Coudurie, M., 'L'espace commerçiale marseillais au XVIIe et XVIIIe siècles' in *Aires et structures du commerce française au XVIIIe siècle* (Paris 1973)

Cavaignac, J., *Jean Pellet, commerçant en gros 1694-1772* (Paris 1967)

Charbonnel, N., Commerce et course sous la Révolution et le Consulat à la Rochelle (Paris 1977)

Clark, J. G., La Rochelle and the Atlantic economy during the eighteenth century (Baltimore 1981)

Caluse, G., 'L'Industrie lainière rémoise à l'époque napoléonienne (Revue d'Histoire Moderne et Contemporaine), (1970), pp 574-95

Cobb, R.,The police and the people; French popular protest 1789-1820 (1970)

Cotton, Sir Evan, East Indiamen; the East India *Company's maritime service* (1949)

Crouzet, F., *L'économie britannique et le Blocus Continental, 1806-1813* (2 vols, Paris 1958)

Crouzet, F., 'Groupes de pression et politique de blocus: remarques sur les origines des Orders en Conseil de Novembre 1807' *(Revue Historique)*, ccxxvii (1962), pp 45-72

Crouzet, F., 'Les importations d'eaux de vie et de vins français en Grande-Bretagne pendant le Blocus Continental' *(Annales du Midi)*, (1953), pp 91-106

Crouzet, F., 'Les origines du sous-développement économique du sud ouest' *(Annales du Midi)* (1959), pp 71-9

Crouzet, F., 'Wars, blockade and economic change in Europe, 1792-1815' *(Journal of Economic History)*, (1964), pp 567-88

Crowhurst, R. P., 'Bayonne privateering, 1744-1763' (Paper presented at the XV International Colloquium on Maritime History, San Francisco, 1976)

Crowhurst, R. P., *The defence of British trade, 1689-1815* (Folkestone 1977)

Crowhurst, R. P., 'The privateering activities of a Swiss merchant, Benoît Bourcard, at Nantes 1793-1814' *(Revue française d'Histoire d'Outre-Mer)*, lxix, (1982), pp 225-35

Crowhurst, R. P., 'Profitability in French privateering, 1793-1815' *(Business History)*, xxiv, (1982), pp 48-60

French war on trade

Dardel, P., 'Crises et faillites à Rouen et dans la Haute-Normandie de 1740 à l'An V' *(Revue d'Histoire Economique et Sociale)* (1948), pp 53-71

Dardel, P.,*Navires et marchandises dans les ports de Rouen et du Havre au XVIIIe siècle* (Paris 1963)

Darsel, J., 'Aspects juridiques et économiques de la guerre de course en Normandie au XVIIIe siècle' *(Revue historique de droit français),* (1975), pp 191-2

Daudrey, P., *Familles de la marine dunkerquoise* (Dunkirk 1979)

de Curzon, A., *Dr. James Currie and the French prisoners of war in Liverpool, 1800-1801* (Liverpool 1926)

Defoe, D., *A tour through the whole of the island of Great Britain* (2 vols, new ed., 1966)

Dejoint, G., *Le politique économique du Directoire* (Paris 1951)

de Lapouyade, M., 'Voyage d'un allemand à Bordeaux en 1801' *(Revue historique de Bordeaux* (1942), pp 164-81

de Lesdain, L. A. B. and Daudrey, P., *Notices généalogiques sur quelques familles patriciennes de Dunkerque* (Fécamp, 1959)

Delumeau, J., (ed), *Histoire de la Bretagne* (Toulouse 1969)

de Maupassant, J., 'Les armateurs bordelais sous la Révolution et l'Empire' *(Revue philomathique de Bordeaux et du Sud-Ouest)*, (1917), pp 25-36, 65-77, 190-9, 224-43

Devleeshouwer, R., 'Période de "take off" pur l'économie belge?' *(*Revue d'Histoire Moderne et Contemporaine), (1970, pp 610-9

Dillon, Sir William, *A narrative of my profssional adventures (1790-1839)* (2 vols, 1955, 1956)

Dion, R., 'Orléans et l'ancienne navigation de la Loire' *(Annales de Géographie)* (1938), pp 128-54

Duceré, R., *Bayonne sous l'Empire; le Blocus et 1814* (Bayonne 1900)

Dufraisse, R., 'La politique douanière de Napoléon', *(Revue de l'Institut de Napoléon)*, (1974), pp 3-25

Dundonald, Earl of, *Autobiography of a seaman* (1860)

Durnin, J. V. G. A., 'Energy requirements in health' in *Starving sailors; the influence of nutrition upon naval and maritime history* (1984), Watt, J., Freeman, E. J. and Bynum, W. F. (eds)

Earl, P, *Corsairs of Malta and Barbary* (1970)

Ellis, G. J., 'Alsace and the Continental Blockade, 1806-13' (D.Phil., Univ.of Oxford, 1972)

Evans, R., *The fabrication of virtue; English prison architecture, 1750-1840* (1982)

Everaerts, J., 'Les fluctuations du trafic négrier nantais (1763-1792)' *(Cahiers de Tunisie)* xxxiii, (1963), pp 37-62

Everard, F., 'Le commerce des laines d'Espagne sous le premier Empire' *(Revue d'Histoire Moderne* (1937), pp 197-226

Fayle, C. E., 'The employment of British shipping', in *The trade winds; a study*

of British overseas trade during the French wars 1793-1815 (1948), Parkinson, C. N. (ed)
Forrest, A., *Society and politics in revolutionary Bordeaux* (1975)
Foucart, P. and Finot, L. J., *La défense nationale dans le Nord de 1792 à 1802* (Paris 1893)
Friendley, A., *Beaufort of the Admiralty 1744-1857* (1977)
Gallois, N., *Les corsaires français sous la République et l'Empire* (Paris 1847)
Garneray, L., *The French prisoner* (new ed., 1957)
Garitee, J. R., *The Republic's private navy; the American privateering business as practised by Baltimore during the War of 1812* (Middletown, Conn., 1977)
Geggus, D. P., *Slavery, war and revolution; the British occupation of Saint Domingue* (1982)
Goodwin, A., 'Counter revolution in Brittany' *(Bu;;etin of the John Rylands Library)*, (1957), pp 326-55
Havard, O., *Histoire de la Révolution dans les ports de guerre* (2 vols., Paris 1912)
Heils, K., *Les rapports économiques franco-danois sous le Directoire, le Consulat et l'Empire; contribution à l'étude du système continental* (Paris 1958)
Ignatieff, M. *A just measure of pain; the penitentiary in the Industrial Revolution* (1979)
Jeulin, P., *L'évolution du port de Nantes; organisation et trafic depuis les origines* (Paris 1929)
Johnson, W. B., *The English prison hulks* (rev. ed., 1970)
Johnson, W. B. *Wolves of the Channel (1681-1856)* (1931)
Kaplan, J., *Elbeuf during the Revolutionary period: history and social structure* (Baltimore 1964)
Kennedy, P. M. *The rise and fall of British naval mastery* (1976)
Lemaignère, E., *Les corsaires bayonnais* (Bayonne 1856)
Latreille, E., *L'ère napoléonienne* (Paris 1974)
Laughton, Sir John (ed), *Letters and papers of Charles, Lord Barham, Admiral of the Red Squadron, 1758-1813, vol II* (1910)
le Coz, J.-N., 'La guerre de course à Saint-Malo sous Louis XVI' (DES, Univ.of Rennes, 1957)
Lefebvre, G., *The French Revolution from 1793 to 1799* (1967)
Lefebvre, G., 'Les mines de Littry, 1744-An VIII' in *Etudes sur la Révolution française* (Paris 1954, Lefebvre, G. (ed)
Legry, F., 'Les étrangers dans la Cité' *(Bulletin de la Societé archéologique et historique de Nantes et de la Loire-inférieure)*, ci, (1962), pp 79-97
Lemaire, L., *Histoire de Dunkerque des origines à 1900* (Dunkirk 1980)
Lemaignère, L., *Les corsaires sous l'Ancien Régime* (Bayonne 1980)
Lemay, J., 'La guerre de course à Saint-Malo pendant les guerres de Louis XV' (Thèse du 3me cycle, Ecole Nationale des Chartes, 1948)
Léon, P., Vie et mort d'un grand marché internationale; la Foire de Beaucaire (XVIII-XIXe siècles) *(Revue de Géographie)*, (1959), pp 309-28

French war on trade

Lespagnol, A., 'Guerre et activités maritimes: l'example de Saint-Malo pendant la Guerre d'Amérique' (Paper presented at the International Maritime History Conference, Greenwich, 1974)

Leyland, J., *Papers relating to the blockade of Brest, vol 1* (1966)

Lloyd, C., *The health of seamen* (1965)

Lloyd, C., *St Vincent and Camperdown* (1963)

McKee, E., *Working boats of Britain; their shape and purpose* (1983)

Mackesy, P., *The war in the Mediterranean, 1803-1810* (1957)

Maistre, M., 'Les corsaires de la Manche sous la République et l'Empire' (Ecole de Guerre Navale, 1929)

Malo, H., *Les derniers corsaires: Dunkerque (1715-1815)* (Paris 1925)

Manger, J. B., *Recherches sur les relations économiques entre la France et la Hollande pendant la Révolution française, 1785-1795* (Paris 1923)

Manning, T. D. and Walker, C. F., *British warship names* (1959)

Marcus, G. J., *A naval history of England, vol.2; the age of Nelson* (1971)

Martin-Deidier, A., 'La guerre de course à Saint Malo de 1688 à 1814' (thèse du 3ème cycle, Univ. of Paris 1976)

Mathiez, A., *La vie chèr et le mouvement sociale sous la Terreur* (Paris 1927)

May, W. E., *A history of marine navigation* (Henley-on-Thames 1973)

Meignen, L., 'Le commerce extérieur de la France à la fin de l'Ancien Régime' *(Revue historique du droit français et étranger),* (1978), pp 563-614

Melvin, F. E., *Napoleon's navigation system. A study of control during the continental blockade* (New York 1919)

Merrieu, J., 'La course, romantisme, exutoire sociale, réalité économique: essai de methodologie' *(Annales de Bretagne),* lxxviii, (1971), pp 307-44

Meyer, J., *La noblesse bretonne* (2 vols, Paris 1966)

Meyer, J., *Une agence de commerce extérieur dans la Convention* (Paris 1946)

Meyer, J., *L'armement nantais dans la deuxième moitié du XVIIIe siècle* (Paris 1969)

Miquelon, D., *Dugard of Rouen; French trade to Canada and the West Indies 1729-1770* (Montreal 1978)

Mitchell, B. R. and Deane, P., *Abstract of British historical statistics* (1971)

Morel, A., 'La guerre de course à Saint-Malo de 1681 à 1715'*(Mémoires de la Societé d'Histoire et d'Archéologie de Bretagne)*, xxvii, (1957), pp 5-103, (1958), pp 30-109

Nicolas, L., *La puissance navale dans l'Histoire* (3 vols., Paris 1958, 1960, 1963)

Nussbaum, F. L., *Commercial policy in the French Revolution. A study of the career of G. J. A. Ducher* (Washington 1923)

Orceau, R., 'Les pelloutier indienneurs' *(Bulletin de la Societé Archéologique et Historique de Nantes et de la Loire-inférieure)*, (1945), pp 26-35

Pares, R., *Colonial blockade and neutral rights* (1936)

Pares, R., *Merchants and planters* (1955)

Paris, R., *Histoire du commerce de Marseille, Tome V, Le Levant* (1957)

Pariset, F. G. (ed), *Histoire de Bordeaux; Bordeaux au XVIIIe siècle* (Paris

1968)
Parkinson, C. N., *Edward Pellew, Viscount Exmouth, Admiral of the Red* (1968)
Perrotin-Dumon, A., 'Les corsaires jacobins de Carthagène des Indes (1811-1815)' (Unpublished paper, Dartington Conference on Maritime History 1976)
Pfister, C., 'Le port de Dunkerque sous l'Ancien Régime français (1662-1729): étude économique' (Thèse du 3ème cycle; Univ. of Lille, III, 1981)
Phillips, W. A. and Reade, A. H., *Neutrality, its history, economics and law, Vol.II. The Napoleonic period* (New York 1936)
Mémoires de Plucket (Pierre-Edouard) de Dunkerque; ancien lieutenant de vaisseau et Chevalier de la Légion d'Honneur (Paris 1843, new ed., Dunkirk 1979)
Razzell, P., *The conquest of smallpox: the impact of inoculation on smallpox mortality* (1977)
Reinhard, M., 'Bilan démographique de l'Europe, 1789-1815' (Paper read at the XII Congress of Historical Sciences, Vienna 1965)
Rhodes, A. J., *Dartmoor Prison; a record of one hundred and twenty six years of prisoner of war and convict life 1806-1932* (1933)
Rice, C. D., *The rise and fall of black slavery* (1975)
Richard, R., 'Le fiancement des armements maritimes au XVIIIe siècle. Un approche: le cas du Havre' *(Bulletin de la Societé d'Histoire Moderne)*, xiv ser., (1969), pp 8-14
Richard, R., 'La flotte de commerce du Havre (1751-1816); Etude statistique d'aprè les archives des Classes de la Marine' in *Aires et structures du commerce français au XVIIIe siècle* (Paris 1973), Leon, P. (ed)
Roustit, Y., 'Raymond Durand, commerçant à Barcelone (1808-1814)' *(Estudios de Historia Moderna)* (1956-9), pp 313-409
Rozzell, P., *The conquest of smallpox; the impact of inoculation on smallpox mortality in eighteenth century England* (1977)
Ruppenthal, R., 'Denmark and the Continental System' *(Journal of Modern History)*, xv, (1943), pp 7-23
Ryan, A. N., 'Trade with the enemy in the Scandinavian and Baltic ports during the Napoleonic War: for and against' *(Transactions of the Royal Historical Society)*, xii, (1962), pp 123-34
Schnerb, R., 'La dépression économique sous le Directoire' *(Annales Historique de la Révolution Française)*, xi, (1934), pp 27-49
Scott, W., *Terror and repression in revolutionary Marseilles* (1973)
Sée, H., 'Le commerce de Marseille à l'époque napoléonienne d'après la correspondance d'Honorat l'ainé' *(Revue d'Histoire Economique et Sociale)*, xxi, (1933), pp27-50
Stein, R., 'The French sugar industry in the eighteenth century: a quantitative study' *(Business History)*, xii, (1980), pp 3-17
Surcouf, R., (ed), *Un captive corsaire, Robert Surcouf* (Paris 1925)
Taillefer, C., 'La guerre de course à Saint-Malo de 1793 à 1802' *(Provincia)*, v,

(1963), pp 113-5
Tarrade, J., *Le commerce coloniale de la France* (Paris 1972)
Thesée, F., *Négotiants bordelais et colons de Saint-Dominque 'liaisons d'habitations'; la maison Henry Romberg Bapst et cie, 1753-1793* (Paris 1972)
Toussaint, A., 'Un corsaire normand dans l'Océan Indien au XVIIIe siècle *(Annales de Normandie),* (1977), pp 19-36
Toussaint, A., 'La guerre de course dans l'Océan Indien pendant la guerre d'Amérique' (Paper read at the XIV Conference of the International Commission for Maritime History, Greenwich 1974)
Toussaint, A., *Histoire des corsaires* (Paris 1978)
Veraghtert, K., 'The Antwerp port, 1790-1814' in *The interaction of Antwerp with the Baltic Region 1400-1800* (1983), van Winter, J. M. (ed)
Viennet, O. (ed), *Le voyage du hambourgeois Philippe-André Nemnich (1809)* (Paris 1947)
Vignols, L., 'La course maritime; ses conséquences économiques, sociales et intérnationales' *(Revue d'Histoire Economique et Sociale)*, xv, (1927)
Watt, Sir James, 'Some consequences of nutritional disorders in eighteenth century British circumnavigations', in *Starving sailors; the influence of nutrition upon naval and maritime history* (1984), Watt, J., Freeman, E. V. and Bynum, W. F. (eds)
Wismes, A., *Jean Bart et la Guerre de Course* (Paris 1965)

Index

adm = admiral; capt = naval captain; lt. = naval lieutenant. All ship names are those of French privateers unless otherwise stated. More than one vessel may have the same name. Names of captured merchant ships are usually shown in a French form as recorded in the original documents.